Word for Word

A Daily Lexicon for Your Spiritual Journey

Hal Hammons

Word for Word: A Daily Lexicon for Your Spiritual Journey
© 2012 by DeWard Publishing Company, Ltd.
P.O. Box 6259, Chillicothe, Ohio 45601
800.300.9778
www.deward.com

All rights reserved. No portion of this book may be reproduced in any form without written permission from the publisher.

Cover design by Jonathan Hardin.

Unless otherwise indicated, Scripture quotations taken from the NEW AMERICAN STANDARD BIBLE® Copyright © 1960, 1962, 1963, 1968, 1971, 1972, 1973, 1975, 1977, 1995 by The Lockman Foundation. Used by permission.

Any emphasis in Bible quotations is added.

Reasonable care has been taken to trace original sources for any excerpts and quotations appearing in this book and to document such information. For material not in the public domain, fair-use standards and practices were followed. Should any attribution be found to be incorrect or incomplete, the publisher welcomes written documentation supporting correction for subsequent printings.

Printed in the United States of America.

ISBN: 978-1-936341-53-5

To Tracie,
For everything

Foreword

Have you even gotten up on a cool crisp autumn Saturday morning, pulled on a fuzzy turtle-neck sweater and an old pair of faded blue jeans, turned on some quiet-time music, situated yourself just right in a big, over-stuffed chair, supped on a hot cup of coffee, and settled in for a couple of hours of just taking mental trips to any place you wanted to go, guided by a good book? It's a great way to spend a Saturday morning in the fall.

I like books. I know—electronic books are convenient, easy to read, handy to have. But it seems to me that there's an aesthetic quality to just plain ole library books. Just to be able to manually turn the pages, go back and read what you read three or four pages back, mark a certain passage with a pencil, turn over a little tab at the top of a page so you won't lose your place—all those things, and more, just make them special to me. And what a joy to just leave the book open, lay it gently on your chest and take a short nap. It's not very comfortable to lay an electronic device on your chest when you lean back to take a little nap—it's apt to slide off and break.

Hal Hammons' *Word for Word* is a fall-Saturday-morning type of book. It's all about who we are—every one us. It's about our feelings—our ins and outs, our joys and sorrows, our times of weakness and failings. Hal takes us on visits to special places—like family fun, and bad drivers, and thoughts about how foolish we all are sometimes. He takes you down a melancholy street by suggesting some pensive moments—moments of love, heartache, and down right, belly-laughable humor—special feelings, all.

The vignettes in *Word for Word* wander aimlessly from *Sunglasses* to *Soccer*, from *Pendulums* to *Pain*, from *Biathlons* (as if someone cared about *biathlons*) to *Fingerprints*, from *Cannibals* to *Crosswalks*, from *Itching* to *Ignorance*—one word at a time.

The book is serendipitous. Hal's observations of life all spring from unexpected places—ranging from theatre marquee signs, to out-dated movies, to observations about Max the dog. It's about simple things—family and friends and failure and stuff.

Fact is, you don't know from one piece to the other where you're headed next. There's no theme to the book. But that's the strength of his work. It takes you on little jaunts that are totally disconnected from one another. He lets you think along just as he thinks, he allows you to be a part of his observations of life. It's rather disjointed, but it comes together nicely.

Actually, it's not so that there's no theme. Every little snippet of information is intended for only one purpose: to take you to the Bible. The Biblical references are wisely located, and strongly applicable. Hal Hammons shows in every sketch an undying, indefatigable faith in God's message. While it's interesting the routes he takes, you have to read but a few pieces to see where he's going. He's headed all the while toward the Bible. And it's a nice ride.

You can just let the book fall open where it will and you'll find you can start right there. In fact, I dropped the manuscript and never did know what page I was on. I just knew every page was good. Enjoy *Word for Word*.

Dee Bowman
September 2012

Introduction

A brother in Christ recently asked me, "Where do you get your analogies?" Caught a bit off guard, I said the only thing that came to mind—"I pay attention."

With the benefit of a bit of time to think about it, I can't come up with a better answer than that. Life is full of lessons the Lord is trying to teach us. And if we are of the right mind, we can pick up on a few of them. (And I'm not really all that observant. Trust me—if I can do it, anyone can do it.)

That is the message of Deuteronomy 6.4-9—not that the people of God were to literally write quotations from scripture on their doorposts or tattoo them onto their hands, but rather that they were to look around every day and in every situation for opportunities to think about God's law, apply God's law, teach God's law. Did you not quite make it through the green light? There's a lesson there. Did your food arrive at your table cold? There's a lesson there. Was it a particularly starry night? You get the idea.

That's basically how these articles are created. Things happen in my life, and I try to find a practical application. These articles, presented more or less in the order they were written, will take you through the Life of Hal in 2010, spent as the gospel preacher for the church in Bay City, Texas. You will learn about Tracie (my wife), Taylor and Kylie (my daughters), and Max (my miniature schnauzer). You will go with me through the Winter Olympics, the World Cup, various extracurricular activities, and pretty much everything else that happened in my life that year. You may choose to read the articles slowly, living the year out with us. Or you can read them all in one sitting. Or anything in between. Your choice.

Sometimes the lessons may overlap. But this is not intended to be a comprehensive look at Bible doctrine. It's simply the encouragement I received from living in God's world, thinking about God's things. The hope is that the reader will find the same benefit.

All Bible quotations are from the New American Standard Bible unless otherwise indicated.

A word about the title: The concept of "The Final Word" was conceived a few years ago when I had a blank half-page on the back of my weekly bulletin, and it occurred to me that a short personal note from me on a Bible theme would be a good way to close. Before long I decided to give each one a one-word title—literally, "the final word."

The deeper meaning, of course, is that Jesus Christ always gets the last say, and that all considerations should end with His revelation on the matter. As He said in John 12.48, "He who rejects Me, and does not receive My sayings, has one who judges him; the word I spoke is what will judge him at the last day." That's as final as it gets. Great pains have been taken to distinguish between my personal opinions (of which I have many, and have included many) and His truth.

Oh, and I'll confess to a bit of ego on this matter as well. I don't get "the last word" in all that often in everyday life. (I'm married. What can I tell you?) And I'm okay with that. But I'll admit, it's a bit satisfying knowing I'll always get it when I'm the sole editor and contributing writer.

I would be remiss in not thanking my wife, Tracie, and my daughters, Taylor and Kylie. I wouldn't have nearly as much to write, or the courage and strength to write it, were it not for them. I also want to thank my Christian brethren in Bay City for their encouragement and for putting the building blocks in place to make this work possible. Also, thanks go to my friends on Facebook, who helped me share these messages from coast to coast and around the world. And of course, in all things I thank my Creator and ultimate Benefactor, who makes all things possible for me.

Hal Hammons
September 2011
Bay City, Texas

Resolve

I resolve in the coming year to "Praise the Lord! Sing to the Lord a new song, and His praise in the congregation of the godly ones" (Psalm 149.1).

I resolve in the coming year to "Give thanks to the Lord, for He is good; for His lovingkindness is everlasting" (Psalm 136.1).

I resolve in the coming year to "long for the pure milk of the word" (1 Peter 2.2).

I resolve in the coming year to "Rejoice in the Lord always; again I will say, rejoice!" (Philippians 4.4).

I resolve in the coming year to "preach the word; be ready in season and out of season; reprove, rebuke, exhort, with great patience and instruction" (2 Timothy 4.2).

I resolve in the coming year to "examine everything carefully; hold fast to that which is good; abstain from every form of evil" (1 Thessalonians 5.21-22).

I resolve in the coming year to "fear God and keep His commandments, because this applies to every person" (Ecclesiastes 12.13).

I resolve in the coming year to "pray without ceasing" (1 Thessalonians 5.17).

I resolve in the coming year to "keep seeking the things above, where Christ is, seated at the right hand of God" (Colossians 3.1).

I resolve in the coming year to "not love the world nor the things in the world" (1 John 2.15).

I resolve in the coming year to tell my readers, "Go and do the same" (Luke 10.37).

Cookies

It's not like I really wanted the cookie. I didn't. Really. Cookies are not on my post-holiday dietary regimen. And cookies don't tend to be very filling. I don't recall ever eating a cookie worth eating and not wanting another one.

But see, it was a gift. A holiday gift, prepared by a fine Christian woman who I respect deeply. The subject of the cookie is bound to come up. And it was the last one of the batch. Just cluttering up the counter, really. And with two daughters in the house, it's not pleasant thinking of arbitrating this cookie's pending custody battle. So basically, I had no choice. I had to eat it. Chomp, chomp.

It has been my experience that where there is a cookie, there is a rationalization. People are going to do what they're going to do, and there's not a lot anyone can do about it. And if they want a cookie, and they know they shouldn't have a cookie, they'll find a reason to justify taking the cookie.

Every deviation from Bible truth I can think of can be traced back to one of two thoughts: "I like it," and, "I think other people will like it." Keep the people happy, and we can keep the ball rolling.

Of course, that shows a lack of understanding on two points. The first is that God's happiness should be the priority, not our own. The second is that it is not up to us to achieve success in God's venture, but rather He who gives the increase (1 Corinthians 3.7). We convince ourselves the cookie is for God. But somehow "God" keeps picking around the cookies we don't like. Funny how that works.

Editing

The worst part of writing, for me, is editing. I love the discovery process, just sitting at the keyboard and finding out what pops up on the screen. I enjoy the first stages of tweaking, finding exactly the right word or phrase to convey my point. But going back over it days later, checking for grammatical errors, redundancies, factual errors, extra spaces—that's just plain boring.

But as is the case with many boring activities, it must be done. Far too often I have found a major error upon my eighth or ninth read-through. If I'd only read the article seven or eight times, it likely would have gone uncorrected. And that's just unacceptable.

If God has chosen to bless this "earthen vessel" (2 Corinthians 4.7) with the knowledge of the gospel and an opportunity to share it, then I must take seriously the responsibility that comes with that blessing. And first and foremost, that means getting it right. If I use two commas instead of one, or I misspell "propitiation," or my analogy leaves something to be desired, that reflects on me. I don't like looking bad, but I can live with that. But if I refer someone to the wrong verse, or misstate a text's meaning, or get my merds wixed so as to confuse the reader, that reflects on the gospel. That, I can't live with.

My job is to "preach the word" (2 Timothy 4.2). If someone is going to go astray, it's not going to be because I didn't take an extra five minutes to preach it right. If I deliver my own soul first, maybe I'll be in position to deliver someone else's.

Advice

With apologies to the late George Carlin, in today's culture there appear to be twelve words, not seven, that you cannot say on television, and here they are: "Turn to the Christian faith and you can make a total recovery." This was the advice that news anchor Brit Hume offered famous Buddhist and satyr Tiger Woods recently on the air. And as you might expect, within hours the firestorm had burst all across the nation's media.

Of course, atheists can offer all the advice they want to Christians, who they see as flat-earth, extra-chromosome, neurotic serial killers in training. Clearly they think we need plenty of it. But offer them advice from the Bible, and the air raid sirens start going off. They'll graciously allow us to believe what we want, but we'd better keep it to ourselves. "No advice from you weirdoes, please." The new, revised First Amendment appears to promise not freedom *of* religion, but freedom *from* religion.

Calls are already ringing for Hume to apologize. But for what? For suggesting that Jesus could be a way of changing a person's life for the better? You could put a much longer list of success stories together for Jesus than you could for, say, yoga. Or Dr. Phil.

Tiger ignored God's "advice" (which is to say, "command") on marriage (Hebrews 13:4). Now his marriage is over. That's no coincidence.

A wise man once wrote, "The fear of the Lord is the beginning of wisdom" (Proverbs 9.10). Please forgive me if I love you enough to pass that bit of advice along.

Word for Word

Microbes

Let's say you own a microscope. You fill an eyedropper with ditch water. You put a drop of the water on a slide and take a look at it through the microscope. You see hundreds and hundreds of microbes—so far beneath you in size, strength and intelligence as to defy description, but yet real and very much alive.

Let's say you develop an attachment to one particular variety of microbe. You decide to devote your life to it. Everything you do is in its interest. You are determined to create the best possible world for it, even if it should cost you everything. You are that devoted to the microbe.

You probably think I'm making a comparison between the microbe as we see it and mankind as God sees us. But that doesn't do God justice. And really it doesn't do us justice either. You didn't make the microbe. The microbe has nothing in common with you. The microbe goes where the eyedropper takes it. But man is God's most special creation, made in His image and given all of creation in trust (Genesis 1.27-28). All of creation glorifies God by its nature. Only man glorifies God by choice.

David, no doubt under a starry sky at the time, wrote, "What is man that You take thought of him, and the son of Man that You care for him?" (Psalm 8.4). His point was not to minimize man in the great scheme of things, but rather to magnify him. With all the creation before Him, God focuses on man.

What a blessing to know I'm not just a microbe under God's microscope. I am the center of the universe. I am the crowning glory of creation. I am His child.

Understand

It happens all the time. A friend is in the process of making a tragic decision. Maybe he's selecting friends who have no interest in the things of God. Maybe she's in love with someone who is abusive. And you intervene in love, trying to get your friend to see the light. And the friend just smiles and says, "You just don't understand."

I greatly fear that people say "understand" when they really mean "agree with me." They tell you their story, ostensibly so you can offer advice. But they don't want advice. They want confirmation. They don't want to change. They just want to be told they're okay as they are.

Often people assume that only someone in the center of the issue, who is acquainted with all the back history and personalities, can render a valuable opinion. But that perspective can cloud one's judgment rather than informing it. Myopia can set in, rendering the person incapable of seeing the big picture. *I see what you're saying,* they tell you, *and ordinarily I would agree. But my situation is unusual. You just don't understand.*

People take the same attitude toward God's rules. They don't want to hear about sin. They would rather explain why God should give them a pass, and why you should be more understanding about their circumstances.

Well, what I understand is this: God issues the passes. And "there is no partiality with God" (Romans 2.11). Getting a friend to "understand" and getting God to "understand" are different considerations. Even if we get the one, we can't afford to assume we're getting the other.

Bookmarks

I read everywhere. In restaurants, on planes, in the car (not usually while I'm actually driving—you have to draw the line somewhere). So I wind up using all sorts of bookmarks. A receipt. A paper chopsticks sleeve. A boarding pass. Anything relatively flat will do. So when I pick the book up again years later (if this tightwad spends good money on a book, he's going to read it more than once), it's like opening a time capsule. *That's right, I read this in that diner that made those great burgers. That explains these yellow stains, too.*

Most of my Bibles have ribbon markers built in, so I don't need bookmarks. But I have placed "mental bookmarks" in all sorts of passages. And looking back at them again, I can recall how much of a difference God's word made at critical junctures in my life.

Philippians 3.15—"Let us therefore, as many as are perfect, have this attitude; and if in anything you have a different attitude, God will reveal that also to you." I remember the first sermon I ever heard on that verse, and being overwhelmed with confidence that God was watching out for me, knowing He truly wants me to succeed.

Philippians 4.6—"Be anxious for nothing." "That's why worry is a sin," the preacher said. "Of course!" I said.

Philippians 4.4—"Rejoice in the Lord always; again I will say, rejoice!" On "one of those days," when there wasn't much to be happy about, God reminded me I was required to be happy anyway.

And that's just at a single opening. I can only imagine how many mental bookmarks are in the whole Bible.

Excuses

Mark Twain was once asked by a neighbor for the use of Twain's ax, and Twain refused. When asked for a reason, Twain responded, "I plan to eat my soup with it." The neighbor said he thought that was a strange reason to give, that axes weren't usually used for eating soup. Twain replied, 'I know, but if you don't want to lend out your ax, one excuse is as good as another."

Sometimes it seems like quality control goes out the window when we are looking for excuses. Any old reason will do. Of course, we have to come up with something good if our boss wants to know why we missed work, or if our parents want to know why we skipped school. But if we are answering to God about why we missed worship services one Sunday, anything goes. My alarm didn't go off. I had a sore throat. It was the first weekend of hunting season. I got in late the night before. The dog ate my car keys. Okay, I made that last one up. But I've heard all the rest, and dozens more besides.

Jesus dealt with excuse-makers in the parable of the great dinner (Luke 14.16-24). Clearly when the invited guests begged off with claims of land that needed checking and livestock that needed testing, they were telling the host how little regard they had for his invitation. Aren't we saying the same thing when we refuse His invitation to worship (Hebrews 10.25)? Or His invitation to holiness (1 Peter 1.15)? Or to service (Ephesians 5.21)?

Maybe instead of looking for new and better excuses, we should be looking for a new and better attitude.

Word for Word

Trophies

I had two really good seasons in Little League baseball. (That is, I played on two really good teams. I stunk.) One year I played for the Angels. We lost to the Bandits in the championship game—the game I got hit in the same shoulder twice by the two hardest throwers in the league. I hated the Bandits.

The next year I got to play on the Bandits. We won the championship. Hey, forgive and forget, I say.

I got trophies both years. I remember being a bit surprised to get something for finishing second. I would have had a stroke if they handled things like a lot of leagues do today. These days, everyone gets a trophy. Even the team you beat 33-2.

Personally, I think the new way stinks as bad as my old batting average. A trophy should be more than an acknowledgment of participation. It should be a prize to which all aspire but only few may claim. The quest for victory can be overemphasized, especially in children's sports, but that doesn't mean we ignore its virtues.

I greatly fear that many Christians expect God to hand out trophies based on participation instead of performance. Paul said he expected to receive "the crown of life" for fighting the good fight and finishing the course (2 Timothy 4.7-8)—not for accepting the fight and starting the course. He wrote in 1 Corinthians 9.24, "Do you not know that those who run in a race all run, but only one receives the prize? Run in such a way that you may win."

I would love to have had Paul on my baseball team. That kind of no-quit, no-excuses attitude wins trophies.

Messy

Some people are absolutely comfortable in their church home. They know their seats will be empty and waiting for them every week. Everyone knows everyone, and always has. The preacher will preach the same sort of lessons he always preaches, the same sort they've always heard. Everything is neat and tidy. Everything is in its place.

I feel sorry for those people. I really do.

I prefer messy churches. I want to be surprised constantly. I want to be inconvenienced. I want a different stranger to steal my seat every week. I want to trip over kids. I want to have to speak up so an older person can hear me. I want to battle through tough accents, burrow into tough Bible texts, field questions that have no easy answers. I want personal, social and spiritual challenges.

I know some of the issues in messy churches will be bad; some will even be tragic. Factions will arise and require exposure (1 Corinthians 11.19). Morality will grow lax and require correction (Galatians 5.16-21). It's a hassle, no doubt about it. Lots of angst, lots of disappointment. But at least messy churches are alive. At least they have growth potential. I'd rather try to stave off false doctrine in a church than try to raise a church from the dead.

Proverbs 14.4 reads, "Where no oxen are, the manger is clean, but much revenue comes by the strength of the ox." A lifeless church is a lot less trouble than a lively one, but you aren't going to get much spiritual reward from working with a group like that. If I have the choice, I'll exchange a clean manger for a sloppy one any day.

Printing

I do a weekly bulletin. The articles are the main focus, of course, but I like to add some graphics to spruce it up a bit. I think it makes the reader a bit more likely to read, a bit more likely to remember.

When I put the final polish on my bulletin from my laptop, I get it to look exactly the way I want it. Then I take it to my printer and put it on paper. But it's not the greatest printer. The graphics get a bit grainy, especially the ones I had to enlarge. And since I'm not going to publish in color, I don't bother printing it in color

Then I take it to the copier. And that's not a perfect process either. Some of my best-looking graphics disappear entirely. Sometimes not even I can tell what the finished product was supposed to look like.

I sometimes wish I could show people the original—give them an idea of what the finished product looked like in my head. But that's just not how the publishing process works. They'll just have to be satisfied with the copy.

I hope and pray that people see my articles for what they are—my feeble efforts to relate my understanding of God's word and its applicability in our lives. They are not Scripture, not infallible. I believe they are true to the text; I would not publish them otherwise. But I've been wrong before. I'll be wrong again. I may be wrong now.

I promise to be as faithful to the truth of God's word as I can be. I ask that my readers imitate the Bereans, who were "examining the Scriptures daily to see whether these things were so" (Acts 17.11). If Paul's efforts called for that kind of scrutiny, mine certainly do.

Milk

One of the first "Hal-improvement" tasks Tracie took upon herself after we got married was getting me off whole milk. She was pretty clever about it, I must say. We switched to two-percent milk first. Then we started cooking with skim. Then one day we ran out of two-percent and I was "forced" to drink skim. And eventually buying two gallons of milk got to be obnoxious, and I told her I'd probably be okay drinking skim. She had me at "I do."

Last week she accidently bought one-percent milk, and I could hardly choke it down. It appears that, instead of lactose-intolerance, I have milkfat-intolerance. It's the same principle that makes me feel bloated just by catching the aroma from a fried chicken stand.

Christians can train themselves to be intolerant of sin, too. The longer we stay away from things that are bad for us, the less we miss them, the more we appreciate how much we were hurting ourselves by indulging in them. The more we "abstain from every form of evil" (1 Thessalonians 5.22), the stronger our taste for the "fruit of the Spirit" (Galatians 5.22-23) becomes.

And we need to appreciate that people who do not know Christ, who do not have our values, will not understand the choices we are making. They love their "excesses of dissipation," and they will think we are strange that we don't join in (1 Peter 4.4). And certainly we will do what we can to bring them into the light. But in the meantime, we certainly shouldn't feel bad about staying away from things far more dangerous than unsaturated fat.

Word for Word

Foam

Root beer floats are a conundrum. If you put the root beer in first, it splashes over the edge when you put in the ice cream. But if you put the ice cream in first, you have to deal with all that foam. Sure, the foam is exciting—kind of like one of those science experiments where you make a volcano with baking soda. But root beer float foam isn't like regular soda foam. It doesn't die. It looks great, but it's actually a problem. It keeps the glass from filling up. It winds up taking longer to make the float than to drink it.

I don't know about you, but I've met some pretty "foamy" Christians over the years. You know the type. People who make a big deal about things—mainly about themselves. They draw attention to themselves and their (alleged) righteousness at every occasion.

Jude writes of troublemakers in the church that fit this description. He describes them as being "wild waves of the sea, casting up their own shame like foam" (Jude 13). They put on a big show, but that's all it is. And at the core of it, the things they are showing off about themselves are things of which they should be ashamed.

In the same sermon Jesus tells us, "Let your light shine before men" (Matthew 5.16) and, "Beware of practicing your righteousness before men to be noticed by them" (Matthew 6.1). The difference between the two is attitude. If we show people the substantive change Jesus has made in us, well and good. If we only "talk the talk," we may put on a good show, but ultimately we will only make a mess that someone else will have to mop up.

Burns

Pizza sauce comes out of the oven at around 425 degrees Fahrenheit. After a few minutes of cool-down time, it has probably dropped a few degrees. But not much. So, for instance, accidentally sticking a knuckle into the pizza while cutting it is a bad idea. You really need to take my word on this point.

I have been burned on pots, oven racks, and various other hot items—mostly in the kitchen, it seems, which is Reason #162 why I'm glad to be married. But unless you count scalding my upper palate, I don't think I've ever been burned on so much as a square inch of area at any single time. God is good.

I cannot imagine the pain, the horror, of actually being on fire. I suppose that, for the average human being, it is just about the most terrifying image imaginable.

I am confident that this is the reason that fire is the most consistent image used in the Bible in connection with hell (Isaiah 66.24, Matthew 3.12, Matthew 18.8-9, etc.). I doubt seriously that the Bible paints an exact picture, just as I suspect heaven doesn't really have gates of pearl and streets of gold. God is trying, in as perfect a way He can with human images, to convey what eternity will be like—unspeakably wonderful for the saved, unspeakably horrible for the lost.

The thought of eternal glory in His presence should be enough to motivate us to serve Him in this life. But if, for whatever reason, it isn't, the thought of eternal punishment for rebellion should suffice.

Adult

When exactly did "adult" become synonymous with "sinful"? I can remember as a child thinking the only thing reprehensible about being "adult" was that you had to pay full price at the movies. Now, of course, when you see the words "adult" and "movies" in the same sentence, it is generally in a very different connotation—typically the video emporiums on the side of the highway with the parking lots hidden behind the building, or else the pay-per-view movies that the parents of teenage boys find mysteriously appearing on their cable bills.

As a movie buff and a parent of a teen and a teen-to-be, I find myself constantly re-evaluating my favorite films to see if they're appropriate for the girls. Some films *(Citizen Kane,* for instance) are legitimately over their heads. Others *(Butch Cassidy and the Sundance Kid, The Dark Knight)* focus on themes they're not quite ready for. Those are the films I would like to call "adult."

But if we shelter our children from lewd or otherwise ungodly entertainment and still watch it ourselves, we leave the impression that such things are privileges reserved for grown-ups. We give it a certain prestige, turning it into "forbidden fruit" that is just that much more attractive.

Being an adult doesn't mean "cleared for sin." Adults should be those who "because of practice have their senses trained to discern good and evil" (Hebrews 5.14). That means being better at identifying and avoiding sin, not identifying and engaging in it.

Nicknames

Most of us picked up at least one nickname in our lives. Some are just derivations of our given names; I've always been "Hal" instead of "Harold" to distinguish me from my father. Guys called "Fridge," "Slim" or "Frodo" probably picked up theirs because of physical traits. Jacob's brother, Esau, picked up the name "Edom" (meaning, "red") because of the red lentil stew for which he sold his birthright—and perhaps also for his abundance of red hair (Genesis 25.25-30).

But some of the best nicknames are given for character traits. My favorite was given to a man named Joseph in Acts 4.36-37. Joseph was so given to charity and selflessness that the apostles started calling him Barnabas, which literally means "son of encouragement." Essentially they were saying that "brotherly love" placed in human form would look just like him.

Barnabas encouraged the needy saints in Acts 4. He encouraged Saul of Tarsus after his conversion and helped him become the apostle Paul (Acts 9.27). He encouraged John Mark to resume his work as a preacher (Acts 15.37). Personally, I would love to be the kind of person that others would feel compelled to call "Barnabas."

What nickname are you in the process of earning for yourself? "Happy"? "Sleepy"? "Grumpy"? "Dopey"? We have a great deal of control over the one that will be chosen. Hopefully the characteristic that most defines us will be one worthy of Christ. Hopefully it will distinguish us as much as the hair on Esau's arms.

Word for Word

Invisible

If you were a superhero, what superpower would you like to have? I have always wanted to fly. I'd give super-strength to Tracie; that way she could open her own pickle jars. I would like my girls to have super-hearing; clearly regular hearing isn't enough.

I know plenty of Christians who would want the power to be invisible. I know that because they are trying their hardest to be invisible now. They miss chances to gather with their brethren. When they do come, they arrive late, sit in the back, and leave as soon as possible.

Ironically, such ones in my experience usually claim to "not fit in" with other Christians. They don't feel like they are a part of things. They don't think anyone at church has gotten to know them. Sort of like one piece of the jigsaw puzzle doesn't "fit in" with the rest when it remains in the box, I suppose. I have, half-jokingly, suggested in the past that churches assign a "wrangler" to each exit to hog-tie the folks who want to skedaddle before we can "love on 'em" a little bit. (Sorry, all you Yankees; the Texan in me sneaks out sometimes.)

Jesus didn't save me so I could be invisible. He saved me so I could be "a city set on a hill" (Matthew 5.14) to the world, and a "true companion" (Philippians 4.3) to my spiritual family. I know "standing out" is more comfortable for some people than for others. But I also know that the obligation to "encourage one another day after day" (Hebrews 3.13) isn't just for extroverts. Maybe something as simple as making conversation can be the first small step into noticeable, visible service.

Distractions

Some of my best ideas come when I'm watching television. And some of my best work is done there, too. But not much of it. And not too much of it at a time, either. There are too many distractions. After all, if I didn't find the show interesting, I wouldn't be watching it in the first place. So an article that might take a half-hour of office time to write will still be unfinished after watching a two-hour movie.

What's more, I find that my work distracts me from the movie as well. (Not that that is such a terrible thing in and of itself, but Tracie is getting tired of me asking her to explain things.)

It's not that we can't accomplish things without focusing on them. But there is no doubt that distractions lower our chances of productivity considerably. Without focus, it's like trying to juggle chainsaws while eating a burrito—if we want to be successful in the one, we would do well to say no to the other, or else be prepared to deal with a pretty big mess.

I fear that many Christians fully intend to succeed in their efforts to serve Jesus, but they allow far too many distractions to clutter up their lives. In the parable of the sower, Jesus warns us that some will be "choked with worries and riches and pleasures of this life, and bring no fruit to maturity" (Luke 8.14). Such Christians become habitual underachievers, bearing little fruit for the Lord because they refuse to put themselves in position to succeed. Jesus has great things planned for us; but to achieve them, we have to start planning for greatness ourselves.

Word for Word

Knots

Okay, this will tell you how much a part of my everyday thought processes this column has become: My daughter Taylor put two of her necklaces in the same drawer, and they became incredibly tangled. I spent the better part of an hour getting them separated, and the entire time I was thinking to myself, "I'd better at least get an article out of this!"

Well, it looks like I did. Thanks, Taylor. I guess. But really, it is astonishing to me how knots can just appear somehow when no one is there to tie them. Jewelry is the worst, but the same thing occurs in hoses, cables, extension cords, basically anything long and stringy. Entire books are written on the tying of knots, when all you really need to do is pile the item up in the corner of the garage. Logic says (at least, *my* logic says) you should be able to put something down, wait a few weeks or months, then pick it up and continue without skipping a beat. But apparently, it doesn't work that way.

Relationships are even worse than necklaces. It's easy to think you can leave them untended in a drawer somewhere without them suffering, but it's just not true. Friendships, marriages, relations with brethren—all human associations must be nurtured if they are to prosper.

Far more important, of course, is our relationship with God. We cannot afford to be content with measures we have taken in the past to draw close to Him, nor should we want to. "Draw near to God and He will draw near to you" (James 4.8). If we invest in the relationship, it will pay great dividends. Sow sparingly, reap sparingly.

Election

No one sounds more humble than a politician who has just been elected to office. In his or her acceptance speech, you are likely to hear repeated references to "you the people, who have the real power," and "my worthy opponent," and (less and less frequently these days) "prayers on our behalf." It's all about the ones who did the electing.

Far too often, though, the humility is either fake or temporary. The politician revels in the perquisites of power—enthusiastic audiences, attentive reporters, face time on national television. And in his mind (I've decided our "politician" is male; I hate typing "his or her" constantly), all of it is deserved—after all, he was elected.

But the election isn't (or shouldn't be) about the one elected, but rather about the ones doing the electing. In a representative republic, elected officials answer to the people daily—and ultimately, they answer in the next election. If they don't perform as the electorate wishes, the election may be reversed.

Christians, as "God's elect" (Romans 8.33), should take heed. Instead of being puffed up with pride after having been chosen to "reign upon the earth" (Revelation 5.10), we should see our exaltation as an opportunity to praise the One who exalted us, and the marvelous system of grace that made it possible. And we should devote ourselves to dutiful service—"make your call and election sure, for if you do these things you will never stumble" (2 Peter 1.10, NKJV). Just because we're "elected" doesn't necessarily mean we'll stay elected.

Word for Word

Sheep

My grandfather, a few years before he died, bought a couple of sheep. Looking back, it was a strange thing for an old cattleman to do. About all they were good for was keeping the grass short and just standing around looking, well, sheepish.

Sheep are stupid. I racked my brain for a more delicate way of phrasing that, but accuracy and conciseness ultimately win out over delicacy. "Stupid" is the word I am looking for. Sheep are stupid.

And as much as it pains me to say it, of all of the animals in God's creation it is the sheep that is so frequently used as a metaphor for God's people. The first time in the New Testament is in Matthew 9.36—"Seeing the people, [Jesus] felt compassion for them, because they were distressed and dispirited like sheep without a shepherd." Of the 39 times afterward that the word "sheep" is used in the New Testament, 31 refer to Christians.

And sheep are stupid.

That's why we so desperately need the "Shepherd and Guardian of [our] souls" (1 Peter 2.25) to point us in the right direction. That is why we need the "Good Shepherd," who "lays down His life for the sheep" (John 10.11). That is why we need the "Chief Shepherd" who will reward us for good behavior in due course of time (1 Peter 5.4). And that is why it is unthinkable that we as His sheep would ever think that our approach to life or any part of it would be preferable to His.

But then again, sheep are stupid.

Cobwebs

If a television or film director wants an indoor setting to look abandoned, cobwebs are a must. Dust is good too, but things can get dusty through regular activity. To give the real, honest-to-goodness look of inattention and neglect, you need cobwebs.

Now, by "neglect," we mean human neglect. Actually, gargantuan activity has been going on. Cobwebs, of course, are nothing more than spider webs ("cob" being an old term for a spider). And spiders work. They work hard. Anyone who's ever read *Charlotte's Web* knows that. But even though scientists keep telling us how strong spider webs are, we have yet to come up with a practical use for them.

Sometimes we can find ourselves in what we might self-diagnose as a "holding pattern" in regard to our faith. We're not denying God or engaging in any gross immoralities. We're just not making much of a positive effort. Our faith is in a state of neglect.

Unfortunately, Satan is not idle. "Your adversary, the devil, prowls around like a roaring lion, seeking someone to devour" (1 Peter 5.8). We may declare a cease-fire in our personal war against evil, but that doesn't mean he will abide by it. He will interpret our passivity as weakness, and do his best to exploit it.

Being inactive is the best way to encourage Satan's activity. He can tell when we have not been "keeping house" for God. A life not consciously filled with the things of the Lord will, consciously or not, eventually be filled with the things of the devil (Matthew 12:43-45).

Word for Word

Conjunctions

I am in a constant quest for new conjunctions for my writing. As "Conjunction Junction" taught me many Saturday mornings ago, "And, But and Or get you pretty far." But (there's one right there) bombarding the reader with the same handful of conjunctions can become wearing. So I shake it up a bit. "Now." "Consequently." "Meanwhile." "However." (Some of those may be adverbs posing as conjunctions, but this isn't English class. Or "Schoolhouse Rock.")

Conjunctions provide flow. Ideally, the reader will gently drift from phrase to phrase, sentence to sentence, paragraph to paragraph, until my overall point is not only iterated, but also placed in a clear and practical context.

Life flows too. It is not lived in years or days or even minutes, but rather in an infinite series of moments strung together by our choices. When we "wake up" in a situation we would have thought unimaginable, actually we have allowed our lives to flow one way by not directing the flow in some other way. David and Bathsheba may not have planned for their tryst to get as complicated as it did; still, a few bad choices later, a husband and a baby had died (2 Samuel 11-12).

Life will continue to flow until we reach Christ's judgment seat (2 Corinthians 5.10). And our fate will be determined by the choices we made all along the way. Each one takes us closer to glory or to destruction.

Good choices tend to beget more good choices. Bad begets bad. The sooner we take command of the flow, the better our chances of getting where we want to go.

Useful

Many years ago, the king of Siam (now Thailand) was celebrating his birthday. One citizen, wishing to do something special, gave him a rare albino elephant. But instead of being flattered, the king was upset. Albino elephants were considered sacred, and therefore not permitted to work. Instead of being a valuable asset, it was simply a burden. And we've been laughing at "white elephant gifts" ever since.

Presents should be useful. I'm not saying they all have to be in the vacuum cleaner category. "Useful" can mean decorative, or comforting, or tasty. The present recipient has many needs; we really don't have any excuse for not hitting one of them when we select a gift.

We need to think in practical terms when we present ourselves to the Lord as "a living and holy sacrifice" (Romans 12.1). The transaction isn't completed when we agree to live in His service; we must also show ourselves to be worthwhile to Him. After all, that's what "service" is supposed to be—ministering to the needs of someone else.

But somehow, some Christians manage to get the gift-giving process reversed in their minds. They're like the man with the white elephant. They think they deserve credit for the gesture they are making, that somehow the King is now in their debt. They forget that they were subject to the King long before they went shopping. He, not we ourselves, judges the adequacy of our gesture.

Are we going to be useful to Christ? Or are we more interested in just focusing on what He can do for us?

Gourds

Hungry people are driven to eat some crazy things. During the famine of Elisha's day, some men grabbed some wild gourds and made soup out of them, making themselves violently ill in the process (2 Kings 4.38-41). Elisha and the power of God had to intervene to save them.

(My marriage tip of the day: Husbands, the next time the wife cooks up some unusual soup or stew, give it a taste and then start writhing on the ground screaming, "There's death in the pot! There's death in the pot!" You'll both get a big laugh out of it. Trust me.)

The same principle applies to spiritual hunger. We have people all over the world who are dying for something, anything, that will fill the spiritual void in their lives. University professors try to convince us that God is a myth. Entertainment moguls try to convince us that God is irrelevant. Government officials try to convince us that God is dangerous. It doesn't work. Telling people how bad the food is doesn't make them any less hungry.

Tragically, seekers often satisfy themselves with any old gourd they find on the side of the road. They don't investigate it for nutritive value. They don't take sample-size bites. They just dive into the pot headfirst, often making their situation worse instead of better.

God provides real sustenance. Those who hunger and thirst for righteousness will find it, and be truly satisfied with it (Matthew 5.6). But "trickery of men" (Ephesians 4.14) will fail us every time. May God give us the patience and courage to hold out for the real thing.

Multitasking

My job is pretty straightforward. Study the Bible, make an outline, preach the lesson. Each component is done in its turn. My wife's job as a homemaker is totally different. Being a homemaker is all about multitasking. Put laundry in the machines, start cleaning a room, plan dinner, check the laundry, brainstorm about Bible class material, all with one brain and two hands. I stand in awe.

Of course, if one task is particularly important, she will focus her energies on just that. But focusing on one task can't be an excuse for ignoring a more pressing one.

Over the years I have watched many parents intentionally neglect their children's spiritual welfare, choosing to show preference to a particular carnal need such as education, making friends, or the ever-popular "staying off drugs." They tell me that they understand and regret the short shrift the Lord is getting in the short term, but that they really need to concentrate on the other issue—an issue they see as more pressing, more urgent.

Well, far be it from me to tell a parent to let their children get on drugs. But if we can manage to multitask well enough to walk and chew gum at the same time, we can figure out a way to serve God's interests and our children's interests simultaneously—especially since they are (or should be) the same. But tragically, in an effort to "save the children," parents choose instead to neglect their divine mandate to rear them in "the discipline and instruction of the Lord" (Ephesians 6.4)—ironically, the one tactic that is guaranteed to "save the children." Shameful.

Word for Word

Rhinos

Protecting my home and family is a top priority for me. That is why I buy rhino repellant. One can (for only $19.95) applied monthly around the perimeter of the house is guaranteed to keep all rhinos at bay. I've been doing it for two years. Not one attack. I'm telling you, this stuff really works.

Now, before you all get in your cars to come over and hold an infomercial intervention on my behalf, let me assure you that the above story is fictional. To my knowledge, there is no such product as "rhino repellant" available in the United States. And we all know why. American consumers (most of us, anyway) know an absence of rhino attacks can be attributed to other, more likely causes. Such as, for instance, the absence of rhinos.

We have a nasty habit of measuring the appropriateness of our actions by the results that follow. One baseball player recently made the news with his insistence that wearing gold lamé thong underwear helped his hitting. Now, perhaps a "good luck charm" can put our minds at ease and thus help us do well. Then again, maybe it's just a coincidence. And not a little bit weird.

Successful ventures are not necessarily the result of successful tactics. Abraham lied twice to protect himself, and twice it worked (Genesis 12 and 20). Was it because lying is sometimes okay? Revelation 21.8 says otherwise. No, his lies were a shocking failure of faith. We too must be careful not to congratulate ourselves for actions that only appear to have been successful, and that may in fact have been serious, soul-endangering mistakes.

Management

While driving through a small town last week, we happened to see a store with a sign posted that read, "Under New Management." Not knowing the place at all, we still jumped to a few conclusions. One, the place had a bad reputation. Two, different people had taken over. Three, the new folks hoped the locals might give it another chance if they knew about the switch.

Management makes all the difference. I get far more upset at a manager who won't take responsibility than I do at the worker who actually made the mistake. Good managers can turn dysfunctional operations and operators into functional ones. Or at least, they can try.

In the age-old argument over whether people are inherently good or inherently bad, I vote "none of the above." Quality isn't a factor of the people themselves, but rather of management. Literally billions of people out there in the world would be, under the proper Manager, perfectly fine, noble examples of what humanity ought to be. As it is, they are just flailing around aimlessly, perhaps having some concept of how their life ought to be but having no idea whatsoever of how to make it so.

They've hired themselves as manager of their lives. And they need to fire themselves. Immediately.

Jeremiah wrote long ago, "I know, O Lord, that a man's way is not in himself; nor is it in a man who walks to direct his steps" (Jeremiah 10.23). The sooner we put God in charge, the sooner He can start making something productive out of our lives.

Word for Word

Chips

In Texas, the first choice for barbecue is mesquite wood. I'm not saying it can't be done with oak or pecan or some other hardwood. I'm just saying it can't be done right.

So let's say I'm out back of the house chopping mesquite wood for barbecuing. (Quit laughing, Tracie!). The chips are flying left and right. Not one to waste good mesquite, I pick up the chips and store them in a dry place. Later, when I'm grilling (a very different process than barbecuing—I'll elaborate another time), I can put the chips in the grill to supply some extra flavor.

Mesquite wood yields mesquite chips. The chips have the same texture, the same smell, and produce the same flavor as the original wood. That's where we get the phrase, "a chip off the old block." We expect the by-product to have the same properties as the original.

The same principle applies with people. The older I grow, the more of my father I see in myself. The same mannerisms, the same preferences, the same tastes. I knew I was in trouble the first time I put a fried egg *and* maple syrup on my pancakes. (Hey, don't knock it until you try it.) You spend formative years in the presence of someone you respect, the characteristics start rubbing off.

It should work that way with our heavenly Father too. Taking after our Father means loving the Son He loved (John 8.42). It means emulating Him as fully as the Son did (John 5.19). If we find ourselves in constant rebellion against everything He stands for, then maybe we're not really "chips off the old block" after all.

Done

I have a "high-speed" Internet connection. At least, that's what the people who draft my bank account every month keep telling me. And I suppose it's faster than driving down to the library and looking things up for myself. But sometimes I wonder.

I hate it when a page is loading, and the green bar at the bottom gets bigger and bigger as the page slowly gets more and more discernible. Then suddenly the green bar vanishes and the word "Done" appears. But the page isn't "Done." It isn't "Close To Done" either. Why doesn't it just say, "Thinking About Being Done In The Not-Too-Distant Future"? At least be honest.

Like former President Bush, we are often eager to shout, "Mission Accomplished." But then, that depends on the "mission" to which we refer. If we are celebrating our citizenship in "the kingdom of His beloved Son" (Colossians 1.13), that's fine. But if we just sit back and sing "Safe in the Arms of Jesus," confident the dangers that plagued us while living in Satan's realm are dangers no longer, we are confusing the battle and the war. Satan is not done with us yet. And neither is God.

The spiritual conflict over our soul has just begun. That's why God tells us to "walk in a manner worthy of the calling" (Ephesians 4.1). That's why He tells us, "Test yourselves to see if you are in the faith" (2 Corinthians 13.5). That's why Paul himself was concerned about being "disqualified" (1 Corinthians 9.27).

If you've given yourself to Christ, you've made a good start. But you're not done. Not by a long shot.

Word for Word

Destiny

After watching *Lawrence of Arabia* again recently (I think that makes six or seven times), I found myself thinking about destiny. Lawrence's attempt to unite the Arab people into a cohesive, democratic union failed in the end because the Arabs didn't want to be united. They hated and distrusted each other more than they did the Europeans. It was a destiny they had not chosen for themselves, and so ultimately they rejected it.

It's flattering to see ourselves as the focal element of a grand scheme—perhaps to save a particular soul near and dear to us, or to grow a church to self-sufficiency, or to plant the seed in virgin soil and watch it grow. But what we may call dedication is in reality the height of arrogance. Moses saw himself as ideally situated to free Israel (Acts 7.25); God said in effect, "Go tend sheep for forty years, and then we'll talk." Any time we see ourselves as "destined" to accomplish something in someone else's life, we can be sure we're on the wrong track.

Perhaps it is easier to work on other people's futures than our own. It makes the downside of failure a lot more acceptable. We can beat our heads against the wall trying to "save the world," and then console ourselves in failure, thinking, "At least we tried." But why not stake out our own destinies instead? Paul wrote that Christians are "predestined to become conformed to the image of His Son" (Romans 8.29). It would be a shame to miss out on the greatest destiny imaginable because we were too lazy or too arrogant to claim it.

I

When I first started doing this column, I decided to start each one with a typographical feature called a "drop cap." Instead of trying to describe it, I refer you to the first letter in this article. That's a drop cap.

When I started putting a collection of these articles together, I noticed that a remarkable number of them began with the letter I. Of course, plenty of perfectly good words begin with I. Still, it sort of gave the impression that these articles are all about me. And in a sense, they are. My experiences are what give me the material for the articles. It's only natural that I personally come up in conversation from time to time.

The thing is, I don't like talking about myself. That's largely because I know people who absolutely *love* talking about themselves. And I don't like those people very much. And I really, really don't want to be one of them.

To a certain extent, though, being a preacher is all about drawing attention to yourself. After all, if you don't get people's attention, they won't listen to you. And the same principle applies to all Christians; we are all supposed to be cities set on a hill (Matthew 5.14), shining for all the world to see. But how do we shine our lights without being arrogant? I'm still working on that.

I think the biggest key, though, is telling people that whatever "light" we have is reflected from Jesus, the true "light of the world" (John 8.12). If we make sure they see Jesus when they look at us, hopefully they'll hear us singing His praises and not just us blowing our own horns.

Word for Word

Grounding

We may finally have gotten to the extreme edge of the "animal rights" movement. I have heard that there is an actual movement to replace Punxsutawney Phil, the famous weather-forecasting groundhog, with a robot. That's right, it's apparently cruel to oust the world's most pampered rodent from his burrow against his will one day a year for a few minutes before letting him go on vacation for another 364 days and 23½ hours.

Needless to say (why do people say that right before they say the "needless" thing anyway?), having a robot check its shadow and make a bogus weather prediction completely misses the point. We don't need a robot to predict the weather; as a matter of fact, we don't need the groundhog either. We *want* the groundhog. The groundhog is cute. The groundhog is fun.

I am in no way in support of animal cruelty. I love animals. But animals are not people. They do not have the "inalienable rights" to which Thomas Jefferson alluded in the Declaration of Independence. They are ours to subdue and rule (Genesis 1.28; Psalm 8)—and if we so choose, eat (Genesis 9.3). God is concerned for animals (Psalm 36.6; Jonah 4.11), but not nearly as much as for man. He didn't send His Son to die for groundhogs.

If you want to feel pity for baby seals, I'll join you. If you want to choose salad over steak, I'll support you. But save some energy for your fellow humans. When Jesus said, "preach the gospel to all creation" (Mark 16.15), He meant the two-footed, lost-in-sin, need-a-Savior creation.

Tires

The only part of a car that actually comes in contact with planet earth is its tires. At least, that's the way it's supposed to work; if something else is touching, you almost certainly need to get it checked out.

If the tires lose touch with the road, so does the car. And unless your car flies or swims, that's a bad thing. So the manufacturers design tires to shunt away water and other material that might accumulate on a hard surface, as well as provide traction for driving on a softer surface.

So in a nutshell: First, have tires; second, keep from driving in puddles, potholes and other less-than-ideal road surfaces; third, remain alert when driving in case the conditions are worse than they might first appear.

Let's try to apply that concept in regard to God. The only thing connecting us to God is our faith (Hebrews 11.1). Evidence abounds for those who are willing to look for it and consider it, but it will wind up coming down to faith. So job one is getting faith, which comes from "hearing by the word of Christ" (Romans 10.17).

Then we try to avoid putting ourselves in spiritual harm's way; enough challenges to our faith will come naturally without us seeking them out.

Finally, we don't allow ourselves to be shaken when things go poorly. Trials can be a joy if we allow them to be (James 1.2-4). It's a thrill to know we have developed the spiritual stamina to emerge from difficulties with our faith intact. With every hardship survived, we find ourselves better equipped to weather hardships yet to come.

Word for Word

Groundwork

My late uncle took me on a tour of one of his construction projects one Christmas morning many, many years ago. I can remember being impressed with the amount of work that had to be done at ground level. Foundation piers had to be sunk as deep as twenty feet to provide stability. And then pumps needed to run around the clock to keep water out of the holes. Without the proper groundwork, the foundation would have no hope of supporting the structure. It would be like building on sand, to coin a phrase from the Lord (Matthew 7.26).

The same is true for our spiritual groundwork. Paul writes that God's people are to be "a holy temple of the Lord … a dwelling of God in the Spirit" (Ephesians 2.20-22). But the temple must be built, he writes, "upon the foundation of the apostles and prophets, Christ Jesus Himself being the corner stone." No other foundation will do.

But efforts to build on the foundation are pointless if the foundation is not secure. If we do not begin with a true, committed faith in Jesus, our efforts are all for naught. We may become, in the eyes of our neighbors, the most impressive Christian on the block – only to abandon the Lord in the end because of poor groundwork.

Paul says the "spiritual man" is the one who accepts in faith that God's way is best and thus agrees to be led by the Spirit instead of his own "natural" impulses (1 Corinthians 2.12-16). If we insist on trusting our instincts on God's construction site, we are setting ourselves up for disaster. Such a project cannot possibly succeed.

Marquee

I can't help wondering about the stability of a movie theater whose marquee reads, "Yes, we are open." No starting times, not even movie titles. Just "Yes, we are open." Such is the case for the only theater in my town. In fact, it has been so for several weeks now.

I know it was closed for a while, thanks to the health department. Ick. But now, if we are to believe the signs (or the sign, as it were), it is open for business again. My curiosity finally got the better of me today, and I drove by the box office for a closer look. Sure enough, times are posted for some relatively recent films. So maybe it is open. But it seems to me the theater owners would get more interest, and by extension more business, if they put real information on the marquee and not just a simple assertion that they are alive and kicking.

It made me think of the church in Sardis, as described in Revelation 3.1-6. I know of many churches who take great pains to tell the world how alive they are. They put up a sign. They keep it maintained. They cut the grass and tend the shrubbery. The outside looks fine. But they don't draw much attention to what's going on inside—perhaps because there isn't much of it.

"As he thinks within his heart, so he is" (Proverbs 23.7). The same could be said of churches. Spiritual vitality is measured by activity, by "walking in truth" (3 John 3)—not by names, labels and outward trappings. As the Lord told the church in Sardis, "Wake up, and strengthen the things that remain" (Revelation 3.2). A nice suit doesn't breathe life into a corpse.

Ownership

In case you haven't met Max yet, allow me to introduce you. Max is our family's miniature schnauzer. He recently had his first birthday. He's a bit off-color for a schnauzer, but otherwise reasonably attractive and pretty adorable all the way around.

Now, when I say "our family's miniature schnauzer," I mean mine. My daughters are quick to claim partial ownership. But I've noticed that when his bills need paying, or his fur needs grooming, or his bodily functions need collecting, they are nowhere to be found.

Ownership implies responsibility. I would be responsible if Max were to maul someone on one of our walks. (Yeah, right—Max runs and hides from blowing leaves.) I would be blamed if he dug up a flower bed or kept the neighbors awake with his barking. Me. The owner.

It's easy to accept ownership when praise is being doled out. *"What a cute dog! Is he yours?"* But when blame is seeking a resting place, it's a very different situation. Blame will find the true owner.

Often we hear of someone "accepting ownership of his flaws." We understand that to mean a person is not going to blame someone else for his failings; he will shoulder the responsibility himself as David did in Psalm 32.5—"I acknowledged my sin to You, and my iniquity I did not hide; I said, 'I will confess my transgressions to the Lord'; and You forgave the guilt of my sin." God is more than happy to forgive His children. But first we have to "own up" to our mistakes. God won't shift the blame, so we shouldn't either.

Idioms

William Shakespeare is generally acclaimed as the most influential writer in the history of the English language. He told us, "A rose by any other name would smell as sweet." He told us that "the question" was "To be or not to be." He knew poor Yorick well (alas). Prominent idioms show influence.

So what will we say of the One who taught us how to be a good Samaritan (Luke 10.30-37)? Or how to go the extra mile (Matthew 5.41)? Or how to be the salt of the earth (Matthew 5.13)? Surely we must acknowledge His impact on the world. And yet many continue to marginalize Him; they would rather strain at gnats (Matthew 23.24) than recognize the King.

For such a one, the writing is on the wall (Daniel 5.5). He will reap what he has sown (Galatians 6.7). If he repents, he may escape by the skin of his teeth (Job 19.20). But if he continues to have feet of clay (Daniel 2.33), then it's fire and brimstone (Revelation 20.10) for him.

If I love my neighbor (Leviticus 19.18), I will continue to hope that the leopard will somehow change his spots (Jeremiah 13.23). But I am at my wits' end (Psalm 107.27) as to how to convince him to forget his sour grapes (Ezekiel 18.2) and swallow his pride—which truly goes before a fall (Proverbs 16.18). It's a real fly in the ointment (Ecclesiastes 10.1).

But God still cares for such ones. They are the apple of His eye (Zechariah 2.8). So I'll keep doing to others what I would want them to do for me (Matthew 7.12).

Life

I have an office where I go to work. It's quiet. The phone doesn't ring too much. I get away from the children and the dog. I can hole up with my Bible and my laptop and get far more done than I would anywhere else.

But that's not where I go to think. I don't get my ideas in the office. I get my ideas from life. I can't tell you how many times I've sat in my office frustrated to no end at my lack of vision for the week's lessons or the day's article, only to go volunteer at Kylie's school or go shopping with Tracie and get ideas faster than I can scribble them down.

I get the impression that Solomon walked through life with writing material in hand, looking for more snippets of wisdom to add to his book of Proverbs. I think David saw every trial and every starry sky as potential subjects for psalms. Of course, they had God's inspiration guiding their hand (2 Peter 1.21), but that means God guided their pen as they wrote, not their feet as they walked. Jude clearly already had pen in hand when the Spirit came upon him to write his epistle (Jude 3).

Although God won't move us to write by inspiration as He did these men of old, we can still make ourselves receptive to the lessons that everyday life has to teach us. If we have God's word always in our hearts—and, ideally, not too far from our hands—we can be permanently on the alert for opportunities to grow. If the Lord can open our hearts to understand His words (Acts 16.14), He can do the same when we look for ways to apply them.

Slippery

When the office cleaning crew puts up those yellow signs that say the floor is slippery, it's for a reason. A very good reason. Fortunately I do not have a sore tailbone as I type. But suffice it to say I recently experienced what it was like to be a completely unqualified applicant for a position with the Ice Capades.

There's no feeling in the world like not having any confidence in the earth beneath your feet. Ever since I was a toddler, I have assumed that my feet would stay where I put them. And the overwhelming majority of the time, my preconceptions have been valid. But every once in a while—like when walking on wet tile, or skating, or like those three wonderful days on the ski slopes back in college—I fall flat and hard, right on my preconceptions.

To Christians who think they are on the most solid of ground, who take their faith and future for granted, Paul writes, "Therefore let him who thinks he stands take heed that he does not fall" (1 Corinthians 10.12). We may not be as grounded as we think. And even if we are, eventually we will wander into one of the devil's potholes.

Ultimately our safety depends not upon the stability of our footing, but rather upon whether we have a remedy in place for the day when we stumble. I love the assurance of Psalm 37.24—"When he falls, he will not be hurled headlong, because the Lord is the One who holds his hand." God's word is our foundation (Matthew 7.24), and His grace is our safety net. If we hold on firmly to both, we won't have to worry about slipping.

Scooters

What's with all the motorized scooters these days? They're everywhere. They're scooting down the sidewalk. They're scooting down the grocery aisle. Have we have had a 1,000-percent (rough estimate) increase in the number of impaired citizens out there?

No, I figure the increase is because scooters are free now. You see advertisements for them on television all the time. (Oh, I forgot that one. Scooting on TV.) Qualified buyers can have their scooters paid for in their entirety by government programs. Which is to say, by me.

I don't want to sound like a total cynic here. I know that people have genuine health issues. I sympathize; really I do. But I also know that a significant number of scooters are driven by people who are just plain lazy—worse, by people who would be benefited greatly by going for a walk once in a while.

It's easy to convince ourselves we are being compassionate by ministering to people in their discomfort. But sometimes consolers are nothing more than well-meaning, self-congratulatory enablers. The goal should not be helping people feel better in their unfortunate condition; it should be changing the condition for the better.

I don't enjoy preaching about sin in the presence of sinners. But how can I do otherwise? They may say, "Speak to us pleasant words" (Isaiah 30.10), and they may love me for doing it. But I'd feel a lot more guilty about watching someone miss out on heaven (1 Corinthians 6.9-10) than about hurting their feelings for a minute or two.

Great

Usually when people ask me how I'm doing or how it's going, I respond, "Great!" Not "Fine," or "Pretty good," or "Not too bad." I do that for several reasons.

One, I really am great. Not in an "Alexander the Great" sort of way, but in a "couldn›t ask for more out of life" sort of way. After all, Jesus is Lord of my life—enough cause right there for me to "Rejoice always" (1 Thessalonians 5.16). I have a wonderful family, terrific friends, blessings aplenty, and a home in heaven waiting for me. It would be deceptive if I *didn't* say I was great.

Two, I love the reactions I get from people when I do it. Lots of times those sort of questions are intended to elicit a cursory response—i.e., "Acknowledge that I greeted you, and let me get back to my life." And when I actually *answer their question*, it throws them for a loop. Some people look confused. Even resentful. *"What's with him? Why's he so chipper?"* After a few of those exchanges, they learn either to adopt my positive attitude or get grumpier and stay away from me. (That's what I call a "win-win" situation for me.) But most people really light up. They love enthusiasm. It's infectious. They realize, *"Hey, you know what? I'm great too!"* And just like that, you've made their day.

Paul wrote, while in prison, "Finally, my brethren, rejoice in the Lord" (Philippians 3.1). If I can catch his positive attitude, I can pass it on to someone else, and they can keep the ball rolling indefinitely. Surely anyone who is "in the Lord" ought to feel great. If not, why not?

Word for Word

Hedge

As a Christian, I have innumerable blessings in this life. (I have even more in the next life, but that's for another article.) Bear with me as I give you a small sample:

I am called to a lifestyle that is most suited for me; after all, I'm following the Owner's manual. I have perfect lungs, a perfect liver, no drug-addled brain cells (just the regularly addled ones).

I am surrounded by a loving spiritual family. They supply instruction, moral support and the occasional binge of saturated fat. Best of all, my good brethren provided a good woman for me to marry and share my life with.

I have gainful employment doing work I love and that benefits others. I am able to supply the physical needs of my family as well as most folks, and far better than many.

It's quite a hedge of blessings that God has built for me—perhaps not quite as nice as Job's (Job 1.9-10), but then again, Job didn't get to watch the Super Bowl in high definition. And so the question Satan asked regarding Job has just as much relevance for me: *Does Hal serve God for nothing?* If the hedge were gone, would it make a difference? What if, say, I caught a horrible disease? Or my brethren turned on me? Or my wife wouldn't support me?

God does not owe us a *quid pro quo* for our service; "we have done only that which we ought to have done" (Luke 17.10). That's why we stay faithful when blessings seem few and far between. We're grateful for the hedge, but we don't serve Him for the hedge. We serve Him because He is God. That should be enough.

Vindictive

When I read *Peanuts* growing up, I always felt sorry for Charlie Brown. Every year Lucy would hold the football for him. Every year he would try to kick it. Every year Lucy would pull it away at the last minute. Pretty pathetic, huh? After all, how many times does life have to kick you in the teeth before you figure out that you're backing the wrong horse? Accept reality, already.

But in my adult years, I have come to look at Charlie Brown as a heroic figure, possessing an indefatigable faith in humanity, believing the best of Lucy and the rest of us despite the barrage of rocks metaphorically aimed at his head (and literally placed in his Halloween candy sack).

However, clinging to faith in times of trial requires confidence in one's ultimate vindication. If Charlie Brown knew for a fact that he'd never connect with the football, he'd quit trying. Likewise we, Christians in a sea of worldliness, require vindication for the choice we have made to serve God. As sin continues to reign, we continue to hope. But as we hope, we pray as David prayed in Psalm 43.1—"Vindicate me, O God, and plead my case against an ungodly nation; O deliver me from the deceitful and unjust man!"

But even if we do not see relief in this life, by faith we know we have made the right choice. Hope springs eternal (Romans 8.24-25). And we finish our prayer as David did: "Why are you in despair, O my soul? And why are you disturbed within me? Hope in God, for I shall again praise Him, the help of my countenance, and my God."

Valentines

When I was in elementary school, we would have an annual Valentine's Day party. I always looked forward to it, and for a number of reasons. For instance, less school time spent on schoolwork. And those icky little hearts with the messages printed on them ("Be Mine," "Hugs," etc.)—hey, candy is candy. But more importantly, I got to give a cute, sappy little note to the pretty little girl in the second row I was too shy to talk to. Even better, I could have a reasonable expectation that I would get one from her in return.

But when virtually interchangeable cards are passed between every person in class, genuine sentiments tend to get lost. If the pretty little girl in the second row gave me the same card as the kid who was always trying to take my lunch money, that didn't mean they felt the same way about me. At least, I certainly hoped they didn't.

There are niceties that are exchanged in polite society and there are genuine, heartfelt displays of affection. And it doesn't take Dr. Phil, Dr. Laura or Dr. Ruth to tell the difference. We are not lulled into thinking one pretty piece of paper is a substitute for 1 Corinthians 13-style love. And yet, when we are commanded, "Be devoted to one another in brotherly love; give preference to one another in honor" (Romans 12.10), our gestures often look far more like the former than the latter.

Do the important people in your life know you love them? If you are picking one day out of the year to tell them, there's a good chance they don't.

Chase

My dog Max's inability to verbalize interferes with our game-playing. It has ever since we brought him home. But I think I've just about got it figured out. Turns out the game we were playing that I have been calling "Fetch" is actually called "Chase." What I have been interpreting as an obstinate refusal to drop his toy rope has actually been an attempt to teach me how the game works. While chasing him around the living room tonight, I could almost hear him. *"Finally, he's starting to get it! He may not be that dumb after all!"*

I wonder how often God thinks that way about us. We're down here on earth, playing our version of the game, thinking we are having some sort of bonding experience with the Almighty—a bonding experience that would work better if only He would hold up His end of the bargain. And up in heaven God is just shaking His head, amazed at the energy we are willing to expend to play our game, not realizing His game is entirely different.

As difficult as it may be to accept, God's goals for us may not be the same as (and may in fact be completely incompatible with) our goals for ourselves. Claiming God is in the game with us does not make it so. Over the years we have tried to get Him to play Charity (John 6.26), Fairness (Luke 12.13), Revolt (John 18.36), and many other popular earth games. All the while, He has been trying to teach us Salvation (Luke 19.10). The sooner we realize that, the sooner we can start learning the rules, the sooner we can learn how to win.

Word for Word

Disclosure

In markets of old, pork was sold "on the hoof" in bags. An unsuspecting shopper might simply trust the integrity of the tradesman and buy a pig without taking a peek at it first. Later, the shopper might find that the tradesman had simply bagged up an alley cat instead of a pig. The secret would be revealed, much to the dismay of the shopper. And if the cat were still alive, it would be a very unpleasant revelation. Thus we learn the hazards of "letting the cat out of the bag," as well as "buying a pig in a poke."

"Full disclosure" is a tricky concept in evangelism. We don't want to scare or discourage someone who appears to have a genuine interest in the things of Christ. But then again, we do them no favors by hiding the less pleasing aspects of service in His kingdom.

How would we respond if someone came to us out of the blue and said they were ready to give up everything and follow the Lord? Jesus Himself said, in so many words, "Don't talk too fast; that's just exactly what you may need to do" (Luke 9.57-58). When the "rich young ruler" showed interest, Jesus scared him off by giving him a condition few people would have expected him to even consider (Matthew 19.21).

I'm not suggesting we bombard new and potential converts with horror stories. But we do them no favors by ignoring the price they will be expected to pay. Counting the cost of discipleship (Luke 14.28) requires knowing the cost is there. Lies and implicit lies will eventually do more harm than good in the spread of the gospel.

Agendas

Hollywood really annoys me sometimes. I just spent 90 minutes watching a film with my children that was promoted as wholesome family entertainment, but which was in truth a thinly disguised combination of (1) an attack on the United States military, and (2) propaganda for the radical environmentalist movement. Now, if those positions sound like bumper stickers on your own car, that's fine. I mean no disrespect. But I have to wonder about the credibility of a cause that has to sneak its message in edgewise to an audience of unsuspecting teenagers.

Everyone has an agenda. I get that. And far be it from Hollywood to be an exception to the rule. But there's something nefarious about hidden agendas. The message itself may be a good one, but I get suspicious when ideology is promoted under the guise of entertainment.

But then, I could say the same thing about many Christians in their attempts to spread the borders of Christ's kingdom. Paul said of his readers, "He called you through our gospel" (2 Thessalonians 2.14). But apparently God has gotten hoarse over the years. His call, we are told, isn't effective anymore. And so they call with basketball, and ski trips, and world record attempts, and pretty much everything else imaginable—thinking, once the crowd is assembled, they can "bait and switch" them.

Paul wasn't ashamed of the gospel (Romans 1.16). I have to wonder why some Christians act as though they are. God has always been able to reach the hearts of truth-seekers. And He has never needed our "help" to do so.

Word for Word

Free

I have heard my entire life that there are no free lunches. But once a year or so, a prominent restaurant chain offers a free breakfast. I thought about taking them up on it this last time but decided against it. One reason is that I'd have to drive an hour or so both ways to get to one of the restaurants. (Gas, unfortunately, isn't free.) Another reason is that the breakfast they were giving away has roughly the same amount of saturated fat as my wife allows me for the entire week.

So I guess there are no free breakfasts either. Whether in the form of fuel costs, new pants or marriage counseling, there will be a bill to pay somewhere.

Freedom comes at a cost, if that's not too oxymoronic. We must behave responsibly in a "free society" if we are survive as such. We understand the guarantees of "life, liberty, and the pursuit of happiness" are perfectly compatible with law—in fact, law protects those freedoms.

The same concept applies in regard to our freedom in Christ (Galatians 5.1). Being "free from the law of sin and of death" does not mean Christians have no moral or spiritual obligations. That is why the gospel is called "the law of Christ" (Galatians 6.2, 1 Corinthians 9.21, etc.). It's why Jesus emphasized law-keeping so strongly (Matthew 5.19-20, 19.17, etc.). Law-keeping is mandatory, even for freemen.

Jesus offers freedom from debt, not obligation. We are free to become what He wants us to be—what we want for ourselves. But we can only achieve it by living our lives under "the law of liberty" (James 2.12).

White

Every year I go sneaker shopping. Every year I get white ones. Every year I try to talk myself out of it. Every year I fail. I think a big part of it is the feeling of amazement when I get something that is truly white in exchange for something that once was white, something I've been calling white, but clearly is white no longer.

It reminds me of Isaiah 1.18—"Though your sins are as scarlet, they will be as white as snow; though they are red like crimson, they will be like wool." Sin is a deep, permanent stain on our souls. No bleach, no scrub brush, no dye job can remove it. That is why I get frustrated at those who claim "dear old grandma" must be saved in heaven because of all the wonderful things she did. We're saved by grace, not works (Ephesians 2.8). Our actions don't get us to heaven. Our actions get us to hell.

The only thing we can hope for is a straight exchange—our life for His (Matthew 16.25). If we give up our vain attempts to be "good enough" and embrace His salvation, He will wash us truly clean (Acts 22.16). Some people have recovered from unbelievably sinful lives, only to hear, "but you were washed, but you were sanctified, but you were justified in the name of the Lord Jesus Christ and in the Spirit of our God" (1 Corinthians 6.11).

But no white is white forever. Thankfully, our new lives will whiten again when we return to the Lord, no matter how much mud we stomp through. If we ask, He will "cleanse us from all unrighteousness" (1 John 1.9) yet again. And again. And again.

Word for Word

Biathlon

I've long held that the Olympics ought to return to its roots and be merely a demonstration of athletic prowess, not excellence in a sport. Running, jumping, throwing—these disciplines exalt athletes as fit to protect themselves and serve others in real-life situations. Plenty of other disciplines are pretty useless. Admit it—if you were in a pickle, you'd much rather have an archer with you than a synchronized diver.

That's why I have an appreciation for the biathlon. I admit it's more exciting to watch snowboarding, or bobsledding, or even figure skating. (Ladies only, please. Male figure skating would be illegal if I had my way. Don't make me explain.) But skiing cross-country over a great distance and then hitting a target with a rifle—that's something that could actually be useful.

I think that we often lose sight of the practical motivations behind some of our behaviors, particularly in the cause of Christ. We send our little children to Bible classes, for instance, with the intent (ostensibly) of getting them to love God's word and meditate upon it constantly (Psalm 119.97). But once we get them there, what do we actually teach them? Coloring inside the lines? Cutting and pasting? These are entertaining lessons for toddlers, certainly, but they are hardly instructive in the ways of the Lord.

If "Bible Hangman" and similar activities can be used to emphasize Bible lessons, I'm all for it. But if we are to have them compete and excel in God's games (1 Corinthians 9.24-27), they are going to require real training in God's word. And that means real Bible study.

Results

Statistically, the worst preacher in the history of the world would have to be Noah. After 120 years in the pulpit, all he had to show for his efforts was a giant boat in his backyard and eight willing passengers—himself, his three sons, and their wives. I cannot imagine how discouraging his efforts must have been.

But then, through those efforts the entire world was repopulated. Without Noah, there would have been no Abraham, no Moses, no Elijah, no Paul. His ministry must have seemed to him at the time to be a colossal failure—seven conversions, all family, in a world some believe may have been populated with as many as a billion people.

But percentages and short-term results have never meant as much to God as they have to us. He looks at the big picture—the long-term good that Noah's work would accomplish. And He also sees the small picture—the significance of a single soul in an incalculable crowd.

For my entire preaching career, I have stated that I will consider my life's work a success if I manage to help four particular souls get to heaven. Anything I achieve beyond that is gravy. That mission keeps me from obsessing about numbers, which may be misleading in the short term and/or irrelevant in the long term. I think that's what Paul meant in 1 Corinthians 1.17—"For Christ did not send me to baptize, but to preach the gospel." I would love to see more conversions come from my work. But it's not a numbers game. Success is in the work, not the results.

Word for Word

Chameleons

In Woody Allen's film *Zeleg*, the title character (played by Allen himself) literally transforms himself to become more like the people around him. He is "the human chameleon." He changes not only aspects like accent, language, philosophy and occupation, but even his physical characteristics. He changes skin color, grows facial hair, gets taller, gains a hundred pounds—all literally right before his neighbors' very eyes. He is not even aware of the changes; the entire process is governed by his subconscious.

It's not the most subtle point in the history of American cinema, but a valid one nevertheless: People will do anything to fit in. We all have an intense desire to be accepted, to be liked. And we know that people will tend to like people who are similar to them. So without even realizing it, we alter our speech, our clothing, our preferences, and anything else that isn't genetically forced upon us. We are chameleons, eager to blend into our surroundings, even at the cost of our own identities.

The problem is, most of the people around us, including most of the strong personalities, do not care much for God or the Bible. They may do lip service to spiritual things, but ultimately they will do what they want to do. And they want us to join in. They may very well ask, beg, bribe, cajole or force us to do so.

It is against our natural urges to "come out from their midst and be separate" (2 Corinthians 6.17). But we must find a way. If we must "blend in," let's blend in with a group of people who are going to heaven.

Pets

I blew the mind of a brother in Christ recently. We were discussing heaven (one of my favorite topics) and the rather carnal picture that many have of it. I mentioned that some have asked me about whether their pet will be in heaven with them, implying (or just stating outright) that it wouldn't be "heaven" otherwise. I said my stock response in such situations is this: "If heaven wouldn't be perfect for you without your pet there, I'm sure God will figure out a way to make it happen."

I say that for a couple of reasons. One, it's a good way of describing heaven to someone who may not have a deep understanding of the Bible—unspeakably glorious, and I do mean "unspeakably" (2 Corinthians 12.1-4), for everyone there, including pet owners. To be perfectly honest, I *very* strongly suspect that complete, eternal fellowship with the Father, Son and Spirit, as well as the saved of all ages, will be so great a reward that we won't be thinking about Rover, or golf, or fishing, or whatever your personal earthly passion may be. But if God wants to reunite me and "Hal's Best Friend," who am I to argue?

Two, it gets me out of a conversation I don't want to have. If you want to discuss the Biblical depiction of heaven and what God requires of those who want to go there, I'm all yours. But if you just want to speculate endlessly about details beyond our comprehension, I have better things to do. It's enough for me to know I have a place prepared (John 14.3) if I live in faith. So I'll content myself with just "hastening the coming of the day" (2 Peter 3.12) and leave it to God to sort out the details.

Word for Word

Vests

Winter months in Texas means it's time for me to break out my sweater vests. The fashionistas in my house don't care much for the trend I'm trying to start, but I'm still holding out hope that I can retain a bit of control in areas of judgment in my house—at least where it directly affects only me. If I can't pick my own art or linens or cutlery, at least I can pick my own clothes. Mostly.

I like vests because they're good middle ground between short sleeves (not warm enough) and sweaters (too bulky). I can be comfortable inside the house at 68 degrees or outside walking the dog at 40 degrees.

Vests work because the body is warm when the core is warm. Insulate your internal organs, and the heart will be able to supply enough 98.6-degree blood to the rest of the body to keep it from freezing. You heat yourself from the inside out.

I think sometimes we would do well to think of our service to Jesus as being an inside-out proposition. I'm not suggesting that externals are unimportant. We need to make sure we live "worthy of the gospel of Christ" (Philippians 1.27). But like Jesus explained to Peter in Matthew 15.19, sins in the body originate with sins in the heart. A heart devoted to God will govern the body's actions in a way that will give Him glory.

Ultimately, sinful behavior isn't the problem, but rather the symptom. If we can sing with David, "Unite my heart to fear Your name" (Psalm 86.11), we will find that our sinful behavior will start taking care of itself.

Triumph

Ancient conquerors would march with their armies into their home cities in a parade called a "triumph." Great archways built for such occasions still stand all over Europe. In the triumph, the conqueror would display the booty he had claimed in battle, strange animals from the distant lands, and enslaved foreigners who had unsuccessfully waged war against him. For some, the triumph was simply an exercise in self-glorification. But for others, like the Romans, it was a celebration of their culture. They genuinely believed their victory was for the greater good—even, ultimately, the good of those who were enslaved.

Reading 2 Corinthians 2.14, I thought of God's successful war with Satan over our souls—"But thanks be to God, who always leads us in triumph in Christ, and manifests through us the sweet aroma of the knowledge of Him in every place." He has taken us prisoner to serve Him in Jesus, as the Psalmist prophesied—"You have ascended on high, You have led captive Your captives" (Psalm 68.18). Our submission to Him is testimony to the transformational power of the gospel. The fiercest warriors in Satan's army eventually learn they must yield or perish. Even Saul, Jesus' staunchest enemy, finally gave up the fight after years of kicking against the goads (Acts 26.14) and became His slave (Romans 1.1).

It is our privilege to walk behind our Lord and Master in His triumph. But as we exult in the improvement of our state, let us not for a moment think that the parade is in our honor. The honor is His and His alone.

Word for Word

Gold

Have you noticed that everyone and his brother are trying to convince you to buy gold these days? That's because gold is seen as the ultimate safe bet for investors. Unlike stocks, bonds and baseball cards, gold has intrinsic value. And when uncertainty reigns in the financial world, people want something more secure. That's why gold goes up in value when everything else goes down.

Ironically, in times of genuine disaster (nuclear strike, month-long power outage, Hurricane Katrina, etc.), gold is about the most worthless thing you can have. You can't eat it. You can't drink it. You can't fuel your car with it. With nothing to buy, gold is just a paperweight.

And such is the case, ultimately, with anything of physical value. No matter how safe financial "securities" may make us feel, they can and will betray us when we need them most—if not in life, then certainly in death. There's a reason why they don't put trailer hitches and luggage racks on hearses.

That's why Jesus says, "store up for yourselves treasures in heaven, where neither moth nor rust destroys, and where thieves do not break in or steal; for where your treasure is, there will your heart be also" (Matthew 6.20-21). He wants you to invest in your souls—a truly secure investment. Then, no matter what happens in this life, good or bad, you have the only real "security" there is. And you will find that the more treasure you put in heaven, the more dear heaven grows in your heart, and the more you look forward to collecting on your investment.

Cool

Tracie and I are determined to be "the cool parents." You know the type. The ones who connect with the younger generation. The ones with the house where our girls' friends want to hang out. The ones who serve as chaperones on class field trips and are actually greeted with enthusiasm. *Yea! We get to ride on the Hammons bus!*

But we're learning that what constitutes "cool" for a 10-year-old may be the very thing that brands us as "uncool" with a 14-year-old. I can bring lunch to Kylie at school and she will practically sit on my lap while we eat it together. If I show up at Taylor's school, it had better be in disguise.

One reaction might be more appreciated than the other, but both are valid. No amount of cajoling, threatening and bribery will get Taylor to change her perception of my behavior. Ultimately, if I want to be "cool" in her world, I will have to do the changing.

Plenty of Christians could take a lesson from this in regard to their approach to God. They want God to accept them, and they will knock themselves out trying to make it so. And they will assume that, since they are making the attempt, God will (or at least, should) acknowledge and reward them. But it doesn't work that way. "He has mercy on whom He desires" (Romans 9.18). And effort spent convincing God of our worthiness is effort wasted.

"He has told you, O man, what is good" (Micah 6.8). You can either listen to Him and be approved, or follow your instincts and reap the consequences. Your choice.

Peaches

They call them "cling peaches" for a reason. A peach doesn't want to let go of its pit. You have to pry it out. And when you do so, the pit leaves an indelible impression in the flesh of the peach. Nothing but that particular pit will fit that particular indentation. And if the peach-eater were so inclined, he could put the pit back and it would nestle into place as though it had never left.

That is the kind of impression Jesus is supposed to be leaving in our lives and hearts. As Christians, we derive our life, our mission, our very name from Him. Serving Jesus creates a void in our hearts that He alone can fill. Of course, the void was there long before we knew the Lord—even long before we realized there was a void. But the more we cling to Him, the more we realize how much we need to cling to Him.

Paul writes, "Abhor what is evil; cling to what is good" (Romans 12.9). And what could possibly be more "good" than Jesus, who is good incarnate (Matthew 19.17)? It is as though we have been pieces in a jigsaw puzzle, frantically looking everywhere for a place to fit in. And once we find Jesus, and we realize how perfectly He suits our needs and desires, we want nothing more than to make a place for Him in our lives.

I love Psalm 63:8—"My soul clings to You; Your right hand upholds me." The reason I can have such confidence in Jesus' care over me is that I am making a concentrated effort to hold onto Him. The tighter I cling, the more secure I feel.

Mondays

I love Mondays!

Maybe it's just me. Okay, probably it's just me. But Monday is becoming one of my favorite days of the week. Let me explain.

I work hard over the weekend. My mind is fully occupied with typical Sunday business. And so when I get the urge to write on a Friday night or Saturday afternoon, I usually wind up staring at a blank screen. It's like I'll never get another idea again.

And then comes Monday and my volunteer time at Kylie's school. I start a project on the copier, and then I let my Bible fall open randomly. *"Let's see what God's word has for me today."* Almost immediately, I grab my pen. The ideas come fast and furious. I find my batteries recharged, my mind refreshed, my spirit awakened.

If you dislike Mondays because it signals a return to the work week, try thinking of Jesus as your Boss and His service as your job. Sunday should be the highlight of the week for Christians. (If it isn't, I would suggest you revisit your priorities.) But instead of looking at Monday as a hangover from being "filled with the Spirit" (Ephesians 5.18-19), try looking at it as the beginning of another opportunity to work His works (John 9.4).

If you need a boost, try reading Psalm 119.25 first thing every Monday morning—"My soul cleaves to the dust; revive me according to Your word." Then pray, flip to a random passage, and listen to what God has said. Before long, you will find that the Bible is the best cure for the Mondays ever concocted. Try it. You'll see.

Word for Word

Chance

The weathermen gave us a slight chance for snow today. I weighed the pros and cons and finally decided to tell my daughters. They, of course, freaked. They immediately asked if we would be taking them out of school early. (Yes, my northern friends, we do that in south Texas. Snow is like Bigfoot—at the first sighting, everyone scrambles for their camera phone.)

I tried to impress upon the girls that it was only a slight chance, and that it would likely be mixed with rain if it came at all, and that even if we did get legitimate flakes we almost certainly wouldn't get enough for a decent snowball in the entire county. Did that quash their little dreams? I doubt it. And as I sit in the nasty, wet, completely snow-free parking lot waiting to pick them up at the usual time, I am mentally preparing for the looks of disappointment that will surely be clouding their faces.

Unreal expectations are killers. We get our hearts set on something, and we wind up being disappointed. Worse, we become a little more jaded, less inclined to get excited about a "chance" for exhilaration the next time. We don't want to get our hearts broken again.

That is the wonderful thing about heaven. It isn't a fantasy. It is real. It cannot possibly disappoint. It is a city prepared and reserved for God's faithful (Hebrews 11.13-16; 1 Peter 1.3-5). And you have a chance to go there. Not a Publishers Clearinghouse Sweepstakes chance—a real chance. Do not let past disappointments keep you from taking a chance on Jesus Christ.

Garage

When I was growing up, we parked the car (and yes, for most of my childhood we had only one) in our garage. Even today, I hear people refer to a "two-car garage" or a "two-and-a-half-car garage." I haven't figured out exactly how that last one works, but it's pretty clear that garages and cars are supposed to go together.

Not at Hacienda Hammons. We have too much "stuff." (I know, it's pretty pathetic what we can complain about, isn't it?) So most things that we don't use regularly, and plenty of other things we do, get stowed in the garage. We've actually moved from one house to another and found boxes that we never unpacked from our previous move. There's no telling what we'll find in there once we get in there and start looking.

It reminds me of the short parable Jesus gives His disciples in Matthew 13.52. When He gave them the parables of the sower and the tares, they came to Him for explanations and He was happy to give them. They showed an eagerness to not only listen to the Lord, but also to put His teachings to work in their lives. To such ones He said, "Therefore every scribe who has become a disciple of the kingdom of heaven is like a head of a household, who brings forth out of his treasure things new and old."

The Bible is a treasure trove, waiting to be opened and looted. And no matter how experienced or inexperienced you are, something is in there, waiting to bless your life—something you may have forgotten even existed. It's all for you. But first you have to open the door.

Word for Word

Sunglasses

The sun is big. Really big. And despite being 93 million miles away (literally), it can, on a sunny day, be a bit too much for human eyes. So, many of us choose to wear sunglasses. Sunglasses reduce the amount of light that actually reaches our eyes, taking away the glare and discomfort, and even damage, that can come from looking at a sunny sky without protection. Plus, they look cool.

They serve much the same purpose as the law of Moses did in Old Testament times. In 2 Corinthians 3.12-18 Paul compares our knowledge of Jesus with theirs, saying Israel of old could not possibly see the full glory of Jesus. He was too glorious to comprehend. They were forced to view Him through the veil of the law. And he comments on the tragedy of the Jews' insistence upon maintaining the law as their guide, effectively keeping themselves from knowing Jesus fully. It would be like wearing sunglasses when you didn't need to—pointless, and potentially dangerous.

It is our privilege to bask in the full, unfiltered sunlight of Jesus Christ. We are not forced to speculate about what He would be like, or what He would expect of us. We can "attain to the unity of the faith, and of the knowledge of the Son of God" (Ephesians 4.13). Tragically, many choose to keep on imagining. They would rather speculate about His will than open God's word and have it light their path (Psalm 119.105). It is as if they are wearing sunglasses when they don't need to. Pointless, and potentially—no, *really* and *extremely*—dangerous.

Impatience

I am not a terribly patient person. If things should get done, I expect them to be done right away. Why not, after all? What's the delay? And when they don't get done, I get annoyed.

This trait has been a problem with me ever since I started preaching. I like my sermons to be practical—"putting a handle on the gospel," I sometimes call it. And so if I see an issue that needs addressing in the church, I'll address it. I like to think I do it in love, and I certainly make sure it is the gospel of Christ (not the gospel of Hammons) to which I am appealing. And then I leave it to the listeners to make the application.

But they don't do that. Not right away, anyway. Grrr.

Sometimes people will thank me, tell me, "I needed that!" and tell me they are going to change. But I don't see it. Double grrr. I start questioning their commitment to change, their work ethic, even their honesty. After all, if they really wanted to change, they would change, right?

However, my impatience only flows in one direction. I frequently put off all sorts of self-improvement projects. And yet I consider myself committed to change. I'm working hard. I'm honest. And I pray for God to be patient with me. Not exactly the model of consistency, huh?

Love demands that I be patient with others—it "covers a multitude of sins" (James 5.20). God loved, and loves, me enough to bear with me in my failings. It's reasonable that He expect me to do the same. Yes, they need to "bear fruit in keeping with repentance" (Matthew 3.8). So do I. With God's help, we'll get there.

Curling

I caught a few minutes this week of Olympic curling—a sport (?) just goofy enough to grab my attention. I think I could understand it if I spent some time watching it (I don't think I get The Curling Channel on my TV, though), researching it (maybe write a report—"Great Curlers of the 20th Century: Their Tactics and Strategies"), perhaps even visiting the Curling Hall of Fame in Neverheardofit, Nova Scotia.

But here's the problem. I just don't care that much.

If I cared, I would put forth an effort. I would not be satisfied with just taking a half-interested peek once every four years. I would not be deterred by widespread indifference, historic apathy or multitudes of jokes at my expense. If I cared, I would work through all of that. And my resolve would only get stronger as I met with strange looks and derogatory comments at every turn.

But, again, I just don't care that much.

Behavior follows commitment, whether in sports or in Jesus. Claims of interest can be quickly debunked by a near absence of effort from the "interested" party.

It's easy to claim, like Jesus' would-be disciple in Luke 9.57, that we will follow Him. We can even convince ourselves we are doing so. But for some, pursuit of Him consists of the occasional trip to the church house, maybe saying the Lord's Prayer when they want something. When Jesus said of a prospective disciple, "let him deny himself, and take up his cross, and follow Me" (Matthew 16.24), He was requiring more than just lip service. Carrying a cross requires effort. Lots of effort.

Opportunity

If you were in line to compete in the Olympic Games, would you keep your cell phone turned on?

Not if you are Germany's Patrick Beckert. No point. After all, Beckert was just the fourth alternate in the 10,000-meter speed skating event. Not the first. The fourth. What would be the likelihood of someone backing out of his chance to compete, and then having three other competitors unavailable to fill his slot? One in a million? Less?

Well, it happened in Vancouver in 2010. And I'm sure that every excuse and rationalization in Beckert's mind is falling somewhat flat today. Bottom line, he could have competed in the Olympics. He could have gone for the gold. And he didn't have his phone on.

We never know when opportunities for greatness will come. Esther didn't expect to one day have a chance to save her people. Nor did Gideon. Or Jephthah. But the day came for each of them. And in that day, the character they had been building over a lifetime was revealed.

Greatness is not scheduled. Greatness is achieved in brief moments of time. Split-second decisions (the good ones, anyway) are not made randomly. They are made out of instincts that have been carefully honed over years in preparation for the opportunity.

What would happen if your phone call from God came today? What if today you had an opportunity for greatness? Would you be ready to answer the call? Listen to the Lord—"Be on the alert then, for you do not know the day nor the hour" (Matthew 25.13).

Word for Word

Squirrels

I don't know exactly what miniature schnauzers were originally bred to do, but clearly it wasn't chasing squirrels. Max has many wonderful attributes, but a hunting instinct is not one of them.

I'll give you an example. Just today, Max and I saw a squirrel in our yard. Well, let me rephrase that: *I* saw a squirrel in our yard. Max was oblivious. So I tried to lead him toward the squirrel. He still couldn't see it. He only clued in when the squirrel dashed around a tree to get away from us. Max quickly ran after him around the tree, where (from Max's perspective) the squirrel had vanished into another dimension. He looked left. He looked right. He turned around in a circle. He never thought to look up.

It's probably not his fault. He very well may never have seen a squirrel climb a tree. And certainly climbing a tree is way outside of Max's own experience. He just naturally assumed his quarry could be found on earth because he didn't know there was another option.

Humans are different. We are "without excuse" when we refuse to look up toward heaven (Romans 1.20). And yet so often we stubbornly insist on remaining earthbound in our thoughts. God wants us to look up for help (Psalm 121.1-2), for guidance (Psalm 119.105), for purpose (Ecclesiastes 12.13), indeed, for everything. But we are not trained to think that way by living in this world.

Paul writes, "Set your mind on the things above, not on the things that are on the earth" (Colossians 3.2). The more we think about God, the easier it will be to see Him as the answer to our questions, the means to our best end.

Hockey

Growing up in central Texas, I never had much opportunity to acquire a taste for ice hockey. I rarely saw a piece of ice that wouldn't fit in a tea glass. And I still don't follow it too much. But I will say this about hockey—it's tough to watch it casually. If you miss a couple of baskets in a basketball game, more will follow soon. Big gaps in the action allow you to flip between a baseball game and a football game and not miss much of either.

But with hockey, you have to stay focused. Action is constant. You don't generally see a situation develop and think, "Okay, now things could get interesting." Scoring opportunities are created almost instantaneously; if you're not paying attention at just the right moment, you miss the moment you've been waiting for. Not a good sport for napping. That's a big reason my interest in hockey tends to be extinguished along with the Olympic flame.

You can give the devil half your attention and be a first-rate sinner. But as with hockey, Christianity requires our full attention. Paul advises, "it is already the hour for you to awaken from sleep; for now salvation is nearer to us than when we believed" (Romans 13.11). As we grow in faith, and get closer to glory, we appreciate more and more how vital it is to pay attention. Lack of focus at exactly the wrong time can mean missing a chance for teaching or service that may never come again. The time for rest will come soon enough. "Therefore, let us fear if, while a promise remains of entering His rest, any one of you may seem to have come short of it" (Hebrews 4.1).

Laundry

First, sort the clothes according to color. Then put one pile in the washer, soap 'em up, and turn on the water. Dry them. Fold them. Put them away. Five steps. It's called "laundry."

Now here's what I want from you, my readers. I want five volunteers for each of my daughters, ten total. Each one is responsible for teaching one of these tasks to one of my daughters. Perhaps the ten of you can succeed where their two parents, as yet, have not.

It appears the girls have gotten the impression they can do any combination of these tasks, and the ones left unaccomplished will be taken care of by laundry elves. And if you wonder how they could have gotten that impression, I'm afraid Tracie and I must plead guilty.

It's not necessarily a problem when parents cover for their children's failings. That's what parents do. But children should never be allowed to develop the impression that their personal development is unnecessary. Yes, parents forgive. Yes, parents extend grace. And yes, parents expect their children to get better.

As recipients of grace ourselves, we should never grow impatient with others—even our children. But we do them no favors by continuing to cover for them as they wallow in mediocrity. In the same way, God is pleased to save us by grace (Acts 15.11). But grace is not license. He expects us to "grow in the grace and knowledge of our Lord and Savior Jesus Christ" (2 Peter 3.18). And if we fail to "press on to maturity" (Hebrews 6.1), we have no one to blame but ourselves.

Signals

Fourteen years ago I was run over by an eighteen-wheeler.

How's that for an attention-grabber?

It's true. I was driving home late one night, alone (thankfully), when a truck turned left directly in front of me. At 50 miles per hour, there was no way I could stop in time. My car wedged underneath the truck's fuel tank (not his wheels, thank God). I was dragged about a hundred feet before it finally stopped. The car, of course, was totaled. Even scarier, my infant daughter's empty car seat was covered in automobile glass.

So you'll excuse me if I make a point of distinguishing between hazard lights and a turn signal. Two blinking red lights on a truck veering to the left means he's pulling off onto the left shoulder—*not* that he is sweeping wide to his left to make a sharp right turn. You need a right turn signal to convey that particular message.

Hopefully the truck driver learned a lesson from that particular incident. I know I did, and it is this: The signals you are getting from someone may not be the signal he thinks he is sending. And even if you can assign 100 percent of the blame to the other party, you may still have to deal with consequences that might have been avoided if you had been a bit more circumspect.

Paul tells Titus to be "sound in speech which is beyond reproach" (Titus 2.8). It should be enough to say the right thing with the right attitude. But realistically, that is often not enough. We need to be considering how our message will be received, not just how we are sending it.

Jeans

Should teachers wear jeans? I asked myself that question as I realized the "student" in front of the junior high was not a student after all. I finally decided it was an authority issue, not a fashion issue. What do I mean by that? Glad you asked.

Teachers are in charge. And they must be seen to be in charge. They get the big desk. They get to be called Ms. X or Mr. Y. They talk when they want to talk, and they require others to listen. If they blend in with their students, the students will intuitively try to treat them like peers instead of authorities. And that's a problem.

Young children's teachers avoid this just by being tall. Finding the teacher in a fifth-grade class is no great feat, regardless of what she's wearing. But in junior high, the kids start looking more like grownups. And right about the same time, they start thinking they are smarter than grownups. Trust me on this one. I know whereof I speak.

Being the children's "buddy"—wearing their clothes, discussing their music, using their slang—bridges the gap between the generations. And that's not a good thing. That's a bad thing. It's an abrogation of responsibility.

Children learn authority from teachers, preachers, and especially parents. Then they are in position to submit to God when the time comes. That's why in Titus 2, the older generation is tasked with teaching the younger. Verse 15 reads, "These things speak and exhort and reprove with all authority. Let no one disregard you."

If you have charge over children, don't be a friend. Be a grownup.

Today

Every day I drive past a butcher shop with a posted special—"Today Only!" At the time of this writing, we have been passing that butcher shop for about fifteen months. The sign has been up every single day during that time. I'd cry "False advertising!" but then, I'm not sure what would be gained by that, except for maybe getting them to cancel the special. And where's the benefit in that?

And as far as that goes, it's not false advertising. Every day the sign has been up has been "Today." And that will continue to be the case no matter how long it stays up. And the store manager would be perfectly within his rights to take the sign down and cancel the special whenever he wants. The special is for "today," not necessarily for "tomorrow."

Jesus offers a "special" on salvation today, and today only. "Behold, now is 'the acceptable time,' behold, now is 'the day of salvation'" (2 Corinthians 6.2). The Spirit says, "Today if you hear His voice, do not harden your hearts as when they provoked Me, as in the day of trial in the wilderness" (Hebrews 3.7-8). Today, and today only, He offers you a chance to "work out your salvation with fear and trembling" (Philippians 2.12). Today, and today only, He offers you a chance to edify and be edified by like-minded souls devoted to His cause. He says, "encourage one another day after day, as long as it is still called 'Today'" (Hebrews 3.13). There is no "someday." There is no "tomorrow." There is only today.

Accept His invitation. Today.

Word for Word

Stiff

Don't you just hate waking up with a crick in your neck? It's like the day is making a bad first impression. Maybe it doesn't feel so bad if you keep your head straight. But almost any movement from side to side is uncomfortable.

What do you do? Well, most of us intentionally inflict minor pain upon ourselves in an effort to get more freedom of motion in our necks. Working through the stiffness is unpleasant at first, but it doesn't take long before you get results. And the renewed flexibility is more than worth the temporary discomfort.

Of course, you could just stay stiff. You could convince yourself that anything worth looking at is right in front of you, and that other people should move to accommodate your condition. But most of us realize that attitude is silly, selfish, and potentially self-destructive.

And yet people persist in their "stiff-necked" approach to life. Stubborn refusal to accept the flaws in their view of the world doomed Israel of old; Hezekiah warned them, "Now do not stiffen your neck like your fathers, but yield to the Lord and enter His sanctuary which He has consecrated forever, and serve the Lord your God, that His burning anger may turn away from you" (2 Chronicles 30.8). Yet the attitude grew worse. It moved the Jews to crucify Jesus, and eventually stone Stephen (Acts 7.51).

Stubbornly clinging to our perspective will hurt us in the end far more than bending our necks to His will. "Let God be found true, though every man be found a liar" (Romans 3.4)—even if that "liar" is me.

Drops

We saw a program on The Food Network the other day (honestly, I think I put on half a pound every time I watch that channel) where the host actually made "liquid smoke." You know, the dark liquid in the little bottle that makes your meat taste like it was cooked all day over hardwood. Amazing stuff. Anyway, if you think I'm going to spend a hundred dollars in equipment and wood, not to mention hours of hard labor, to save 79 cents, you obviously don't know me at all. Hi. Hal Hammons. Cheapskate and lazy bum. Good to meet you.

But if somehow I were convinced to go through this procedure, you'd better believe I'd gather and store every drop my work managed to produce. It would be like liquid gold. And no doubt, I'd immediately jump on the computer and write an article to tell all you fine folks about my struggle and ultimate triumph.

I thought of that today while reading Psalm 56.8—"You have taken account of my wanderings; put my tears in your bottle, are they not in Your book?" God is intimately aware of every drop of tears that falls from our eyes because of unfairness and pain, every drop of sweat we shed in His service. He bottles every one. And He records them in His book. And one day He will judge us by what is written, for good or ill (Revelation 20.12).

Nothing is wasted that is spent in His cause. Every drop of toil, pain and sacrifice go toward our heavenly account. And by faith we patiently wait for the day when we get to enjoy the final fruits of our labors.

Word for Word

Alarms

There are two kinds of alarms: the kind you set, and the kind you don't set. You set an alarm clock; you know what time your daily routine begins, and you know how much time you will need to get ready. Simple subtraction. You don't set a burglar alarm; you want it to go off automatically under certain conditions, which could arise at any time.

Trying to put a timer on a burglar alarm is folly. The burglar could come at any time, including and especially times when you are not prepared for him. If you plan to leave your house unattended, you don't scour newspaper records to determine the hours of the day or night most favored by burglars, and then program your alarm system to arm itself at "the right time." No, you want to be ready at all times. Any rational homeowner would.

Paul and Peter both use this analogy in reference to the return of Jesus Christ. He will come "as a thief," they write (1 Thessalonians 5.2; 2 Peter 3.10). If that means anything, it means that He will come when least expected, catching unawares those who have not made preparation.

And yet we have wave after wave of predictions, allegedly based on the Bible, as to when the time—and even when the exact day and hour—of His coming will be. What kind of burglar does that?

Jesus' point is that we must make ourselves ready at all times. If we had an ETA, we could rationalize loafing until zero hour drew near. As it stands, He wants us to be vigilant always, "for you do not know which day your Lord is coming" (Matthew 24.42).

Burglary

The church building here in Bay City was burglarized over the weekend. And it was pretty weird. Broken glass was on the floor by the window the burglar broke to get in. Cabinets and drawers were open everywhere. He clearly took a look at some relatively expensive equipment. But as far as I can tell, he didn't actually take anything.

We figure he was looking for cash and only cash. Our bank deposit bag was open and lying in the middle of the floor. But for obvious reasons (even more obvious now), we don't keep money in the church building. It seems he dug around a while, looking for our "secret stash," and finally quit. All in all, it could have been much worse.

The tragedy is, of course, we had abundant wealth lying out in plain view all over the place. And he didn't have to resort to burglary; we would have given it to him freely, with smiles on our faces. The word of God is the greatest treasure man has ever been given (Matthew 13.44, 2 Corinthians 4.7, etc.). The psalmist writes in Psalm 119.72, "The law of Your mouth is better to me than thousands of gold and silver pieces." And again in verse 127, "Therefore I love Your commandments above gold, yes, above fine gold."

It all depends on what you value. You can pursue earthly wealth, perhaps illicitly, and "store up your treasure" in a way you will eventually regret (James 5.3). Or you can treasure His word in your heart (Psalm 119.11), and in so doing store up "treasures in heaven" (Matthew 6.20). Not much of a choice, I'd say.

Word for Word

Zucchini

When Taylor was 2 or 3, we would ask her, "What are you afraid of?" She would respond, "Monsters and spiders and zucchini." We never could get a solid answer from her as to why tubular green vegetables would be inherently terrifying. Perhaps she was afraid they would overpower her and force her to eat them. (Come to think of it, that is sort of scary, isn't it?)

That all changed when Tracie found a recipe for zucchini bread. I don't know what role the zucchini plays in the deliciousness process, but I say don't mess with a winning game plan. Taylor is just as averse to eating straight zucchini as ever, but she waters at the mouth at the aroma of zucchini bread. As do we all in Casa Hammons.

Packaging makes all the difference. Put the nutritious food on a plate raw and unseasoned, and they run screaming. But shred it, mix it with other ingredients, bake it up and slice it up, and they will beg for seconds and thirds.

I worry sometimes that we do that with sin. Christians should have an instinctive aversion to evil things. We say, "Get behind me, Satan!" when approached frontally. But if he mixes in some extra ingredients that look appetizing, we start rationalizing. After all, the TV show is really funny. The film is really exciting. The outfit is really trendy. So we take a big bite. And another. And another.

Paul writes, "abstain from every form of evil" (1 Thessalonians 5.22)—not just the forms that look scary. Satan's clever enough to camouflage his monsters. We need to be clever enough to see them anyway.

Spiritual

Have you noticed how the word "religious" has been largely replaced in our lexicon with the word "spiritual"? I think I first noticed it when an avowed atheist in a movie I was watching described herself as a "spiritual person."

As best I can tell, a "spiritual" person is simply a person who acknowledges personal needs beyond the five senses—i.e., a person of character, a moral person. Of course, pretty much everyone except out-and-out sociopaths qualifies under that definition.

It's obvious why the average person in the world would like that more than being "religious." "Religious" implies structure, boundaries, obligations, rules written by someone other than ourselves. Even (gasp!) believing in God. The modern "spiritual" person doesn't worry about such things. He only concerns himself with holding to his own personal code, and then congratulates himself for doing so as well as anyone else does.

But God's idea of "spiritual" is considerably different. A "spiritual blessing" (Ephesians 1.3) is one that pertains to our relationship with God. The same goes for "spiritual songs" (Ephesians 5.19), "spiritual service of worship" (Romans 12.1), and "spiritual sacrifices" (1 Peter 2.5). You cannot have a consideration of spiritual things and leave out the "Father of spirits" (Hebrews 12.9).

The truly spiritual person will seek out the things of God (1 Corinthians 2.14-16). The worldly, "natural" man will not. He thinks truly "spiritual" things are nonsense. Well, we will see about that.

Word for Word

Treasure

Back in the olden days, pirates roamed the seas looking for ships to plunder. And when they were successful in their illegal ventures, often they would find an island in the Caribbean where they could hide their loot from the prying eyes of governments. (That part hasn't changed much.)

Today, treasure hunters work diligently to determine where such pirates may have stored their loot, thinking that the pirates may not have been able to return and recover it. If it sounds like a lazy man's way to a fortune, it absolutely isn't. They spend hundreds of hours in libraries and museums, hundreds more scouring possible treasure trove sites, thousands of dollars spent on equipment and travel—all with the full knowledge that the treasure might not exist at all.

But they gladly do it, because they know that the treasure they could discover would be worth more than they could possibly find any other way. And they truly believe, despite the lack of absolute proof, that the treasure is there, that they will eventually be rewarded.

Solomon characterizes wisdom and knowledge as such treasures. "For if you cry for discernment, lift your voice for understanding; if you seek her as silver and search for her as for hidden treasures; then you will discern the fear of the Lord and discover the knowledge of God" (Proverbs 2.3-5). If we ask for help from the right Source and truly open our ears to the guidance He offers, if we truly value the prize He has hidden, then no amount of effort on our part could possibly be too much.

Language

Ah wahn foah paahbaw. Or something like that, at any rate. That was what the man in front of me at the gas station in Louisiana (or was it Mississippi?) said. Honestly, it sounded like he had a golf ball in his mouth.

And then the checker peeled off four lottery tickets. And the light went on. *I want four Powerballs.* I felt like Napoleon uncovering the Rosetta Stone, or James Spader in *Stargate* when he decoded the alien symbols that opened the passage to another planet. And I mean no disrespect to my friends in Louisiana and Mississippi when I say that.

But seriously, do you ever feel like the people around you speak a different language? Your words "give grace to those who hear" (Ephesians 4.29). You speak truth (Ephesians 4.25). Your words are "seasoned with salt" (Colossians 4.6). And your neighbors' language is salty, all right, but in a completely different way.

It's a return to Babel, where God confused the languages of men (Genesis 11.9). But the root cause wasn't God; it was sin. Mankind was unable to speak the same language because mankind rejected God's language.

Have you ever asked, "Why can't we all just get along?" This is why. We don't speak the same language. Christians speak God's language, and others are either confused, amused or enraged. And vice versa. All we can do is keep praising Him with our tongues, praying that others will follow, and hoping for the day when we won't have to listen to Satan's clamor and vulgarity anymore.

Word for Word

Cannibals

We've all heard horror stories about people trapped in extreme circumstances who are moved to employ extreme measures to stay alive, even to the point of cannibalism. The Bible even describes an instance in 2 Kings 6.24-31, and passages such as Jeremiah 19.9 and Ezekiel 5.10 describe cannibalism as the ultimate sign that a culture has hit absolute rock-bottom.

And we know there have been cultures over the years that have practiced it by choice. (Perhaps they do even today—I haven't been to New Guinea or Melanesia lately.) But you would think that most of us would be too reasonable and compassionate to resort to such behaviors.

But Christians do it. We've always done it. And we don't need extreme situations. A preacher gets a bit too well known? Take a bite. Paul was a popular chew toy in his day (Philippians 1.17). Or maybe a young Christian has trouble adjusting to his new lifestyle? Take a bite. After all, he has to toughen up sometime, right?

I'm not discounting the importance, even the necessity, of "tough love." The Lord chastens the ones He loves (Hebrews 12.7), and we should be no different. But there is a vast difference between necessary discipline and unnecessary brutality. As my dad likes to say, the Lord has the only army in the world that shoots its wounded.

We cannot preserve our fellowship by picking fights with one another. As Paul says in Galatians 5.15, "But if you bite and devour one another, take care that you are not consumed by one another." Good advice.

Weeds

Spring has sprung, and so has the ugly head of yard work. So after mowing the weeds (funny how they start growing so much faster than the grass), I paced back and forth with weed-killer, thinking to myself, "You know, from a distance, a lawn of weeds doesn't look that different from a lawn of grass."

But I trudged on. And as a result, it very well may be that (in two to four weeks, according to the label) I could be looking at a yard with big patches of yellow and brown on a field of green. Or maybe big patches of green on a field of brown and yellow.

Is it worthwhile? Should I knock myself out improving my lawn, and in so doing temporarily (I hope!) make it look worse? Or should I learn to be content with a well-maintained version of the lawn I already have? Fortunately for my marriage, unfortunately for my aching hands and back, I chose the former.

I know lots of "weedy Christians" (read Luke 8.14 for a description) who would love to be stronger in the faith but are just not prepared to do what it takes to make it so. They know their earthly interests (work, school, hobbies, entertainment) are a problem, but they are not ready for the upheaval and chaos that would result from a massive restructuring of their lives. So they settle.

God has no place in His kingdom for mediocrity. He tells us, "Run in such a way that you may win" (1 Corinthians 9.24). Accepting the weeds' victory means you have given up on winning your battle against the devil. And second prize in that race is no prize at all. Literally.

Word for Word

Banner

In the days before cellular phones (or even radios), armies sent messages to their soldiers by banners. The soldier entrusted with carrying the banner had to grip it tightly and hoist it high so everyone could see whether they were to advance or retreat. This became especially important when the battle was going poorly. Any hope of staving off pending defeat depended on the army's ability to act as one. And this could only be accomplished by looking to the banner.

David describes such a situation for the people of God in Psalm 60. Hardship had come upon the people of God; in fact, it was God's will that it be so (v.3). As always, the problem was that they had neglected to follow His instructions—to look to the banner, as it were. In such situations, God gives a banner to the faithful and expects them to lead the way in His cause (v.4-5). *It is not too late to salvage the day,* He is saying. *Even at this late hour, the battle can still be won—if you will heed My directions.* David ends his psalm with confidence in his God and his people; "Through God we shall do valiantly, and it is He who will tread down our adversaries."

God bless you if you are such a banner-bearer. But remember Israel's battle with Amelek in the wilderness. Israel prevailed when Moses' hands were raised. But the credit did not go to Moses, nor to Aaron and Hur for supporting him. Moses named the memorial altar "The Lord is My Banner" (Exodus 17.15). God shows the way, and He gets the glory. We are only privileged to carry His flag, going where He says go, staying where He says stay.

Compromise

My wife's birthday falls right in the middle of March Madness. This was not my idea. I'd write to the NCAA, but I'm confident they will not move the tournament just for her. After all, it would just interfere with some other poor slob's wife who doesn't like basketball.

The only reasonable option is for her to celebrate her birthday on a different day in the years it doesn't fall between Monday and Wednesday. Believe it or not, she would do that. But Taylor and Kylie would pitch a fit.

After seventeen Marches together, we have learned to compromise. Either I go an evening without basketball and hope I don't miss a really good game, or she gets a really, really good present. This year she got concert tickets for her favorite band. Enjoy the show, hon.

Relationships are all about not getting your way and not minding that much. If you want to have your way all the time, buy yourself an island somewhere. If you want to deal with people, you have to learn to compromise. And you do it gladly, because you know the relationship you are building is worth the liberty you are sacrificing.

I think that's a big part of what Paul means in Ephesians 5.21—"and be subject to one another in the fear of Christ." Being Christians gives us a bit of an advantage here; we're already used to elevating Him above ourselves (or at least, we certainly ought to be). Now we need to channel that attitude of selflessness toward our brethren. Our relationship with Jesus is more than worth it; our relationship with our brethren is too.

Word for Word

Underdogs

Tracie can never understand why I get excited watching games in which I have no vested interest. I am not a fan of the athletic programs of Wofford, or Louisiana-Lafayette, or Murray State. But I get all worked up when one of them threatens to knock off a prominent program.

It's the thrill of the underdog. There is something noble, something heroic about defying the odds and achieving greatness, however transitory it might be. Watch *Hoosiers*; if you don't get it then, I can't help you.

The classic underdog tale, of course, is David and Goliath. An untrained youngster shakes his fist in the face of a heavily armed, battle-tested giant, telling him, "This day the Lord will deliver you up into my hands, and I will strike you down and remove your head from you" (1 Samuel 17.46). And he takes into battle only his shepherd's sling and five river stones—which, as it happened, turned out to be four stones too many.

David's story resonates with Christians because we feel like the underdogs ourselves sometimes. We see the forces of evil surrounding us, we see them succeeding at every turn, and we sense fear in the hearts of our brethren in arms. The giant looks powerful beyond belief.

But the truth is, we're not the underdogs. We're not even favorites. For practical purposes, the game is over. We've already won. We've peeked at the end of the book. We know how the game will end. God "gives us the victory through our Lord Jesus Christ" (1 Corinthians 15.57).

We're winners. Let's think and act like winners.

Empty

The letter "E" is a fine letter—the most common one in the English language, in fact. And my dictionary says it can stand as an initial for thousands of words. My wife, on the other hand, insists that the one on our dashboard must stand for "empty." Never mind that it could just as easily stand for, let's say, "extra"—as in, "you have a little *extra* gas left, so feel free to continue down the highway in search of a station that will sell it a penny a gallon cheaper."

Clearly she's wrong. The needle had reached the "E" line, and we still had gas. It has dipped below the "E" line, and we still had gas. She's been in the car when it happened, and she still doesn't believe.

Then again, she's never run out of gas in her life. And I have. Many, many times. So I guess she has a point. And I guess the point is this: A situation doesn't have to be critical to be worthy of attention.

Lots of people want to know what they need to do to go to hell, so they can make sure they come up just short. Like, if it takes ten pounds of sin, they want to weigh in at nine and a half. I try not to look at sin that way. In the first place, God doesn't describe sin in terms of critical mass; He just says, "the wages of sin is death" (Romans 6.23). But more than that, allowing ourselves a "token vice" (or vices) teaches us to tolerate sin, precisely what God cannot do and what He requires us not to do. "Hate evil, you who love the Lord" (Psalm 97.10).

We need to drain the tank. Get rid of "all that remains of wickedness" (James 1.21). Immediately.

Word for Word

Profile

I have a friend online. She's a Christian. She attends worship services. She's a good person in pretty much every way you would define a "good person." She's a joy to be around. I like her.

But her online profile concerns me. She uses nine lines to describe herself. That's not much, but it's enough to tell me who she is. I can identify her best friend, her job, her schooling, her hometown, and some of her favorite activities.

She doesn't mention Jesus at all. Or the Bible, or the church, or anything else that has to do with spiritual things.

That bothers me. I have a tough time understanding how a Christian could describe herself and not mention Christ. After all, Paul said of himself, "to live is Christ" (Philippians 1.21), and of us, "Be imitators of me, just as I also am of Christ" (1 Corinthians 11.1).

How about this profile:

My name is Hal Hammons. I'm a Christian.

My best friend is Jesus Christ.

My job is serving Him. I work 24/7. I love my job.

I study the Bible at His feet. Working on my master's.

My home is heaven. I'm not moving in yet, but I'm making payments on my place there, and I hope to make a permanent move there soon.

I enjoy marveling at God's creation, basking in God's grace, and worshiping with God's people.

That's a profile worth posting—if not online, then at least on my heart, on my sleeve, and on my life.

Itching

I itch. Bad. I think I must have come in contact with some poison ivy when I replanted our garden a week or so ago. (That'll teach me.) I finally broke down and bought some cream, and I think it's starting to feel better. But there for a while, it was just about all I could think about.

That's what itches do. They don't necessarily threaten our lives. They don't endanger our long-term health. They just bug the daylights out of us until it becomes impossible to concentrate on the important issues of life. And giving them the good scratch they're begging for tends to make the problem worse instead of better.

Our lives are full of poison ivy. Personal slights. Name-calling. Rudeness. They may be minor compared to our personal trials of faith and struggles with sin. But they are real. And they are irritating. And they make us want to scratch. But scratching won't make the itch go away. And it may make our own situation far worse. Maybe the itch will cause us to act inappropriately in the short term—losing our temper, speaking unkindly or vulgarly, etc. It may even have long-term effects on our attitude, souring us on the offensive ones in particular and people in general, robbing us of the joy and peace that should come with living in Christ (Philippians 4.4-7).

Paul had a "thorn in the flesh" (2 Corinthians 12.7-9) that caused him no end of consternation. But he knew that the big things going right in his life far outweighed the little things going wrong. If he could put up with his nuisances without scratching them, we can too.

Word for Word

Helpers

My daughters love to help Tracie in the kitchen. Well, let me rephrase that. They love to *participate* with Tracie in the kitchen. Exactly how much "help" they are is a judgment call. They're both getting better, but still, I suspect Tracie could do the job better and quicker without all the "help" she's getting.

I like to think that the help I offer as her husband is an actual blessing to her. That's the whole point, after all. Woman was created as "a helper suitable" for man (Genesis 2.18), and Tracie more than fits that description; it's only fair that I should return the favor. And I don't mean in the kitchen primarily—although I do skin a mean chicken, if I do say so myself.

No, primarily husbands and wives should be helpers in the same way God is our helper—getting us through life's challenges, keeping us focused, showing us the joy life has to offer. He is "a very present help in trouble" (Psalm 46.1); husbands and wives should be as well.

Unfortunately, God is often seen as the source of the trouble instead of the solution. Some people expect His "help" to consist of removing their problems, and oftentimes in His wisdom He doesn't. We treat spouses the same. But generally, accusing a spouse of not being the right kind of "helper" in tough times is not so helpful either.

The psalmist said of God, "You have turned for me my mourning into dancing; You have loosed my sackcloth and girded me with gladness" (Psalm 30.11). May we be called that kind of helper in our marriages.

Litter

I cringed as I watched the little boy throw his napkin on the ground. I mentally applauded his mother as she said, "Don't litter!" Littering is a real pet peeve of mine. But when the boy asked why, the mother said, "It's bad for the environment." She lost me there.

Understand, I'm all in favor of taking care of the planet God has entrusted to us. But one white paper napkin is not going to deplete the ozone layer, poison our drinking water or slaughter native species. There are far better reasons not to litter.

Most obviously, it's ugly. A splash of man-made white on a field of green is just ... *wrong*. It's the blight of man upon God's perfection. But more than that, it's the principle of the thing. Like my camp counselors always told me, "You always leave a place cleaner than you found it." If the area is to look like it should, someone will have to clean it up; who better than the one who trashed it out in the first place?

It's a little thing, to be sure. But Jesus said, "He who is faithful in a very little thing is faithful also in much" (Luke 16.10). Littering shows an attitude of heart. Are we the sort of people who do whatever we like and expect others to fix it or deal with it? Or are we the sort of people who take responsibility for their actions?

Jesus went on to say in that same passage, "And if you have not been faithful in the use of that which is another's, who will give you that which is your own?" (Luke 16.12). I'm not suggesting you have to clean up after yourself to go to heaven. But it couldn't hurt.

Word for Word

Handwriting

I scribble little notes to myself constantly. I've written sermon outlines on napkins, receipts and envelopes. I've used markers, crayons, maybe even an eyebrow pencil once. Whatever's available. If I don't get the idea down quickly, I'll likely forget it. And on the rare occasion I get a good one, I'd like to keep it.

Unfortunately, my handwriting is pretty bad at its best. In situations such as those described above, it's downright atrocious. I've stared at my scrawl for what seemed like hours, trying to make some sense of it. No dice. And trust me, if I can't decipher it, no one can.

God's word is often accused of being like that. Readers often complain that it is too deep, too long, too complicated, too something. Pick one. Impossible to understand, anyway. And how can God hold us to a law that is beyond our capacity?

Well, that line of reasoning won't work with the IRS, and it won't work with God. Yes, God's word can be difficult; Peter even said so by inspiration (2 Peter 3.16). But God's basic expectations of His people have always been straightforward and simple. In consideration of the (ostensibly) ponderous and overly difficult Law of Moses, God asks in Micah 6.8, "what does the Lord require of you but to do justice, to love kindness, and to walk humbly with your God?" That's not too tough, right?

He told the prophet to write so clearly that people could read it while they are running (Habakkuk 2.2). And why not? God wants us to be saved (2 Peter 3.9). Why would He give us the words of salvation in code?

Supper

Today I saw a study of religious art over the years, particularly depictions of the Lord's Supper. Leonardo da Vinci's is the most famous, but there have been many others. The study indicated that the pictures of food have gotten proportionally bigger over the years. The author half-jokingly blamed our culture's obsession with fast food; everything has to be "supersized."

Well, far be it from me to pass on a chance to blame McDonald's for anything. And I don't doubt that our portion sizes are generally bigger today than they were in Jesus' day. But allow me to play amateur psychologist and suggest a deeper implication. I think over the years we have come to expect more and more out of Jesus. The old plate of salvation, if you'll pardon the expression, isn't big enough anymore. Today we expect Jesus to educate our youth, feed the hungry, house the homeless, cure the sick, basically fix every societal ill we may be able to identify.

Just as paintings have taken to depicting a meal comprising whatever the author thinks is appetizing (one even puts pork on the Lord's table—an odd choice for a Jew), so also today people impose upon Jesus their vision of what His mission should be.

Supper with the King means eating what He serves. And as concerned as He was with the plight of man on earth, He focused on getting us ready for heaven, giving us "the food which endures to eternal life" (John 6.27). The church, His body (Colossians 1.18), needs to serve the same meal He served. No more. No less.

Gangs

I recently asked the church teenagers why so many of their school-mates join gangs. They confirmed the reasons I had in my own mind: profit from criminal activity, and camaraderie with peers.

I did not know this from personal experience (thankfully). I knew it because that was why teenagers joined gangs in Solomon's day. You don't believe me? Read Proverbs 1.10-19 and tell me it doesn't sound like a modern father trying to keep his son out of a gang. The group says, "Let us lie in wait for blood, let us ambush the innocent without cause" (v.11). The group says, "Throw in your lot with us, we shall all have one purse" (v.14). Profit and camaraderie. As Solomon said elsewhere, "there is nothing new under the sun" (Ecclesiastes 1.9).

So I suggested to them, as I do to you now, let's start a gang of our own. We'll leave out the criminal behavior, certainly. Our club will be better, safer, more stable.

And we would offer the same thing the gangs offer, only bigger and better. After all, anyone can see that the benefits of gang membership are short-lived; Solomon writes in Proverbs 1.18, "they lie in wait for their own blood." Joining our gang won't get them killed. We'll promise them a treasure that cannot be stolen or ruined, that will keep its value despite threats, violence or economic downturns. We'll promise them friends who will never, ever desert them or turn on them, who will have their back under any and all circumstances.

Or better yet, they could join a gang like that already in existence, founded 2,000 years ago by Jesus Christ.

Holes

The 2010 Daytona 500, the biggest event in NASCAR, was interrupted by a pot hole. A *pot hole*. That kills me. Hundreds of people put in thousands of hours of work and spend millions of dollars trying to get everything ready for the event. You would think that at some point some one would think to, I don't know, maybe *pave the track*.

Life's pathway is full of holes. And with a little forethought and planning, we can avoid them. But often we would rather just drive pell-mell down the road blindfolded, having a blast, just trusting that things will work out okay when any rational person would know it won't—in fact, that it can't.

I have never understood the attitude of so many Christians who seem determined to set themselves up for failure. Paul writes, "Therefore, be careful how you walk, not as unwise men but as wise" (Ephesians 5.15). We have options. We can take the blindfold off. We can slow down. We can enlist help. The vast majority of the barriers in our path are completely avoidable. In fact, plenty of our problems will go away on their own if we don't do anything to feed them. Consider David and Bathsheba in 2 Samuel 11. Don't look. Don't invite. Don't respond. Don't succumb. At any number of times their adulterous and ultimately murderous tryst could have been avoided if one or the other of them had *just done nothing*.

We can do this. We can navigate through the holes. "Walking in truth" (2 John 4) is a challenge, but it doesn't have to be as big a challenge as we make it.

Word for Word

Rewrites

I rewrite articles for various reasons. Sometimes I notice a mistake. Sometimes I find a better approach. And sometimes I have computer problems that result in me *erasing a whole day's work.*

In the case of the third of the three scenarios listed (that happened to me today, but you've probably figured that out for yourselves), it's particularly frustrating. I have difficulty remembering the topics I chose, let alone 300 words of text. But generally I am able to shake it off, sit back down at the keyboard, and put something together that is just as good or better. I credit several factors.

First, I trust in God. By that I don't mean I expect God to guide my pen the way He guided the pen of the inspired writers of old. I mean that His word doesn't change. Jesus is "the same yesterday and today and forever" (Hebrews 13.8). As long as I use His gospel as the foundation for my doctrine, I can't go wrong. It may not be quite as good as my first effort (as I measure goodness). But it will be just as scriptural.

Second, I trust my memory. Not nearly as much as I trust God, of course. But an idea worth preserving is probably going to stick in there somewhere. And if it doesn't stick, well, that just leaves that much more room for good ones. No sense fretting about the lost bad ones.

Going over the same ground twice can foster personal growth, or introspection, or at the very least patience. Or we can value our work and time so highly as to think their loss to be critical. Let's pray that we have enough humility to embrace the former and ward off the latter.

Anointing

The Israelites of old would sometimes keep themselves cool by pouring olive oil on their heads. Ick. I'll keep my air conditioning, thank you very much.

The anointing also had symbolic value. When Aaron was anointed high priest in Leviticus 8.12, that set him apart from all others. No one else, not even his brother Moses, could come into the presence of God to atone for the sins of the people.

Jesus is our High Priest today (Hebrews 2.17); the word "Christ" literally means, "anointed one." But we as Christians are "a royal priesthood" in our own right (1 Peter 2.9). And we have an anointing of our own (1 John 2.20) which guides us in His way. But God doesn't single us out with greasy hair, but rather with obedience. If you are His child, you listen to Him as "His anointing teaches you about all things" (1 John 2.27). The anointed follow God's word; others don't. Simple.

But the anointing also has refreshing connotations. Being in fellowship with God just feels good. We have "the peace of God, which surpasses all comprehension" (Philippians 4.7). And we have the extra blessing of fellowship with likeminded brethren. "Behold, how good and how pleasant it is for brothers to dwell together in unity! It is like the precious oil upon the head, coming down upon the beard, even Aaron's beard" (Psalm 133.1-2). If it's not refreshing to be in the presence of your brethren, you have the wrong brethren, the wrong anointing, the wrong attitude, or some combination thereof.

Word for Word

Castes

Watching *My Fair Lady* with the girls, I was reminded how grateful I am for the opportunities that are theirs as Americans. George Bernard Shaw, the English playwright who provided the inspiration for the famous musical, believed in fundamental class distinctions in society. He thought, as Professor Henry Higgins states, lower castes have "no right to live." It is no accident that Eliza Doolittle and her father see their lives fall apart when they are elevated beyond their "proper" station. (The name "Doolittle" for one of the self-described "undeserving poor" is no coincidence, either.)

Americans have always had contempt for caste systems. Perhaps it is because so many of our great figures have arisen from the lower classes (Alexander Hamilton, Abraham Lincoln, Rosa Parks, Mickey Mantle, etc.). We deeply resent condescension. *He's no better than me,* we may say of the fellow with his nose up in the air.

We need to make sure we do not build a caste system in the Lord's church. Jesus told the parable of the laborers in the vineyard to His disciples after acknowledging that they had passed a test the rich young ruler had failed; "we have left everything and followed You," Peter claimed (Matthew 19.27), and Jesus agreed. But as the parable in Matthew 20.1-16 points out, the one who works long and hard for the Lord is no better than any other disciple.

Elitism has no place in Jesus. The best Christian of all is, at the core, a sinner saved by grace. If Paul was the chief of sinners (1 Timothy 1.15), surely I am no better.

Natural

Some people seem to be "naturals," meaning they seem to have an intuitive inclination toward a certain activity—a natural ballplayer, a natural pianist, a natural orator. We may look at such ones with envy, wishing our own career path came "naturally." But in reality, a person at the top of his or her field gets there, almost without exception, through years and years of concerted effort and sacrifice. Some have advantages from birth, to be sure, but they are wasted if they are not honed and crafted. There's nothing "natural" about hitting a round ball with a round bat squarely.

And there is absolutely nothing "natural" about being a Christian. A person born to Christian parents may seem to have shorter and fewer hurdles to jump. But at its core, being a Christian is antithetical to our instincts. All sorts of things may come "naturally" to us, regardless of our upbringing—losing our temper, speaking rashly, acting immorally, on and on we could go. But the Bible says our nature is what we are trying to overcome, not our unalterable and lifelong destiny. Our "natural" impulses are in direct opposition to God's wisdom, according to James 3.15, and are associated with being "earthly" (that is, not heavenly) and even "demonic."

Only by choosing to reject our "natural" impulses in favor of the guidance of the Holy Spirit can we become the "spiritual man" of which Paul writes in 1 Corinthians 2.12-16. Only when we decide we will do whatever His word teaches, rejecting all of our own preconceived notions, will we have "the mind of Christ."

Word for Word

Breezeway

Back in the "good old days," we didn't have air conditioning. (I think I just contradicted myself.) At any rate, the Texas summers weren't any cooler back then, global warming alarmists notwithstanding. So houses were often built with a breezeway, which was a covered, open space that cut the house in two. Allowing the wind free passage through the house helped alleviate the heat during the summer, which in Texas encompasses pretty much every month of the year that doesn't end in "-uary" or "-ember."

Cooling breezes are great. But if hot air is actually supposed to be exchanged for cool, there must be flow. I learned to appreciate this fact while driving my car at highway speed with the sunroof open and the windows up. The air was sucked in, but it had no place to go. I thought my eardrums were going to meet until I rolled a window down and relieved the pressure.

It is wonderful basking in the glory of Jesus Christ. The Spirit comes to us like a cooling breeze (John 3.8), bringing the innumerable blessings that come to the children of God, including and especially salvation itself (Acts 2.38-39). But we must allow the wind to blow through. He blesses us so we may bless others—our family, our brethren, and our neighbors.

An old hymn compares some Christians to the Sea of Galilee and others to the Dead Sea. We can allow God's blessings to flow on, blessing ourselves and others. Or we can shut off the flow, neglecting others and ending up stagnant and dead ourselves. Not much of a choice.

Hazardous

I mailed one of my books to India today. (India! It is amazing how far the "right hand of fellowship" can reach in the modern era.) As usual with parcels, the clerk asked if I was mailing "hazardous materials." Without thinking much about it, I said, "No."

But then I gave it a bit of thought. I suppose it *is* hazardous, in a sense—just not in a "what's with the white powder" way. (Needless to say, I didn't think it was the time or place to ask, "Exactly what do you mean by 'hazardous'?" I'd like to keep my current streak of cavity-search-free days intact, thank you very much.)

But there's no doubt that God's word is hazardous to the devil. The "sword of the Spirit" (Ephesians 6.17) is designed specifically to wage warfare against him. It is the light of Jesus that, like Himself, "shines in the darkness, and the darkness did not comprehend it" (John 1.5).

It is also dangerous to my ego. God's word slices me open and lays me out naked and without excuse before my Judge (Hebrews 4.12-13). It shows me how inadequate I am without my Savior, and also (thankfully) how completely adequate He is, and how adequately the word equips me "for every good work" (2 Timothy 3.16-17).

But all that assumes that my words are in harmony with His words. If not, then I as a teacher "incur a stricter judgment" (James 3.1). If I do not "retain the standard of sound words" (2 Timothy 1.13), substituting for them my own doctrines and philosophies, shame on me. And shame on you for paying attention. We have both put ourselves in a hazardous position indeed.

Word for Word

Coupons

With the economy the way it is, our family has turned to coupon-clipping as a way to stretch our shopping dollars. It's a hassle, no doubt. Grocery shopping is now a two-person chore. (My job is stacking the cart, grabbing available store coupons along the way.) We have to plan ahead; it makes me feel a bit like Eisenhower on D-Day. We get what is discounted, not just whatever we want. But when our receipt prints, and we've knocked 40 percent off our bill, it's all more than worth it.

However, we were not ready for the strong reactions we would get from other shoppers. Sure, we figured we might get some heavy sighs from people in line who might have to wait an extra 30 seconds or so. But some people get actually *upset*. It's not fair, they say, that we get to save so much money. Of course, virtually every avenue we pursue is available to virtually every other shopper. It's not that they *can't* save money; they just don't want to do what it takes to make it happen.

I think a lot of people in the world look at Christians the same way. They covet the joy, peace and purpose we find in Jesus. But they know the cost, and being a "living and holy sacrifice" (Romans 12.1) appeals to them not a bit. So they content themselves with trying to drag us down to their level of misery.

Sorry, Satan. If your people insist on choosing misery, that's too bad. But they won't choose it for me. The best transaction of my life was when I traded my life for His cross (Luke 9.23-24). I refuse to pretend otherwise.

Bragging

Tracie and I determined long ago that we would not be the kind of parents that are always bragging about their children. *"Did you hear? Bobby got straight A's! Did you hear? Suzie made All-Stars! Did you hear? Missy cured cancer!"* Yeah, yeah, you're proud of your kids. We get it.

As our children have grown older, I have found myself modifying my position in this area. We still try not to gush too much. But I do have to say, Tracie and I make great kids. And if you haven't heard, it's time you did.

Atop a long list of Taylor and Kylie's accomplishments is their decision to give their lives to Jesus. I won't pretend Tracie and I were passive bystanders there. But we didn't bribe, badger or threaten them. On their own they came to ask, like the Ethiopian in Acts 8.36, "What prevents me from being baptized?" I pray to one day have occasion to write of them, as John did of Gaius in 3 John 3, "I was very glad when brethren came and bore witness to your truth, that is, how you are walking in truth."

I fear that many Christian parents are bragging with less cause than they think. They go on and on of the success Bobby and Suzie have made in the secular world, proud as peacocks. But when Jesus comes up, they frown a bit and say that, actually, they aren't really serving the Lord very faithfully anymore. And they quickly leave that subject and get back to happier topics—including their grandchildren, who are being reared not to love the Lord.

I ask you, with all the love that's in a father's heart —is that really something to brag about?

Word for Word

Crosswalks

Fact: About 80 percent of automobile-pedestrian accidents occur within 20 feet of a crosswalk. Conclusion: Crosswalks cause accidents. The city planner's determination: Eliminating crosswalks will save lives.

Fact: Elijah asked God to withhold rain (1 Kings 17.1). Conclusion: The drought is Elijah's fault. Ahab's determination: Killing Elijah will bring the rain back.

Both logical progressions fail because of the same principle: Correlation does not equate to causation. Just because crosswalks are associated with accidents does not mean they create them. Perhaps we just tend to put crosswalks at dangerous intersections, and they are not as successful at warding off accidents as we might like.

Likewise, Christians are often portrayed as part of the problem in wicked societies. Stirring up discontent is counterproductive, we are told. So if complaints about humanistic schools, vulgar media and corrupt officials would just go away, then things could get back to normal.

I say, Elijah isn't the problem. Ahab is the problem. And efforts to stymie the work of God's servants in moral causes is no more sensible than taking the white stripes off our streets. God calls us to be "blameless and innocent, children of God above reproach in the midst of a crooked and perverse generation, among whom you appear as lights in the world" (Philippians 2.15). It is our job to shine. Darkness has no say in the matter.

Evil exists, whether or not we talk about it. We might as well talk about it.

Real

I was commended the other day for using the time I spend volunteering at Kylie's school as study time. It was a good idea, the teacher said, for me to "get out there into real life."

I think I know what she meant by that. She meant that God's word takes on new depth when seen in the context of everyday life, as opposed to just sitting in an office and studying it as an academic exercise. I agree; in fact, that premise is what this column is all about. But still, it bothered me a bit to have planet earth described as "real life."

Look at it this way. Say you are dreaming. The world you see is especially vivid and lifelike. It seems to last for hours. But compared to the waking state that follows, it passes in an instant. And the world that replaces the dream state is infinitely more vibrant—brighter colors, sharper tastes, stronger smells.

Which of those two states would you characterize as being "real"?

Well, as different as the dream state is from the waking state, just as different is the physical from the spiritual. The physical world seems real because it is all we see right now. But "our citizenship is in heaven" (Philippians 3.20), even if we have not yet spent a single hour there. To Christians, heaven is real. Heaven is what really matters. Heaven is where our real life will be found.

I just shake my head when I am accused of "not living in the real world" by non-believers who marginalize and ridicule my faith. The fact is, I'm not "living in the real world." Not yet. But that will change one day soon.

Saddle

I've seen my share of unusual things in airports over the years, but I've never seen someone packing a saddle as carry-on luggage. Until today.

You won't be surprised to hear that the traveler in question was wearing a ten-gallon hat. Or that he was wearing cowboy boots. What I found a bit more unusual was that his jacket bore what appeared to be an official PRCA logo. That's Professional Rodeo Cowboys Association, for the benefit of the uninitiated. It seems I was in the presence of a relatively famous person. But he wasn't draped in paparazzi like, say, Paris Hilton or Kate Gosselin would have been (and with considerably less justification, if you ask me). And if I'd nudged a neighbor and asked, "Hey, isn't that Bob Smith, the famous rodeo cowboy?" he likely would not have known or cared.

But being unrecognized doesn't make someone unimportant. People operate in different circles. Plenty of folks wouldn't know the difference between Dale Earnhardt and Dale Evans. That's no reflection on the Dales. That just shows that people know what, and who, they know, and they may not be inclined to change their viewpoint.

Christians are not "known" (that is, acknowledged, valued or appreciated) by the world, according to 1 John 3.1. That's not a reflection on us; it's a reflection on the world—the same world, the text says, that didn't know our heavenly Father either.

I'll never get the credit a child of God deserves from this sinful world. And I can live with that. I'll just say a prayer for them and quietly ride off into the sunset.

Airplanes

I suppose there are still a handful of naysayers out there who deny the viability of manned flight. *How could a huge thing like an "airplane" fly?"* the argument goes. *"What goes up must come down. And surely something that huge could be no exception."*

Of course, this conclusion is based on a limited number of facts within the grasp of the naysayer. Yes, airplanes are heavy. Yes, heavy things sink. It's not difficult to see where the naysayer would get his ideas.

The thing is, there is plenty more information that could easily be within the grasp of the naysayer as well. Like, say, the big silver birds whistling through the sky. He could even go to an airport, board an airplane himself, and prove or disprove the idea once and for all. But he won't do that. His fear of being wrong, of having his entire conception of the world shaken (to say nothing of a controversial and, as it turns out, erroneous position he has espoused), will invariably paralyze him. He would rather be ignorant and wrong than embarrassed and right.

I firmly believe most agnostics are in this position. They claim the existence of God cannot be proven—and I suppose, in a test-tube sort of way, they are right. But persuasive and conclusive evidence abounds, if only they would look. Like the sun, moon and billions of stars flying through the sky, for instance. "The heavens are telling of the glory of God; and their expanse is declaring the work of His hands" (Psalm 19.1). Truly such ones are "without excuse" (Romans 1.20). They would rather cling to their view of the world than reconsider it. Tragic.

Signposts

Our neighborhood has been around for a long time. So long, in fact, that the streets still have concrete signposts at the intersections, with the names of the streets engraved. I don't know why, but it gives me a sense of stability, knowing that the fundamental underpinnings of the world I'm living in have not changed in my lifetime, and likely won't in my daughters' lifetimes.

Of course, years of erosion have worn away the lettering a bit. So some homeowners, or perhaps some city officials, have gone back and reinforced the lettering, either clearing out the collected sediment or actually painting inside the grooves. Those signposts are much easier to read now. Of course, this sort of reinforcing is very different from painting a brand-new street name of the owner's choosing. That would essentially amount to telling all passers-by that they are on the wrong street.

When Solomon wrote, "Do not move the ancient boundary which your fathers have set" (Proverbs 22.28), he was not just concerned with preserving family property. He was teaching a lesson about our obligation to later generations. We owe it to our children, and our children's children, to respect the Biblical heritage passed down to us from generations past, back all the way to the apostles (2 Timothy 2.2).

Dressing the signposts up is fine. Working to preserve them is wonderful. But we must not change their fundamental message of truth; otherwise, we run the risk of future generations unwittingly walking on the wrong road.

Yield

The Texas Department of Public Safety lists thirteen rules for yielding the right of way. Most of them are pretty much common sense. If you are driving on a private road or driveway, you yield to anyone on a public road. Obey signage. Yield to emergency vehicles, school buses and trains. Especially trains. (I kid you not, someone was killed a few weeks ago in a neighboring town trying to beat a train. On a *bicycle*. Alcohol was involved. What a shock.)

Some people are not especially inclined to yield. They would rather do whatever they want and have the rest of us adjust. And we do adjust—or at least, we try. We don't appreciate the inconvenience, but we're not about to ruin our day, or worse, just to prove a person is an idiot. He's working hard at proving that himself anyway.

Obeying the rules of traffic, and of polite society, almost assures us of getting where we want to go a little slower than would have been the case with a bully mentality. Nobody's suggesting that's fair. And if you get a chuckle when the speed demon who passed you on the shoulder gets stuck in the same traffic jam as you, well, give me a wave, because I'm right there with you.

But we yield anyway. And not because we think the person will say, in the spirit of Luke 14.10, "Friend, move up higher." We know he probably won't. We yield because we would rather promote our neighbor's agenda than our own. That's the love that "does not seek its own" (1 Corinthians 13.5), that "will cover a multitude of sins" (James 5.20).

Word for Word

Backpacks

What is the deal with children's backpacks? We didn't need them in my day. But I have to spend $20 every fall for each of my daughters—more if the older one is successful in convincing me that having a big picture of Taylor Lautner is really required for her to pass eighth grade. (Personally, I think anyone who would be associated with any film dumb enough to be entitled *The Adventures of Sharkboy and Lavagirl* should be banned from the industry. But that's me.)

The easy answer to the backpack dilemma is that kids today have a bigger task load. But I don't buy it. They don't do any more homework than I did. They don't take any more classes. Their books aren't any bigger. No, I suspect it's all a racket. The kids don't mind; now their hands are free for easier texting. But then, why would they mind? They're not paying $40 every fall.

It's easy to convince ourselves that conveniences are actually necessities. But my generation, which has never really experienced large-scale reverses (none that an extra credit card wouldn't fix, anyway), is learning the difference. Paul's words regarding contentment in Philippians 4.12—"I have learned the secret of being filled and going hungry, both of having abundance and suffering need"—take on new meaning when the problem is bigger than having to wait for a table at Olive Garden. Perhaps, instead of finding innovative ways to maintain our lifestyle, we can use adversity to hone our faith and build our hope.

Motivation

I would like to think my work motivates people. But I am slowly coming around to the idea that motivation is not as big a part of a preacher's job as some (including me) have made it out to be. My first task is information, not motivation. I need to give my readers and listeners the facts from God's word they need to succeed and prosper in their walk with Christ. With that, they should be able to provide their own motivation.

I'll confess a bit of self-service in that philosophy. Most of my moments of angst as a preacher are caused by my inability to motivate people to do what they need to do—and more often than not, what they know they need to do. My life gets a lot easier when I stop carrying a burden I was never meant to bear.

I'm like the watchman of the analogy God gives Ezekiel in Ezekiel 3.16-21. My job is to see the danger and inform the population. My job is not to sit down with each individual person, consider their own personal life situation, and craft a persuasive argument that will convince them that death and destruction are not in their best interests. (You would think that would be easy. I guess not.) I can try to motivate them, and I do. But ultimately, motivation must be left to the individual.

Being dragged to safety against one's own will didn't work for Lot's wife (Genesis 19.26), and it won't work for people today. Jesus teaches the same lesson in Luke 17.23-33 to those who cling to life as they know it instead of heeding God's warnings. So I need to focus more on doing my job right, and trust my listeners to do theirs.

Word for Word

Traps

It's a scene right out of *Gilligan's Island,* or maybe a Scooby-Doo cartoon. A person sets a trap for an animal. The prey comes and goes, but somehow it is the one who laid the trap who winds up ensnared.

Silly, right? Who would really fall into their own trap? Well, Solomon said the young people of his day were doing it. He writes in Proverbs 1.17-19, "Indeed, it is useless to spread the baited net in the eyes of any bird, but they lie in wait for their own blood; they ambush their own lives. So are the ways of everyone who gains by violence; it takes away the life of its possessors."

Do young people know about the dangers inherent in criminal behavior? Or drug use? Or premarital sex? Of course they do; how could they not? We spend millions of taxpayer dollars convincing public school children to "just say no," but realistically, the children usually have more and better information than the teachers. Seeing the trap isn't the problem. The perception of invincibility is the problem. *Sure, it's happened to millions of others. But it won't happen to me.*

And maybe it won't. Maybe he'll be the one teenager in a hundred who can put his foot in the bear trap and not have his leg crushed. Then again, maybe the trap will work exactly the way it is designed to work.

The psalmist prayed, "Keep me from the jaws of the trap which they have set for me, and from the snares of those who do iniquity" (Psalm 141.9). Stay away from the trap, decrease considerably your chances of stumbling into the trap. Sounds like good advice.

Naps

Researchers have determined that naps are excellent tools in the education and training process. In fact, information taken in just prior to a nap is far more likely to be retained than the same information without the nap. I guess "sleeping on it" is a better idea than we had realized.

I should note that I did not do any personal research to arrive at this conclusion independently. Nor did I get this result from a scientist or read it in a scientific journal written and edited by scientists. In fact, I heard it in passing from a person who had an undisguised agenda of his own, who may himself have gotten the data third-hand, heard it in passing from an unsubstantiated source, or just plain made the whole thing up.

I don't know, and I don't much care. The fact is, I like naps. And this "research" gives me a great justification for taking naps. So it's not tough to convince me of the value of naps, research or no research, facts or no facts.

People will believe what they want to believe. Christians are constantly amazed at the ability of wayward Christians to justify their lifestyles despite mountains of Biblical admonitions. Personally, I've given up being surprised. They are just doing what people do.

The only question of significance is whether one is willing to do what God says to do simply because He says to do it—what Paul calls "being led by the Spirit of God" (Romans 8.14). If you're committed to doing God's will, you'll find a way of working it out. If you're not, you'll find an excuse for rejecting it. It's as simple as that.

Upselling

I want a hamburger with mustard, that's it. *Do you want cheese on that?* No, thanks. Just a burger. *Any fries or tater tots?* No, thanks. Just a burger. *Anything to drink with that?* (Getting a little peeved now.) No, thanks. Just a burger. Nor do I want a chicken sandwich, frosty milk shake, breakfast burrito…

Okay, I made the last part up. But the rest of it happened the last time I sat in a fast-food drive-thru, and pretty much every other time I have as well. I try not to get too annoyed. The person on the other end of the microphone is just doing his or her job; in fact, most of them are required to do exactly what I've described.

It's called upselling. The idea is that the customer may not be aware he is desirous of the various offerings that are available to him (although, for me, if the full-color picture on the menu doesn't close the deal, the gravelly voice on the intercom isn't likely to, either). Either way, they figure I'm more likely to buy if they ask.

It occurs to me that lots of Christians try to upsell God. He has told us the service He requires of us, making us "equipped for every good work" (2 Timothy 3.17). But we keep trying to give Him other things, assuming they're okay with God unless He specifically refuses them. We wouldn't appreciate that sort of attitude; why would He?

And if we don't even like being asked, imagine how God feels when we shove all our extras down His throat without His consent, and then expect Him to thank us and reward us. I wouldn't call that "good service." I suspect you wouldn't, either.

Foreign

I love singing. I wish I were better at it, but still, I am likely at any moment to burst into a tune—perhaps a song I heard over the mall intercom, perhaps an old favorite called to memory by a random word or phrase, perhaps (my favorite) a hymn from my worship that, evidently, I needed to sing more than once.

But some days, I don't feel like singing. I feel like the Jews of old felt when forcibly removed from their homeland, and then asked by their captors to put on a little concert. "How can we sing the Lord's song in a foreign land?" the psalmist asks (Psalm 137.4). It almost seems *wrong* to carry on as if nothing is amiss, when in fact I am overwhelmed with sadness and loss.

The closer I draw to the Lord, the more I am conscious of my status as a foreigner here on earth. It's bad enough that I am not at home in heaven, where lies my true citizenship (Philippians 3.20). That is true even on my best day. But some days on earth seem even more "earthly" than others. Some days I feel swallowed up in a foreign land's depravity, to the point I despair of finding any hope for my fellow man at all. Some days I feel horribly outnumbered by a foreign land's people, even wondering if I could find the 7,000 who had not bowed the knee to Baal in Elijah's day (1 Kings 19.18). Some days I feel myself struggling, and sometimes stumbling, in my battle with foreign spiritual forces that rule here (Ephesians 6.12). Some days, "singing the Lord's song in a foreign land" seems horribly inappropriate.

On those days, I sing anyway.

Apology

You probably have heard the expression, "It's easier to ask for forgiveness than for permission." And often it's true. If we have our heart set on a certain behavior, and we suspect it might not be kosher with the powers that be, we might prefer to go ahead and do the act in question and trust that we can explain our way out of it afterward. After all, most people are forgiving sorts.

But let's say I really need a new house, and I can't afford one. So I rob a bank a day until I have enough. Then I buy the house. And when the authorities catch me, I apologize and ask for forgiveness. But I keep the house. Or take Judas. Imagine Judas seeing Jesus on the cross, saying, "Sorry, Lord!" and keeping his blood money.

An apology is not the same as true repentance. Most of us can squeeze out some alligator tears when it suits our purposes. But when the apology only comes after the fruits of the crime have been harvested, the apology rings hollow. You can't sin now and plan to repent later.

True repentance is a result of genuine regret of past actions, not just regret that past actions were necessary (necessary in the eyes of the one doing the repenting, that is). Paul writes in 2 Corinthians 7.10, "For the sorrow that is according to the will of God produces a repentance without regret, leading to salvation; but the sorrow of the world produces death." Peter's repentance (Luke 22.54-62) drove him to be a better person; Judas' repentance (Matthew 27.3-5) drove him to destroy himself. Which are we more like when we repent?

Fingerprints

Imagine you are an elementary-school janitor. You have a job as difficult as it is thankless. But you do it with a smile, resting your head peacefully at the end of a day in the knowledge of a job well done.

But let's say your job is glass doors one morning. Let's say you leave the first one absolutely spotless. And let's say a crew of fourth-graders come through right afterward and smear their fingerprints (and a fair amount of peanut butter and jelly) all over the door. Would you maintain your positive attitude and keep cleaning? Or would you talk to the principal about instituting waterboarding as an official form of corporal punishment?

It is easy to take God and His forgiveness for granted. We make messes; that's what we do. Romans 3.23 reads, "For all have sinned and fall short of the glory of God." And He cleans them up; that's what He does. According to 1 John 1.9, "If we confess our sins, He is faithful and righteous to forgive us our sins and to cleanse us from all unrighteousness." So if we can keep the confessions flowing, He will keep the grace flowing.

It's a marvelous system, and we thank God for it. But if we are not careful, we can forget about the dirty little fingerprints—our dirty little fingerprints—that should never have been put on God's glass door in the first place, the fingerprints that are an offense to His holiness.

Grace is not a license for sin. We must not "continue in sin so that grace may increase" (Romans 6.1). We owe it to the Father who loved, and the Son who died, to exercise Their patience with us as seldom as possible.

Word for Word

Diamonds

I've been on a James Bond kick lately. My first complete viewing of *Diamonds are Forever* didn't exactly change my life beyond convincing me Jill St. John may challenge Britt Eckland as the most intellectually challenged Bond girl of them all. But the theme song (of the same name) got stuck in my head. The idea is that a woman requires expensive jewelry as a token of her man's commitment. A willingness to spend enormous amounts of money is a sign that he will stay with her. And if he doesn't, at least the diamonds will.

Gloria Steinem can scream about it all she wants, but most women want the security that comes with marriage. And most men are uncomfortable with a plan that extends beyond the weekend. So it is highly appropriate that the hardest substance in nature has come to symbolize the promise a man makes to a woman. Diamonds are forever.

Jesus Christ makes a promise to His church. He intends to make us His bride; in fact, we get a peek at the wedding (Revelation 21.2). He will take that bride to live with Him in heaven for eternity (1 Thessalonians 4.17). Not for fifty or sixty years, not for life. For eternity.

And He has given us the spiritual equivalent of an engagement ring—His inspired word. Paul writes in Ephesians 1.13-14 that the Holy Spirit is "given as a pledge of our inheritance." Any time we have questions about whether Jesus is really committed to us, we can read what the Spirit has revealed—His love, His mercy, His sacrifice, His blessings. With all that in mind, we can have no doubt at all of His intentions. Heaven is forever.

Seekers

It's easy to speak on behalf of God when He's not here in person to speak for Himself. Sure, He speaks through His word, but people can distort the word ("to their own destruction," 2 Peter 3.16), and He's not here to defend it personally.

If someone starts a sentence with, "I know God would want me to ..." you can pretty much take a few things to the bank. One, he has set his heart on a course of action. Two, he has no Scripture to back himself up, and probably quite a bit that argues against him. Three, you are going to have a lot of trouble convincing him to change.

A nation full of similarly headstrong people was sent into captivity in the days of Jeremiah. God's patience with their willfulness, rebellion and compromise finally came to an end. After centuries of refusing to do what they were told, they were placed in a situation where they had no choice. Having rejected God's authority, they were involuntarily forced to accept Nebuchadnezzar's.

It doesn't have to be this way. We, like Israel of old, can "know the truth" and be free as a result (John 8.32). But to be finders, we must first become seekers. God could easily be speaking to us in Jeremiah 29.12-13—"Then you will call upon Me and come and pray to Me, and I will listen to you. You will seek Me and find Me when you search for me with all your heart."

Being a true seeker means being prepared to accept what you find, regardless of the change it requires you to make. But if you have given your heart to the Lord already, it won't be tough to use it to look for His truth.

Word for Word

Speech

My older daughter, Taylor, has taken up speech as an extracurricular activity. I couldn't be more pleased, and for any number of reasons. It's cheap. She's walking in the footsteps of her mother, who was herself quite the debater in her youth. She shows quite an affinity for it. Mainly because it's cheap.

The concept of a fourteen-year-old learning how to speak in public is a bit odd, I grant you. (The saying is true: You spend eighteen months teaching them to walk and talk, and then eighteen years teaching them to sit down and shut up.) But the idea of speech training is not so much the teaching of verbalization, but rather of articulation—choosing the right words, and packaging and presenting them in the most effective manner possible.

We intuitively know the difference between "just talking" and saying something important. When the subject is serious, or dozens of people are hanging on our every word, we tend to be more circumspect about our tone, our diction, our vocabulary, everything. I'm sure Taylor will feel much more at ease when she has a few more speeches under her belt. But even then she will be a bit nervous.

We should never forget the significance of what we say; we should always speak "as one who is speaking the utterances of God" (1 Peter 4.11). Serious speech should be spoken seriously. The more we speak God's word to others, the more comfortable we should get doing it. But when we speak words that pertain to the salvation of souls, it's always a bit nerve-wracking. And that's a good thing.

Stupid

You know how parents spell out words in the presence of their little ones? Well, "stupid" is such a word in my sister-in-law's house. But she has the curse of clever children (as do we), and her son picked up on the significance of that particular sequence of letters quickly. So when she or her husband slipped and said "stupid," they would likely hear a little voice squeal, *"Oooh! You said P-I-D!"* (So he couldn't spell the whole word at the age of three. I didn't say he was Jimmy Neutron; I said he was clever.)

Well, call me an irresponsible parent if you want, but I like the word "stupid." I use it a lot. I've lived on this planet for close to forty-four years, and trust me—sometimes "stupid" is the word you're looking for.

Now, I don't use it in every circumstance. I don't apply it to everyone who acts irresponsibly or without forethought. I certainly don't apply it to everyone who disagrees with me. But I do apply it to some of them. Often.

And so does the Bible. Jeremiah said his contemporaries who worshiped wooden gods instead of the God of heaven were "altogether stupid and foolish" (Jeremiah 10.8). To give the glory due our Creator to something we created ourselves? It doesn't get much more stupid.

Ultimately, any gesture of pride and self-reliance on our part is stupid. When Agur wrote, "Surely I am more stupid than any man" (Proverbs 30.2), he wasn't comparing SAT scores. He was saying anyone who trusts his own wisdom instead of the tested word of God (verse 5, same context) is stupid. Stupid me included.

Tattoos

It is safe to say I will never get a tattoo. I mean, I'm not too keen on using ink to write on paper, let alone my body. I'm encouraged in this attitude by actors whose personal commitments don't tend to outlive their dairy products, and yet they insist on wearing the name of their love of the moment for the rest of their lives. Bummer for their love of the next moment.

If I were to put a permanent mark on my body, it would have to indicate something about me that would never, ever change. I cringe at the idea of having tattoos commemorating my previous attachments. "Fan of OJ." "ABBA Forever." "The Future Mr. Jodie Foster."

A permanent, visible identification. That is the lesson of the "666" mark in Revelation 13.18. It's not a literal mark on the literal forehead of a literal person (like that creepy kid in the *Omen* movies). It's the devil's way of marking his people, just like God marks His people in the very next verse. Jesus Himself even has a tattoo in this vision (Revelation 19.16). Think of the marks as subtitles in the craziest foreign film you've ever seen.

God's message, in Revelation and throughout Scripture, is that the person who is paying attention to the story can tell the difference between the players. "By this the children of God and the children of the devil are obvious: anyone who does not practice righteousness is not of God, nor the one who does not love His brother" (1 John 3.10). Yes, sometimes the wolves will wear sheep's clothing (Matthew 7.15). But you can distinguish between the counterfeit and the genuine article with a little effort.

Fortunes

Allow me to take a brief moment today to comment on the deplorable state of fortune cookies today. (I know, not the most pressing of issues. Maybe I'll deal with terrorism and race riots next week. For now, just hear me out.)

I remember when you used to get *real* fake fortunes in fortune cookies. Now I usually just get some kind of general advice. *"To make a friend, first be a friend."* Or, *"Happiness is found where it is least sought."* What does that even mean?

Maybe it's a lawsuit thing. Maybe some Chinese food aficionado was told, "You are domestically inclined and will be happily married" (a friend of mine got that one twice), and she decided to sue because the fortune gave her false hopes, mental anguish, etc. So now the cookie makers play it safe with some sort of Ben Franklin/Ann Landers/Tony Robbins hybrid.

But that's what happens when you tell people their future. Your credibility rests on your accuracy. I love the simple test in Deuteronomy 18.22—"When a prophet speaks in the name of the Lord, if the thing does not come about or come true, that is the thing which the Lord has not spoken. The prophet has spoken it presumptuously; you shall not be afraid of him." (Anyone out there still reading Hal Lindsay books? Anyone? Just checking.)

The actual word of God, on the other hand, "stands forever" (Isaiah 40.8). We shouldn't worry about the fortune He gives us coming true. Unless, of course, we are not right in His eyes; then we should worry greatly.

Word for Word

Grapefruit

Texans have a reputation (probably deserved) for thinking our state is the best at everything. The best food (Tex-Mex and beef barbecue), the best music (Buddy Holly, George Strait, Stevie Ray Vaughn), the best scenery (the Hill Country, covered in live oaks and bluebonnets), on and on we could go. Personally, I'm open-minded enough to admit most of this is opinion, and nothing more. Others can and do make good arguments for their region's merits. But one specific case brooks no argument whatsoever.

Texas has the best grapefruit. Period. Paragraph.

If you're still struggling through that sour yellow stuff, and you have not yet experienced the ruby red splendor grown in Texas' Rio Grande Valley, well, I weep for you, friend. I really do. Sweet, juicy, just the right amount of tartness. Eat it by the slice, just like an orange. And don't you dare put any sugar on it! It's perfect just the way it is.

And so is Jesus. But you'd never think so, considering the sourpuss attitude some Christians adopt. They live halfhearted, unfulfilling lives. They have no peace, no joy, no purpose. Why would anyone lose his life (Matthew 10.39) for that? I wouldn't.

But I would give everything for "the peace of God, which surpasses all comprehension" (Philippians 4.7), to "rejoice always" (1 Thessalonians 5.16), to eagerly anticipate an eternal home in "a better country" (Hebrews 11.16). Why wouldn't I?

Jesus is sweet, not sour. So get that scowl off your faces, Christian. Your neighbor is watching you.

Debt

A man was hanging from the edge of a cliff, screaming for help for hours. Finally, a man showed up and pulled him to safety. Thankful, the man asked, "What can I give you that will repay the debt I owe you?" His savior replied, "Tell you what, I'll settle for half of what you would have been willing to pay five minutes before I arrived."

Debt is a funny thing. A desperate man may go to a loan shark looking for a quick fix, knowing the usurious terms attached. But when the time comes to repay, the deal he has struck does not look nearly as advantageous. Many a man has been moved to renegotiate a deal once he's already received his half of the bargain.

None of us would argue that we do not owe Jesus a debt—the biggest debt imaginable, in fact. And there is no way we could possibly pay it back in full. But He does require us to try. In 1 Peter 2.24, we read, "And He Himself bore our sins in His body on the cross, so that we might die to sin and live to righteousness; for by His wounds you were healed." It's like a responsibility sandwich. We like the part about Him bearing our sins, and we want our wounds to be healed. But when the subject changes from what He has done to what we must do, suddenly we become a lot less hungry.

But that's not the way our debt works. We can't just declare moral bankruptcy, as it were, and hope Jesus will accept us anyway. If Christ is crucified for us, we should we willing to be crucified with Him (Galatians 2.20)—and to feel honored to be given the opportunity to do so.

Word for Word

Casual

James Michener is one of my favorite authors. I'm currently enjoying *Chesapeake*. I loved *Alaska*. I adored *Centennial*, both the novel and the miniseries (although I think 23 hours is a bit long to be called a "miniseries"). I thought he was pretty fair to Texans in *Texas*, which is a rare thing to say of an outsider.

But I don't read Michener often. If you've ever tried to hoist one of his volumes, you can probably guess why.

Reading Michener takes lots of commitment, and I'm a casual reader. I read when engaged in a task that requires my body but not necessarily my mind—maybe half an hour at a time, an hour a day total. And although I am confident intellectually that spending three weeks of my reading schedule on one Michener book will be worth it, usually it's easier to pick up something smaller. And I mean that figuratively *and* literally.

The Bible, interestingly, is about the same length as a Michener novel—around a thousand pages in most editions. And it, too, is a bit daunting to the casual reader. Some have a sort of passing interest—like the Athenians of old, who "used to spend their time in nothing other than telling or hearing something new" (Acts 17.21). Such ones—"casual Christians," if you will—usually balk at the idea of serious spiritual discussion.

Let us all determine to be like Ezra instead—"For Ezra had set his heart to study the law of the Lord and to practice it, and to teach His statutes and ordinances in Israel" (Ezra 7.10). There was nothing casual about Ezra's commitment to spiritual things.

Coarseness

Watching old movies is like going back through time. Three things particularly jump out at me as having changed radically. One, everyone used to smoke. Two, driving while intoxicated was, if not actually encouraged, at least winked at. Three, cursing was rare, mild, and never done by or in the presence of women.

Smoking is against the law in much of America now. And Mothers Against Drunk Driving has waged a remarkably successful campaign to change our attitude about the dangers of combining cars and alcohol.

But although we've made considerable progress toward what I would call civilized behavior in these areas, we've gone in the opposite direction with foul language. It has gotten considerably more prominent, considerably more prevalent, and considerably more foul. Why the difference? I'm not sure. Perhaps we are able to appreciate the negative impact of smoking and drunk driving, but coarseness is not seen as a necessarily bad thing. Many people like being free to express themselves however they like without worrying about suffering public stigma.

But coarse speech is as damaging to a culture in its own way as anything else. Filthiness is listed with immorality, impurity and greed in Ephesians 5.3-5 as a behavior that disqualifies one from kingdom citizenship. By polluting the air with foul speech, we pollute the minds of everyone who breathes that air. Actions have consequences. We need to accept responsibility for the messes we make, whether they be physical or moral.

Word for Word

Bananas

You know bananas are seedless—at least, the commercial yellow Cavendish strain is. (I didn›t even know they had a name; did you?) What you may not know is, no Cavendish banana seeds exist. At all. They are all grown from cuttings. That means, after countless generations, all yellow bananas are virtually identical, genetically. Literally, if you've eaten one, you've eaten them all.

That's great for now; no picking around pits in my peanut butter and banana sandwich. But it poses possible long-term hazards. Genetic variation is a natural defense against blights and infestations. As it stands, a particularly virulent disease or pest could potentially lay waste to the fourth-biggest cash crop in the world, threatening the livelihoods of half a billion people worldwide. (I know, too much *National Geographic*. I'm working on it.)

Variety is essential in churches, too. Human organizations tend strongly toward homogeneity. And homogeneity stunts spiritual growth. An obvious example: Racism led to "black churches" and "white churches" long ago, and we still have not recovered. Both groups suffer for it.

Doctrinal variation is rebellion and must be considered anathema (Galatians 1.8-9). But personal variation is healthy, even necessary. Being "one in Christ Jesus" (Galatians 3.28) means ignoring cultural lines, and embracing "the unity of the Spirit in the bond of peace" (Ephesians 4.3). Without fresh approaches and viewpoints, we risk inbreeding ourselves into a spiritual stupor, imperiling our souls and those of generations to come.

King

If I were king, I would impose an immediate moratorium on the writing of new "pop" music. (There's nothing "new" about it anyway, so what's the harm?) Anyone not inclined toward country, classical or jazz would be required to subsist on a strictly regulated diet of rock icons, none of which made their debut on the charts later than 1985.

If I were king, no restaurant would be allowed to serve barbecue without a license from a governing board. I would be on the board. Nix that. I would *be* the board.

If I were king, full stops would not be required at stop signs when no other cars are in sight. Speed limits would change automatically based on traffic conditions. Two at-fault accidents in 12 months, ride the bus for five years.

If I were king, public hangings would be re-instituted and imposed for a wide variety of crimes, including but not necessarily limited to murder, rape, drug possession, basing a reality TV show on your own life, and playing a car stereo at full blast with windows down.

If I were king, dissent would be encouraged. Dissenters would be given a half-hour to convince me of the error of my ways. If they are unsuccessful, public hanging.

Of course, I'm not king. Jesus is king. He came to earth for that specific purpose (John 18.37). He Himself said, "All authority has been given to Me in heaven and on earth" (Matthew 28.18). It is submission to His law, not mine, that equates to fellowship with God (2 John 9).

So the question is, am I as enthusiastic about imposing His actual laws as I am my own imaginary ones?

Word for Word

Why

Have you ever had one of *those* days? You know the kind I mean. The car breaks down. The boss yells at you. The wife burns dinner (or the husband gripes about it). Your son expresses his fervent desire to be a full-time rodeo clown. You get the idea.

All of our favorite questions on those days begin with the word *why. Why does this have to happen to me? Why is life so unfair? Why can't I catch a break?*

Job had just such a day—far worse, I'm sure, than any day you or I have experienced. In an instant he lost everything—his wealth, his children, his servants—through no fault of his own (as if that would have made it any better). And his bad luck was just beginning; soon he lost his health, and very nearly his marriage.

That is the story of the first two chapters of Job. And for the better part of the next 35, he asks, "Why?" I suspect we would, too. And God never tells him. Even when He responds to Job at the end of the book, He does not bring meaning to his sufferings; He brings perspective—as if to say, "Job, when your life is in a mess, you don't need answers; you need Me." Job's faith got him through his trials; more faith would have made the trip even easier.

Most "why" questions directed at God are presumptuous. We would be well advised to stick to "what" questions. What is right? What is wrong? What is my purpose in life? And most importantly, "What must I do to be saved?" (Acts 16.30). If we get our "whats" right, we'll find that the "whys" don't really matter that much.

Conclusions

Hooters has a drive-thru. That kills me.

I have never entered a Hooters restaurant, so I'm by no means an expert. I may have seen the only Hooters drive-thru in the world. Or it may be corporate policy. Not the point. The point is, *Hooters has a drive-thru!* Maybe some men really do go there for the food. Maybe some men read *Playboy* for the articles. Maybe some men buy Carmen Electra's workout video for the exercise. Maybe I've been too quick to jump to conclusions all these years.

It's funny how that works. I work hard to preserve my reputation in the neighborhood by avoiding things I find objectionable—like the objectification of women, for instance. And it's easy for me to assume that someone who doesn't avoid the same things also doesn't share the same values. But that's not necessarily fair. Maybe they really are just there for the wings.

There is middle ground to be had. We ought to be slow to believe the worst in others—not being naive, but rather "shrewd as serpents and innocent as doves" (Matthew 10.16). We also ought to want to be "spotless and blameless" (2 Peter 3.14). I should help my neighbor avoid coming to a bad conclusion about me if I can.

Others will not always extend us the same courtesy we are trying to give them. Maybe steering clear of things that are not inherently evil isn't "fair." But if the apostle Paul could stay away from meat entirely for a greater good (1 Corinthians 8.13), surely I can stay away from one restaurant's chicken wings.

Word for Word

Humor

I love a good joke. I enjoy finding a good (and appropriate!) joke to share with my girls on the way to school. And I try to insert a little humor into my writing from time to time. But although joking with the girls is all in fun, I try to keep it limited in my writing. God's word is serious business, and my treatment of it should be as well.

Some have tried to tell me that humor has no place at all in religious discussion. I think such ones should read their Bibles more carefully. Job shows my kind of sarcasm when rebutting his friends' "wisdom" in Job 12.2—"Truly then you are the people, and with you wisdom will die!" And again in Job 26.2, "What a help you are to the weak! How you have saved the arm without strength!"

Jesus Himself shows a sense of humor; I don't know how else to read his analogy in Matthew 7.3-5 about picking a speck out of someone's eye with a log stuck in your own. The same with His suggestion in Luke 11.11-12 that a father might tell his son, in so many words, "Sorry we're out of eggs—here's a nice fat scorpion for you instead!"

Humor can be used to make a point. But when the point is how funny the preacher is, that's bad. Drawing people to oneself instead of the message is arrogant and contrary to the spirit of Christ. To paraphrase John 3.30, He must increase and my ego must decrease.

I hope my readers and listeners find my presentation of the gospel instructive *and* entertaining. I'll continue trying to accomplish both. Please be my friend and chasten me if I start getting the order mixed up.

Baking

Apparently one channel devoted entirely to food is not enough. Now we are told to anticipate in the next few weeks the launch of The Cooking Channel—which appears to be pretty much just like The Food Network, except it has people on it I've never heard of.

Personally, I love cooking shows. I love seeing how a touch of this, a pinch of that, a dusting of the other at just the right moment can turn an ugly mound of ingredients into a masterpiece, exactly the way the cook wants it.

That's precisely why, I predict, we will never have a "Baking Channel." If cooking is art, baking is science. The recipe must be followed exactly. Too much or too little of anything and the entire process is disrupted. It's basically a big chemistry experiment, conducted almost entirely behind darkened glass over a long period of time. And who wants to watch that?

Cooking is a reflection of the mind of the cook. That's the attitude lots of people like to take toward salvation. If you prefer less salt or more sugar, that's fine; just don't require me to do the same, and all is well.

But baking is a reflection of the recipe. Do exactly what it says, and you get exactly what you want. No tweaking allowed. That's what Jesus' salvation is like. He gives us the recipe in the gospel— "the power of God for salvation to everyone who believes" (Romans 1.16). It's perfect just the way it is. No tweaking allowed.

If you tamper with the recipe, you tamper with the results. And if you think a 400-degree oven is hot ...

Vaccine

I believe in the conservation of words. (I don't always practice it, but I believe in it.) But sometimes extra words can be helpful. An example: One pharmacy in our town has signs posted in its parking lot that read, *"H1N1 vaccine available here."* Another pharmacy advertises, *"We have H1N1."* Are they both saying the same thing? Probably. Am I more likely to patronize the one than the other? What do you think?

It made me think, this probably isn't the only situation where what is presented as the vaccine is in reality the disease. After all, medically, a vaccine is little more than a dumbed-down version of the disease—the theory being you can train your body to stave it off by exposing it in small, weak doses.

That sounds a lot like most current efforts at sex education. In theory, we can get children to avoid sexual activity by showing them the extreme consequences. But in practice, we whet their curiosity and actually create the unwanted behavior. Maybe they avoid pregnancy and disease (although a trip to the high school nurse's office may persuade you otherwise). But in any case, the main problem is not social or medical, but moral (Hebrews 13.4). And by declaring victory in the battle against teen pregnancy and STDs, we are sowing the seeds of defeat in a much greater battle—the battle for their souls.

There's no acceptable measure of a bad thing. Common sense tells us it's easier to say no at the beginning than in the middle. The quicker our children learn that lesson, the fewer sleepless nights there will be for fretful parents.

Illness

I am not the world's best patient. I know that. On the rare occasion that I contract some sort of illness, I become intolerable. And not in the way you might think. I don't get whiny and needy. I don't make people run and fetch for me. Very much the opposite, actually. I will sit in my chair and groan a bit, but otherwise I will insist that I'm okay, that I'm not really sick, that no one need bother with my so-called problems.

Of course, my toughness (in my mind, that is—Mrs. Hammons calls it stubbornness) does not change the central issue. I would be better off if I would allow someone to do some things for me—especially since those closest to me delight and excel in rendering aid. (That is, the ones with thumbs excel in rendering aid. Max, bless his heart, tries. But as therapeutic as scratching his belly may be, usually I'd prefer a warm meal and an Advil.)

My pride is actually a bigger and longer-lasting problem than my illness. Although I may portray my bull-headed attitude as self-lessness, an unwillingness to burden others, in truth I am making myself miserable and dragging others down with me. Worse yet, I am denying others the joy that comes from serving those in need.

It reminds me of Jesus washing Peter's feet, despite Peter's best efforts at "humility." Jesus told him, "If I do not wash you, you have no part with Me" (John 13.8). It is Jesus' delight to bestow grace upon those who desire it. If we remain too proud to ask Him for grace, preferring to work through our problems on our own, He very well may grant us our wish.

Word for Word

Undermine

Before gunpowder, cities would build walls of brick to protect their citizens from attack. A city with a fresh water supply and ample food stores could defend itself behind a wall against innumerable hordes with minimal effort for years.

Eventually early engineers discovered they could dig a tunnel underneath the wall, light a large fire, or mine, inside the tunnel and compromise the foundation of the walls. This made the walls crack and collapse, allowing the invading armies to enter—hence our term *undermine*.

No matter what kind of structure we may build, a weakened foundation will threaten it. Satan knows this as well as anyone. That is why he is hard at work trying to undermine our faith, the system of belief we have constructed in our minds and hearts that connects us to God. Paul wrote in Ephesians 2.20 that we are "built on the foundation of the apostles and prophets, Christ Jesus Himself being the corner stone." The same firm base that served to anchor the lives of the saints of old can and will anchor ours if we will build on it as they did.

It is no accident the devil is so determined to erode our confidence in the basics of our relationship with Jesus—His deity (Colossians 2.9) and humanity (1 John 4.2), the inerrancy of the Scriptures He gave (2 Timothy 3.16-17), the single and difficult path to glory (Matthew 7.14), the essentiality of baptism (1 Peter 3.21). If he can cause us to question the fundamental principles of faith, whatever faith we have left will crumble under his siege. We must start strong if we are to stay strong and finish strong.

Intransigent

The "word-to-impress-your-friends of the day" is *intransigent*. Defined: refusing to agree or compromise; uncompromising; inflexible. I'll use it in a sentence—"The children wanted ice cream instead of creamed spinach, but their father was *intransigent*." Or it can be a noun—"The children's father, a true *intransigent*, also ignored their pleas regarding a possible reduction of summertime chores."

Most people see intransigence as a negative. And often it is. After all, getting along with your fellow human being requires a certain amount of accommodation. It is unreasonable to think that I can get my way at the expense of my fellow humans 100 percent of the time.

But I don't have to compromise with my daughters. I can get my way all the time. I can have the last piece of pie, or hog the remote control, or trash any outfits of theirs I don't approve of—just because I want to. They don't have to like it. I don't ask them to like it. But they have to accept it. And you'd be amazed how often they do.

Now, I'm not quite the tyrant that the previous paragraph might indicate. But I do make sure my daughters understand our respective roles. And it's not just so I get the remote (although that's not a complete non-factor). It is so they understand the concept of intransigent authority.

God rules with complete intransigence. All my girls' *yes sir's* and *no, thank you's* are preparing them for when God asks them to submit (James 4.7) and doesn't provide a full explanation why. There is no compromise with God; there is only submission and rebellion.

Word for Word

Spin

In *McClintock!* a young man, in love with a girl who he just saw on an outing with another young man, tells her father, played by John Wayne, "I said what I said, and I'll stand by it to the death." Turns out he had said, "Any girl who would permit a man to kiss her before they're properly engaged is a trollop." He then bends the girl over his knee and spanks her repeatedly, while her father smiles and smokes a cigar. I said to myself, "You don't see much of that these days."

I referred, of course, to the notion of standing behind your words, including and especially the ones that get you in trouble. Today it's more popular to shoot your mouth off indiscriminately, and then spend quality time and effort explaining how you didn't say it, and how you didn't mean it, and how you were taken out of context, and how you weren't, strictly speaking, under oath at the time.

Paul was accused of being a "spin doctor" repeatedly; he writes in 2 Corinthians 1.17, "Or what I purpose, do I purpose according to the flesh, so that with me there will be yes, yes and no, no at the same time?" The phrase, "according to the flesh" is the key. If he had been a man-pleaser, he would have said what was necessary to please men—a different message for every circumstance. But since he was a God-pleaser instead (Galatians 1.10), his yes meant yes and his no meant no.

Spin doesn't work with God, who "tries the feelings and the heart" (Jeremiah 11.20). We shouldn't try to make it work with people. As Mark Twain said, "If you tell the truth, you don't have to remember anything."

Productive

I have a cough. It's not a bad cough. I'm not leaving pieces of lung everywhere I walk. But it's bad enough to be annoying. It recently has become a productive cough, as opposed to a dry, hacking cough. I don't especially prefer one to the other. But at least with a productive cough, I feel like I'm accomplishing something—something more than stripping my throat raw, I mean.

Not that I'm complaining. Life is tough for everyone. Job (and he would know) said in Job 5.7, "For man is born for trouble, as sparks fly upward." The idea is that we are like heated pieces of metal in the blacksmith's shop, sitting on life's anvil, and the circumstances of our lives keep pounding away at us like a big hammer. Not the most wonderful of experiences for the metal, right?

But the blacksmith is not trying to punish the metal. He is trying to turn it into something productive, something to serve the greater good. That's why God gave us metal in the first place. And metal will not reach its full capacity for strength and durability without going through a series of rigorous trials at the hand of the blacksmith.

I can't claim to know what specific purpose, if any, God is trying to work in you with a specific hardship in your life. I do know, however, that we can emerge better than we were before the trial if we allow it to be so. He will teach us patience, if nothing else (James 1.2-4). And if we concentrate on being productive in His cause while we suffer, we may find ourselves not noticing the suffering quite so much.

Washed

I love going outside on a sunny day after a rainstorm. It looks like I feel after a good shower—like the grime that accumulates from day-to-day existence in the world has been washed away. It's the world the way it should be, clean and bright and new.

Invariably it makes me think of the day I was baptized. The New Testament word "baptize" is the same Greek word that would refer to the dyeing process. Cloth is plunged into dye, which permeates every fiber, transforming it from the raw, natural color to the one preferred by the owner. Likewise, we are "buried with Him through baptism" (Romans 6.4) so that we can replace our old, "natural" look with one more befitting a child of the King.

This imagery fascinates me. We are "washed" (1 Corinthians 6.11), we become "white as snow" (Isaiah 1.18), by immersing ourselves in blood; "the blood of Jesus His Son cleanses us from all sin" (1 John 1.7). Clearly this "bath" is like no other we have ever taken.

The grace of God does not make us a cleaned-up version of what we were before; it transforms our very character, changing us from common to holy, vile to exalted, earthly to heavenly. God washes His trees so they can be better-looking trees. He washes me from the inside out, not so I can be a better version of myself but rather be "conformed to the image of His Son" (Romans 8.29).

It's a relief to have my sins washed away (Acts 22.16). But it thrills me even more to see God's word working in my life every day. Please, Lord, help me get out of Your way, so You can have Your way with me!

Magnolias

Magnolia trees annoy me. Seriously. Everything about them. Their saucer-sized leaves. Their huge, noxious blooms. Worst of all, their weird, amorphous shape. A magnolia just doesn't *look* like a tree. More like a hibiscus on steroids.

Now, a live oak—*there's* a tree. A majestic dome shape. Thick branches begging to support a tree-climber or a tree house. Great wood for barbecue. Or a maple—beautiful symmetry, glistening green in the spring, breathtaking color in the fall. Makes great furniture and baseball bats. Or if you like flowers, how about a cherry tree? A beautiful spray of pink in spring, luscious fruit in fall.

You may think this is completely arbitrary, and maybe it is. But let me ask you this: If you don't like the look of a magnolia, what purpose does it serve? You can't eat from it. Its wood is gummy, barely burns, is worthless for commercial endeavors. It's a one-trick pony. And if you don't like the trick, it's a waste of space.

The lesson for us (and yes, there's a lesson) is this: If you have only one task, you'd better be pretty amazing at it. And God says that is precisely the case for each one of us. "The conclusion, when all has been heard, is: fear God and keep His commandments, because this applies to every person" (Ecclesiastes 12.13)—or, as the King James Version renders it, "this is the whole duty of man."

One task. Whatever else we may accomplish in our own pursuits is ultimately vain. If we are not serving God in this life, we're just cluttering up the landscape.

Word for Word

Schedule

My dog can tell time. Okay, maybe that's overstating it a bit. But he definitely knows on school days when it's getting close to 3.45 p.m. He gets antsy. Every little sound outside the house sets him off. He knows the girls are about ready to come home from school. And he knows that when they do, they will take him out and play with him. It's the high point of his day, and if you think he's sleeping through it, you're crazy.

He can also tell the days of the week. He knows one morning out of seven we get dressed up in nice clothes and get in the car, and that he is never, ever allowed to go. So when we grab our Bibles, he slinks over to his cage.

I fear Max has a leg up on some Christians. I have known brethren everywhere I have lived who act like Sunday morning worship services is something new, like they have no idea how long it takes to get dressed, eat breakfast and drive to the church house. I can't help thinking they take a different attitude toward work and school.

Important things get scheduled. They remain written on the calendar in ink; other, lesser activities are worked in around them. And the longer they stay scheduled, the more instinctive they get. If we can train ourselves to be in front of the television on Mondays at 8 p.m., we can train ourselves to be in the car on Sundays at 9 a.m.

Ezra is a great example for us: "For Ezra had set his heart to study the law of the Lord and to practice it, and to teach His statutes and ordinances in Israel" (Ezra 7.10). May God help us all set our hearts similarly.

Improve

Let's say you own some prime Texas pastureland. Once a year the government taxes you a certain amount of money simply because you own that property. (I can't contain what I have to say about taxes in 300 words, so we'll just let that slide.) But if you make an improvement on that land (build a house, dig a well, etc.), the land value goes up. That means you will owe even more in taxes next year.

But "improvement" is a relative term. Building a house doesn't improve the native grasses, which you will have to kill out to make way for your lawn. It doesn't improve the lives of the local fauna, which feed on the local grasses, and which you will aggressively exterminate to protect your flower beds and vegetable garden. No, it's an improvement in human eyes, and human eyes alone.

That's a concept we would do well to remember when we are tempted to "improve" God's plan—His plan for salvation, for worship, for morality, for any aspect of His interaction with mankind. We have all sorts of ideas as to how things could be streamlined or simplified or modernized. But if pressed, we would have to admit that our ideas have nothing to do with God's will, which has already been "once for all handed down to the saints" (Jude 3). It's improved in our judgment, not His.

After extolling the perfection and righteousness of God's law, David writes in Psalm 19.13, "Also keep back Your servant from presumptuous sins; let them not rule over me." What could be more presumptuous than telling God His word needs help from us?

Word for Word

Eyeglasses

In third grade I took my first eye exam. I couldn't read the second line on the eye chart. I remember being astonished. I never knew I had a problem. I'm sure there were all sorts of warning signs—inability to see the chalkboard from the back of the room, squinting to read, etc. But I never thought about it. I never considered the possibility that I might have a problem. And so I never conceived of its solution.

The day I came home with my first pair of eyeglasses was a revelation. I was utterly astounded at being able to see individual bricks on houses we drove past. I could see leaves on trees. Before they had just been blurs. It made me simultaneously thankful at my improvement in life and regretful that I had lived so long ignorant of my problem.

I wonder how many sinners are in similar situations regarding their spiritual vision—and how many Christians, for that matter. It's easy to become complacent, whether with or without God, and never consider the possibility of a much clearer, much more vibrant reality.

I'm reminded of how Israel was facing an army far superior in number and materiel. Elisha's servant was losing hope. And Elisha prayed, "O Lord, I pray, open his eyes that he may see" (2 Kings 6.17). And suddenly he saw a host of spiritual warriors who had been there all along, just outside his limited vision.

God's eyeglasses will help us see possibilities for our lives we could never have imagined. But first, we have to recognize our need for them. Only then can we see the glorious world God has bestowed upon us.

Drive-thru

I am willing to wager that I will finish writing this article before I get to the front of the line in the McDonald's drive-thru. We'll see if I'm right. I like my chances, though. The entire county appears to be in need of an after-school treat.

And thanks to the convenience of battery power and laptop computer technology, I do not have to force myself to just hang out doing nothing, listening to the girls chatter incessantly about the Jonas brothers and why purple is superior in every way to pink (and why I should care).

I'm not doing this just to have something to do, though. I'm doing it because we only have a certain number of hours on earth before we are called to give account for ourselves (2 Corinthians 5.10). And until that time comes, I need to be taking the advice of our Lord, who said in John 9.4, "We must work the works of Him who sent Me, as long as it is day; night is coming, when no man can work." ...

Well, I ran out of time. And I could argue that the folks at the drive-thru work a lot faster than I had anticipated. Or that the front seat of a car is not exactly conducive to typing. Or that the girls were a constant source of distraction. But no excuse would change the outcome.

Thankfully, I can have a second chance. And a third, and a fourth—however many I need, as long as life and electricity remain. Such will not be the case in judgment. As with the five foolish virgins, once the door is shut, it's shut (Matthew 25.10). With that in mind, I'd better take full advantage of the one earthly life God gives me.

Word for Word

Idols

A *Peanuts* cartoon from the 1970s shows Peppermint Patty telling Marcie that tennis legend Billie Jean King was one of her idols. When Marcie told her the apostle Paul warned us about idols, Patty replied, "He never saw Billie Jean King hit a backhand."

Marcie's point, and Paul's, is even more valid today. We have always been drawn to larger-than-life figures who give us hope and encouragement in our own quest for excellence. That's not all bad; Paul himself wrote, "Therefore I exhort you, be imitators of me" (1 Corinthians 4.16). We need role models, especially for our youth.

But the gap between an idol in the Bible and an "idol" in pop culture is shrinking. Teens and pre-teens govern their whole lives, from entertainment choices to clothing to wall art, based on the example of the hottest singer, actor or athlete. The worst part is, their "worship" tends to focus on their idols' least admirable aspects—vulgar lyrics, raunchy clothing, boastful and self-aggrandizing behavior. A pop diva may do admirable works of charity, but that's not why she is idolized. Character doesn't move merchandise; sex and attitude do.

Our young women should nurture "the hidden person of the heart, with the imperishable quality of a gentle and quiet spirit" (1 Peter 3.4). Our young men should "flee from youthful lusts, and pursue righteousness, faith, love and peace" (2 Timothy 2.22). And we adults should strive to be worthy of emulation. After all, they will emulate someone. Better us than Lady Gaga.

Memorial

One of the things that makes this country great is its respect for heroes of the past. Great Americans such as Crispus Attucks, Nathan Hale, Stonewall Jackson, Amelia Earhart, Carole Lombard and Todd Beamer gave the ultimate sacrifice to preserve the freedom that you and I hold dear. Perhaps their vision of America was not precisely parallel to mine or yours. Perhaps we would have lived our lives somewhat differently without sacrificing our patriotism. But there can be no doubt that they continue to provide an example of honor, heroism and service, and that we continue to owe each of them a debt. As God said of Abel, "though he is dead, he still speaks" (Hebrews 11.4).

Abel, of course, died for a cause greater even than patriotism. He died because he thought it was more important to obey God than placate his brother. He offered no apologies for his own faithfulness and no justification for Cain's rebellion. And so he died (Genesis 4.1-8).

And so, as America remembers its fallen, remember also those who have fallen in an even greater struggle—the struggle for the souls of men and women, both of their age and of ours. Hear them call from the tomb, "How long, O Lord, holy and true, will You refrain from judging and avenging our blood on those who dwell on the earth?" (Revelation 6.10), and pray with John, "Amen. Come, Lord Jesus" (Revelation 22.20). And perhaps think of one hero in particular whose sacrifice particularly speaks to your heart, whose life has changed yours.

I have such a one. I wear His name.

Word for Word

Condensation

My friends in Arizona and other places not blessed with 99 percent humidity may not be able to appreciate the constant condensation experiments we cold beverage drinkers run along the Gulf Coast. A soda can fresh from the fridge immediately mists over, yanking water vapor out of the air faster than cellulite out of a Kardashian. Mist quickly converts to droplets, droplets to drops, and drops to circular stains on my end table. It may appear that water just appeared out of nowhere. In fact, the water was there all along, waiting for an opportunity to change forms. All it needed was a chilled conductor.

I wonder how much rebellion lies dormant in a Christian, just waiting for an opportunity to appear. Christians like me, with family members and friends in the common faith as far as the eye can see and the genealogical tree can reach, can find it easy to remain faithful. But what if circumstances changed? I know Christians who have, seemingly overnight, left the Lord to have an affair, or pursue worldliness, or to blend in with new friends who care nothing for Him. Did they change? Or did they just finally have an opportunity to show what they always were?

James 1.15 reads, "Then when lust has conceived, it gives birth to sin; and when sin is accomplished, it brings forth death." The only way we can be sure of disrupting the "sin condensation" process is by stopping it in its tracks—wiping the can at the first sign of mist, as it were, even when it seems harmless. If we do not remain constantly vigilant, we may wake up one day swimming in sin.

Obese

My fitness program has identified me as "obese." *Well, that's rude,* I thought. Sure, I could stand to lose double-digit pounds, there's no arguing that. But to lose 55 pounds like it suggests, I'd need more than Marie Osmond, or even Jillian Michaels. I'd have to do six months in an Afghani prison camp. Or amputate a leg.

But whether the term fits me or not, certainly America has an obesity problem. And you don't have to watch *The Biggest Loser* to notice it. A trip to the local all-you-can-eat buffet should suffice. Some of us have gone way beyond spare tire range. More like spare Volkswagens.

Of course, Americans didn't invent fat. The Bible talks about it at length (or width, if you prefer). And although "the fat of the land" (Genesis 45.18) is a blessing, fat in its people is usually bad. Yes, "Good news puts fat on the bones" (Proverbs 15.30), but too much good news can be a problem. Psalm 73.3-4 describes fat people as wicked in their prosperity. Jeremiah 5.28 says they ignore the plight of the poor so they can remain rich themselves.

Now, I don't think for a moment there is a scale waiting at the pearly gates; Jesus is our judge, not Jenny Craig. But I do think we as the people of God can become so glutted with blessings that we become self-reliant or superior in our own minds. We should pray with Agur in Proverbs 30.8-9, "Give me neither poverty nor riches; feed me with the food that is my portion, that I not be full and deny You and say, 'Who is the Lord?' or that I not be in want and steal, and profane the name of my God."

Spraying

Well, it's springtime again, and for many of us that means it's time to donate blood—not to the Red Cross or the local hospital, unfortunately, but rather to the insect world. Last week my family was bombarded by a horde of mosquitoes that reminded me of Black Friday at Walmart. I think they actually carried Kylie a couple of feet down the sidewalk.

So I started spraying. And I kept spraying. And gradually the carcasses started increasing and the dive-bombers started decreasing. At this rate I may get my front porch back by the time it's too hot to use it.

But unfortunately, Max likes his walks. And my neighbors don't appear to be as diligent with their spraying as I am. And since I'm not inclined to fumigate the entire neighborhood at my expense, I suppose I'll have to spray myself before venturing out into enemy territory.

Dealing with sin can be even more frustrating. I have fits keeping my hands and heart pure—and that's with a steady application of God's word. "How can a young man keep his way pure? By keeping it according to Your word" (Psalm 119.9). And then I go out into the world, among people who are not similarly protected, and I am subjected to even more sin. Paul writes that I'd have to leave the world to get away from sinful people (1 Corinthians 5.10. And one day I will. But for now, I'll have to be content with taking God's word with me everywhere I go, protecting myself as best I can and encouraging others to do the same—for my benefit and for theirs.

Bureaucracy

I was watching the news today and seeing how the folks in Louisiana are trying to build barriers in the Gulf of Mexico to keep the massive oil spill from destroying more of their coastline, and how the government had not yet approved the necessary paperwork. The environmental impact of such a construction has not been adequately studied. I won't even comment.

Then I went out and cut my grass. In the process, I hit an anthill. Within a fraction of a second, the ants began to reconstruct the mound. No forms. No committees. No threat assessments. Just work. Call me cynical, but I have a hunch a bureaucratic ant colony would get a lot less done, meaning I'd spend a lot less money on Spectracide.

You don't have to be part of a particular political movement to believe in the stultifying, paralyzing power of bureaucracy. Long ago Solomon wrote, "If you see oppression of the poor and denial of justice and righteousness in the province, do not be shocked at the sight; for one official watches over another official, and there are higher officials over them" (Ecclesiastes 5.8).

As layers of bureaucracy increase, efficiency decreases. That's why Jesus said, "Give to him who asks of you" (Matthew 5.42), not, "Send him to the nearest charitable institution." It's why we as individuals are to "visit orphans and widows in their distress" (James 1.27). We can't delegate our benevolent duty.

Bottom line: If you see a good deed that needs doing, don't wait for clearance from the government, or even from the church. In the words of Phil Knight, just do it.

Word for Word

Objectify

Bret Michaels seems like a good guy in most respects. Works hard, loves his family, all that. And I'm sure he had no intent of objectifying his friend when, on live national television, he told her husband he was a lucky man to be married to a woman who looked so great in the "baby-maker" of a dress she was wearing.

And yet he did objectify her, I think most of us would agree. Most women want to be judged by something more than a tape measure. And they deserve that.

Now, in fairness to Bret, formerly of the '80s hair band Poison, the rock-'n-roll lifestyle encourages men like him to objectify women. For crying out loud, he had his own reality TV show where women literally lined up to be objectified by Bret Michaels. So it's understandable that he has a tough time looking at a beautiful woman (or her breasts, to be more specific) with an eye for her character. So maybe his culture should get some of the blame.

Perhaps his friend should take some blame, too. I have little sympathy for women who complain about men staring at body parts they are obviously showing off. Paul writes, "I want women to adorn themselves with proper clothing, modestly and discreetly" (1 Timothy 2.9). They should put their good works on display, not the good work of their physical trainers and plastic surgeons.

But the husband shouldn›t go blameless, either. If my wife were going to spend quality time with a hound like Bret Michaels, I'd make sure she wore a big burlap sack. Sorry, Bret. Nobody sees her in a "baby-maker" but me.

Inertia

I am a finisher. If I start a book, a movie, whatever, I have to make it to the end. My wife, not so much. If we watch four episodes of a TV series, she is perfectly capable of saying, "I don't care what happens next," and, just like that, reclaiming an hour of her week.

Unfortunately, I care. Once I find out what's happening, I want to find out what happens next. It's what led to my unfortunate soap opera summer in my teenage years.

It's the principle of inertia—one of the precious few things I retained from high school physics. Things like to stay the way they are. Things that are stationary (like me in front of the TV) tend to stay stationary; things in motion (like me on the way to the refrigerator during commercials) tend to stay in motion. If I get used to a behavior pattern, it tends to be easier to stay in it than to change.

That's one of the main reasons people in the world are resistant to the gospel. Jesus calls us to change virtually everything about ourselves—our likes, our dislikes, our behaviors, our alliances, virtually every connection we have to life on planet earth. And people don't like to change—especially when they enjoy being where they are. As we read in John 3.20, "For everyone who does evil hates the Light, and does not come to the Light for fear that his deeds will be exposed." So most of us resist.

But we can make inertia work for us instead of against us. The more entrenched we get in Jesus' lifestyle, the more we will want to "walk in the Light as He Himself is in the Light" (1 John 1.7). With God's help, we'll dig a rut in that path so deep we'll never be able to get out of it.

Tuna

I love tuna week. Every couple of months I'll whip up a batch of my special lowfat tuna salad and eat at least one sandwich a day until it runs out. It makes me glad to be a carnivore.

My wife hates tuna week. She thinks tuna stinks like dead fish. (I guess she has a point there.) And since I love Tracie more than I love tuna, I try to wait until she leaves the house, or at least the kitchen, before making it.

I'll grant that tuna has an unusually strong scent. But then, so do steaks on the grill. And roses. It's not the pungency of the odor that is objectionable, but rather its quality. And quality is in the nose of the smeller.

The gospel has a certain distinctive "odor" as well. Some love it, some hate it. And although becoming "all things to all men" (1 Corinthians 9.22) has its place, I can't offer an alternative to the fundamentals of God's menu. I can come up with dozens of recipes for tuna casserole, tuna croquettes, tuna burgers, whatever. But if a person doesn't like tuna, I can't do much with that.

Some preachers can't take rejection. They find more palatable messages and dress them up as the gospel, or hide tiny pieces of the gospel in a framework of worldliness. But they miss the point. If I say my lasagna is 100 percent tuna, Tracie won't believe me. And if I say I put some tuna in her chocolate cheesecake, she may shoot me.

I want people to love "the pure milk of the word" (1 Peter 2.2), not just my preaching. If they can't develop a taste for God's cooking, I need to find someone who can, and not "distort the gospel of Christ" (Galatians 1.7).

Correct

All men may be created equal, but all articles aren't. At least, not mine. I take great care to make each one the best it can be, but sometimes it just comes out better than other times. It might be that I just wasn't firing on all eight that day and I'll need a fresh pair of eyes later to tidy up. Some of my analogies are more *apropos* than others.

But my absolute minimum standard is correctness. If it's not correct, it doesn't matter how well constructed my arguments are, or how much I chuckle when I read it, or how good it makes my daughters look. It must be correct.

It's bad enough when I spot an extra period, or a split infinitive, or an incorrect use of the subjunctive mode. But that's not really the kind of correctness to which I refer. I mean Biblical correctness. I mean a proper handling of the word of truth (2 Timothy 2.15), from citing a passage accurately to making appropriate application.

I don't mean to suggest that a person bears no responsibility of his own when he turns to 2 Peter when I should have written 1 Peter, gets frustrated, and quits studying his Bible. Jesus' words will judge him (John 12.48); that would be so even if I had never taken up the pen. But I certainly would like to think I am making the pathway to righteousness easier to walk and not harder. If I'm not, I need to hang up my word processor until I learn better.

I think that's a big part of James 3.1—"Let not many of you become teachers, my brethren, knowing that as such we will incur a stricter judgment." My words need to be a reflection of His words, or I need to remain silent.

Word for Word

Respect

Tracie hates being the center of attention. And that's a bit of a problem for me, since I'm someone who (1) makes his living by standing in front of people and talking, and (2) gets his best illustrations from things that happen in everyday life.

So Tracie lets me talk about our girls all I want from the pulpit, but she wants me to leave her out of it. And I'm happy to do that—not so much because I'm afraid I might wake up one morning with fewer body parts than I had the night before, but because I respect her too much to put her in a position that makes her uncomfortable.

I guess this article might violate that principle. Oops.

Anyway, my point is, if I am truly "one flesh" with my wife (Genesis 2.24), I will show her the respect that I expect to be shown. I don't want people to think poorly of her; that reflects poorly on me. We're a package deal.

I am continually amazed at the eagerness of married people to demean their spouses—especially in a single-sex environment. The boys want to talk about how rotten their wives' cooking is. The girls want to one-up one another with stories about their husbands' idiocy and incompetence. Exactly what is that supposed to accomplish?

I want it to be said of my wife, "Her children rise up and bless her; her husband also, and he praises her, saying, 'Many daughters have done nobly, but you excel them all'" (Proverbs 31.28-29). And it is my responsibility to make sure people know how wonderful she is—or if she doesn't want to have the spotlight, at least I should refrain from dragging her name through the mud.

Evil

Hollywood loves evil. Can't get enough of it. And I don't mean that as a moral judgment (although I could make a good case) but rather as a comment on its preferred subject matter. The more evil, the better. If Robert Mitchum was grotesque in the original *Cape Fear*, make Robert DeNiro even more so in the remake. (And if they can blame religious zealotry for his depravity, so much the better.)

Consider *Monster*. Charlize Theron, one of the most beautiful actresses of her generation, won an Academy Award by donning the ugliest trappings possible to play serial killer Aileen Wuornos. (If you missed it, you're in good company; so did I and a few hundred million other Americans.) I'm not suggesting she wasn't great; I wouldn't know (again, missed it) but that the film industry has a bizarre fascination with society's dregs. It's not enough to point out evil; we must trace it to its source.

Well, I'll tell you the source. And it's not poor schools, or the inequality of classes, or ethnic bias, or any other real or perceived socio-economic problem. It's the devil. And I don't mean in a goat-sacrificing, blood-drinking, Manson family sort of way. I mean the actual, literal devil. The father of all depravity, from lies to murder (John 8.44). The world's ruler (John 12.31), its god (2 Corinthians 4.4). And all those who have not been transferred out of his kingdom and into the church, "the kingdom of His beloved Son" (Colossians 1.13), are still in it.

People choosing Satan over God. That's your source of evil.

Word for Word

Pain

I was telling my chiropractor about an old softball injury the other day. I told him the doctor diagnosed me as having stretched ligaments and gave me a prescription for pain, and that the problem went away in a couple of days. He asked, "Did the *problem* go away, or did the *pain* go away?" I chuckled and said that from my perspective, there wasn't a difference.

But I understood his point. Pain is not, strictly speaking, a problem; it's a symptom of a problem. If you have a broken leg, meds can make you more comfortable. But they won't help you walk; you'll need real treatment for that. In fact, if you think about it, pain is good. It's the mind's way of telling the body about a problem needing attention. The stronger the pain, the stronger the message.

I wish the people of the world would learn that lesson in regard to spiritual pain. God made humans for His purposes. And when sinners live in violation of those purposes and suffer for it, they are "receiving in their own persons the due penalty of their error" (Romans 1.27). Unfortunately, they often ignore the pain instead of using God's cure. Hopefully we Christians can pay better attention to His little messages when we wander off His path.

But also remember, pain isn't always from sin; sometimes it's just a consequence of living in the physical world. The curse brought pain (Genesis 3.16-19), and it will continue until we go to a world that is better. And there's a message there, too. Accept pain, deal bravely with it, but don't forget about it. Use it as a reminder of the things God has waiting for us on the other side.

Chilis

One year for my mother-in-law's birthday, I ate a whole jalapeño pepper. I thought it might provide a little extra entertainment for the occasion. Boy, was I right. I turned beet red. I started sweating profusely. Nothing could put out the fire in my mouth. I've often fantasized about dying in a Mexican restaurant, but this was not what I had in mind.

Turns out, you can actually measure the amount of capsaicin in a particular chili and objectively determine how "hot" it is. (Now they tell me.) Jalapeños max out at around 8,000 Scoville units of capsaicin. But the habanero weighs in at 580,000 Scoville units, more than 70 times the heat of the jalapeño. Ouch.

I have been told the habanero is as hot as it gets. Not so. India's *bhut jolokia*, or "ghost chili," registers more than a million Scoville units. The Indians are currently trying to weaponize it. Literally. That's how hot it is.

And yet people eat them. And, usually, survive. But not for a lack of effort, it would seem.

Why would someone willingly subject themselves to such an ordeal? Showing off, mostly. People (especially men) will do almost anything to get the attention of others (especially women). And we give it to them. Hey, we'll give them their own show on the Travel Channel.

Solomon writes, "Like one who binds a stone in a sling, so is he who gives honor to a fool" (Proverbs 26.8). I wish we would be as good at honoring those who deserve it as we are those who seem determined to destroy themselves in the name of "putting on a good show."

Word for Word

Loners

I don't mind being alone. I prefer company, preferably that of my wife and (when they behave) my children. I love socializing with friends and strangers alike in public settings. But being by myself has advantages. I get the remote control. I get the good chair. If I want to eat the last cookie, I eat the last cookie.

In fact, as I look at the large number of first person singular pronouns in the last few sentences, all of the advantages to being a loner are pretty selfish. It reminds me of Proverbs 18.1—"He who separates himself seeks his own desire." The best way to get your own way is to avoid any competition.

But the disadvantages to life as a loner outweigh the advantages. That's not just Social Hal's judgment; Proverbs 18.1 goes on to read, "He quarrels against all sound wisdom." Common sense should tell us that we need other people in our lives. And if we're lacking in common sense, take God's word for it—"It is not good for the man to be alone" (Genesis 2.18).

Americans, far more than any other culture on earth, crave "personal space." We buy large tracts of land so we don't have to interact with neighbors. We shun public transportation. We revel in our cowboy and pioneer culture. Far be it from us to "need" anybody.

But we do need people. God gave us the church so we could have brethren to love, and who we can love in return. "Now you are Christ's body, and individually members of it" (1 Corinthians 12.27). We all need that connection, "loners" and social butterflies alike.

Lessons

A fundamental premise of this column is that God uses daily activity to teach us about Him, ourselves, and our role here on earth. Sometimes God draws a big circle around the lesson; sometimes He lets us work it out for ourselves.

An example: In 1 Corinthians 9.9, Paul quotes from Deuteronomy 25.4—"You shall not muzzle the ox while he is threshing." A farmer's ox would occasionally want to have a snack while grinding grain. But instead of tying the ox's mouth closed to maximize yield, the owner was to allow the ox to profit from his work. Paul says the purpose of the law was not to promote "animal rights" (more on that bizarre concept another time), but rather to teach a lesson about work, and about common decency.

The same is true for prohibitions on interbreeding livestock, or planting a field with two crops, or blending different plant fibers in a single garment (Leviticus 19.19). He was teaching lessons on purity. Hopefully by keeping the commandments pertaining to mundane matters, the people would be reminded to remain distinct from the pagan nations that surrounded them. Paul teaches us the same lesson in 2 Corinthians 6.17—"Therefore, come out from their midst and be separate."

God is trying to transform our character into that of His Son (Romans 12.2). Some of the steps He asks us to take may seem less central to the overall purpose than others. But we don't see the overall purpose as well as He does. We need to just sit quietly, learn our lessons, and thank Him for the privilege of sitting at His feet.

Word for Word

Enough

Life in God's physical world brings many wonderful joys, and we are blessed to be partakers of them. Among my own favorites are sports, music, thrill rides, and good Chinese buffets. As Solomon wrote in Ecclesiastes 3.12-13, "I know that there is nothing better for them than to rejoice and to do good in one's lifetime; moreover, that every man who eats and drinks sees good in all his labor—it is the gift of God."

But in all of these joyful pursuits, we eventually reach a metaphysical, conceptual place called "enough." "Enough" is the point where the pleasure derived from the activity in question no longer outweighs the disadvantages—the aching, the monotony, the heartburn. And I have noticed, as I wade deeper and deeper into my mid-forties, that "enough" arrives earlier than it did a few years before.

And that's okay. The pleasures aren't any less real or frequent; in fact, they become more so as my children grow and mature in the flesh and in the Lord. But I look forward to the time when I will receive even greater blessings, even greater pleasures. And not getting to "enough."

I love praising God with (and without) my brethren. But my voice eventually gives out. That will not always be the case. One day there will be no "enough."

I love spending quality time with my brethren. But my mind eventually gives out. That will not always be the case. One day there will be no "enough."

I love being a "living and holy sacrifice" (Romans 12.1). But my body eventually gives out. That will not always be the case. One day there will be no "enough."

Socks

On the first day of every basketball practice, the late great John Wooden, coach of the most dominant team in college basketball history (maybe sports history), the man who literally wrote the book on winning, the man who every basketball dad in the country wanted his son to learn from in the boy's formative years, did the same exact thing.

He taught his boys how to put on their socks.

Socks, you see, get wrinkled in a sneaker, especially under the stress that occurs while playing basketball. Wrinkles cause blisters. Blisters cause lost playing time. Lost playing time hurts the team.

The lesson stuck. Bill Walton, one of his greatest players (Wooden would have preferred "student"), recalled years later that it prepared them for "everything we would need to know for the rest of our lives."

Big problems often come from a poorly prepared foundation. When we start poorly, we build poorly, and typically we finish poorly.

Such is the case in our walk with Christ as much as any other endeavor. The most important verse in the Bible is not John 3.16, or Acts 2.38, or Colossians 3.17—although each of those is vital. The most important verse in the Bible is the first verse—"In the beginning, God created the heavens and the earth" (Genesis 1.1). If we start by acknowledging God as Creator, we are in position to appreciate His role as Lawgiver and our own roles as clay in His hands (Jeremiah 18.6). If we miss that lesson, we have no hope of properly applying any of the others.

Word for Word

Punishment

Say a father tells his child, "No." Say the order comes with the promise of a specific punishment. Say the child breaks the rule anyway. And just for my sake, say this isn't my child.

What is a father to do? Well, the obvious course of action is to follow through with the promised punishment. But sometimes he doesn't. Maybe he never really intended to punish the child. Or maybe he found it convenient to change the rules in the middle of the day.

We would probably call that poor parenting (that is, when it's someone else's child in question). And yet we insist on saying God parents that way (that is, when we ourselves are the child in question). Not too consistent.

We have any number of Bible lists of sinful behaviors, but Malachi 3.5 will do—" Then I will draw near to you for judgment; and I will be a swift witness against the sorcerers and against the adulterers and against those who swear falsely, and against those who oppress the wage earner in his wages, the widow and the orphan, and those who turn aside the alien, and do not fear me,' says the Lord of hosts." Now the question is, will God do as He promised? And remember, the very next verse reads, "For I, the Lord, do not change."

And remember Numbers 23.19—"God is not a man, that He should lie, nor a son of man, that He should repent; has He said, and will He not do it? Or has He spoken, and will He not make it good?" He can't lie, so the threat was real. He won't repent, so the rules don't change. It sounds to me like God plans to punish sin.

Ego

I was halfway watching a sports show on TV when a "highlight" showing the near-complete disintegration of a racecar flashed on the screen (hence the quotation marks around "highlight"—the driver likely would have described it differently). The visual was striking enough. But then the announcer asked, "And what does a wreck like that do to a driver's ego?"

That got my attention. I mean, I'm not a professional driver. But if I were, and shards of my vehicle were flying to the four winds while I became increasingly enveloped in flames, I don't think I'd be worried about my *ego*.

But I could be wrong. Ego can be a pretty compelling force. I'm reminded of the story of King Amaziah, fresh off a victory over Edom and eager for more. He challenged King Jehoash, his fellow Israelite who had a much stronger army. Jehoash told him a story: "The thorn bush which was in Lebanon sent to the cedar which was in Lebanon, saying, 'Give your daughter to my son in marriage.' But there passed by a wild beast that was in Lebanon, and trampled the thorn bush" (2 Kings 14.9). Translation: Delusions of grandeur do not an army make. Of course, Amaziah fought him anyway; of course, he lost.

Why do we insist on slaying dragons that don't need slaying instead of just whittling the sharp edges off our own pride? Perhaps the worst defeat we can imagine is the death of our own invincibility. But if Christianity requires anything, it's the death of ego. As Paul writes in Philippians 3.8, we cannot truly gain Christ until we give up any claim of being special in our own right.

Pendulum

I get uneasy when people talk about "the pendulum" of morality. You know the conversations. You're sitting at the lunch table, griping about modern clothing styles, song lyrics, whatever. And someone invariably says, "I'm just waiting for the pendulum to swing back toward traditional values. It always does."

I'm not too sure that's true. Where is the documentation of a society's wild swings between morality and degeneracy? Sure, the movies describe the wild and crazy America of the 1920s, followed by the austere 1930s. But the average American wasn't holed up in a speakeasy for ten years drinking bathtub gin with Al Capone. Basic morality for most of the population, as far as I can tell, went largely unchanged until the 1960s, when a variety of factors (Vietnam, rock-'n-roll and "the pill," notably) pushed an entire generation toward hedonism. I haven't seen any significant drift backward. And I've been watching.

We're using the wrong metaphor to describe sin. It's not a pendulum. It's a snowball. It doesn't reverse itself. It is the fire that never says, "Enough" (Proverbs 30.16). If given a rich environment, it will spread until it not only dominates a society but actually defines it. Many such societies have developed over the years. Babylon. Persia. Rome. The Soviet Union. Seeing a trend, anyone?

True, "Blessed is the nation whose God is the Lord" (Psalm 33.12). But the solution isn't national. It's me and my family, you and yours, saying, "as for me and my house, we will serve the Lord" (Joshua 24.15). It won't save the world. But it might just save us.

Friendships

On Facebook, I don't turn down friend requests. I've wanted to a few times. Some people, frankly, are annoying. Some are total strangers. Some seem rather proud of their immorality. Some aren't "people" at all; they appear to be companies or organizations that I may or may not have heard of, which I may or may not patronize.

But I say yes anyway. It gives me an opportunity I would not have otherwise to share the gospel. I can always "unfriend" them later if it becomes necessary.

(Please note that I do not advise this approach for you. And I expressly forbid it for my daughters.)

It seems to me that the whole point of friendships in the sinful world is to be lights (Matthew 5.14), to show how they can imitate us as we imitate Christ (1 Corinthians 11.1). After all, what better thing could one do for a friend than help him save his soul?

But it also seems to me that many Christians appear determined to keep their friendships and their service to Christ separate. It's as if Jesus is a threat to their friends and their sensibilities from which they must be shielded.

Well, He's a threat, all right. He will shake them to their core. He will challenge every belief, every loyalty, every priority. He tells them nothing they've done to this point in their life matters at all—that they, like Nicodemus, need to be "born again" (John 3.3).

But that's a good thing. Indeed, if you call Jesus your Lord and heaven your home, that's the only thing. What kind of friend would I be if I robbed them of that?

Example

Every parent of more than one child has had "the example talk" with the oldest one at some point. In my house it sounds something like this: "Taylor, Kylie's looking up to you. You need to be an example for her."

Well, the fact is, she's going to be an example whether I tell her or not, whether she wants to be or not. It's a matter of whether she will be a good example or a bad one. Naturally, I'm rooting for good. But actually, Kylie needs both. Actually, so does Taylor. Actually, so do I.

In verses 6 and 11 of 1 Corinthians 10, ancient Israel is described as an example for us. The bad kind. In between those verses, we have their specific offenses. Craving evil things. Idolatry. Acting immorally. Trying the Lord. Grumbling. And we have the specifics of how God responded to the offenses. It's not a pretty picture.

We often turn to Hebrews 11 to see what godly examples look like. And certainly people like Noah, Abraham and Moses can be great sources of encouragement and instruction. But we can learn lessons just as valuable from the villains of the text. Like ancient Israel.

We read passages such as Colossians 3.5—"Therefore, consider the members of your earthly body as dead to immorality, impurity, passion, evil desire, and greed, which amounts to idolatry." We accept it intellectually. But do we give ourselves a pass when we come up short? After all, we are the people of God.

Well, the Israelites were the people of God, too. Consider what happened to them. Learn from their example.

Relevance

At the time of this writing, my Facebook group reaches 24 different nations, touching every continent on earth but Antarctica. (It may take a while to put that particular pushpin on the map.) That excites me. I never thought I'd be able to preach in China, or the Philippines, or Nigeria—let alone all of the above and more, three times a week.

But it's also a bit daunting. I'm very American, and even more Texan. My writing reflects my culture, my surroundings, and my way of life. I'm not sure at all, having lived almost entirely here, that my experiences translate well for those who do not share my background.

That's one of the wonderful things about the gospel of Jesus Christ, though. Its relevance transcends national borders. It connects with people at a level much deeper than ethnicity, native tongue or political ideology. It appeals to our common failings—"for all have sinned and fall short of the glory of God" (Romans 3.23). It appeals to our common ancestry—"and He made from one man every nation of mankind to live on all the face of the earth" (Acts 17.26). It appeals to our common desire—"For indeed in this house we groan, longing to be clothed with our dwelling from heaven" (2 Corinthians 5.2).

I don't know how much in common Peter's listeners had at Pentecost, but it was enough to convince them of their common need for the One who was made Lord and Christ (Acts 2.36). If I stick close to that message, I'm confident my efforts will have more than enough relevance—not because of my work, but because of His.

Burrs

My dog Max loves visiting my folks in the Texas Hill Country. He finds himself surrounded by all sorts of wildlife that he doesn't see in my neighborhood. He's quick to dart into every grass patch, hoping (apparently) to find a deer, mouse or raccoon. Needless to say, he would not have the slightest idea what to do if he found one.

But in the Hill Country, grass means grass burrs. And as fond as I am of following him through the underbrush, I'm not too thrilled with holding him down and picking the burrs out of his coat. (He's even less thrilled than me.)

It's easy for me to get frustrated at the burrs' annoying ability to dig into animal fur. But then, they are doing exactly what God made them to do. Max and a few trillion of his fellow mammals are just laying the foundation for the next generation of pesky weeds. Thanks, Adam.

God's design works. We may not always appreciate or acknowledge that when things don't go our way, but it is working just the same. This is a critical lesson for us—particularly with regard to the spread of the gospel. It may seem that our efforts in His cause are in vain, judging from a lack of visible results. But we must remember the words of Isaiah 55.11—"My word ...will not return to Me empty, without accomplishing what I desire, and without succeeding in the matter for which I sent it."

The gospel doesn't save everyone; it isn't designed to. It's designed to cut us open and reveal our hearts (Hebrews 4.12-13), to appeal to His people and repel others (Matthew 11.25). That's exactly what it does.

Evidence

Driving home from a short trip out of town this week, it quickly became clear that our part of the state had been through a pretty big storm. The evidence was everywhere. All the rice and corn fields had standing water, most driveways had puddles, broken tree branches littered the yards. I didn't need a Ouija board to get the message.

It's the same thought process, natural and instinctive, that God asks us to use in our search for Him. If we intuitively assign a cause to disorder, is it not that much more necessary for us to assign a cause to the underlying order? If we assume something made the tree break, must we not also assume something made the tree itself?

We walk along boardwalks and jetties that maximize our use of the beachfront, and we assume someone built them. But God built the beach (Job 38.8-11). Which is more impressive?

We see a light burning in the house and we assume someone turned it on. But God turns on the sun every day (Job 38.12). Which is more impressive?

We see a falcon leap from its handler's wrist, capture its prey and bring it back, and we assume it has been trained to do so. But God taught it how to fly in the first place (Job 39.26). Which is more impressive?

You do not need me to prove the existence of God. If you are not inclined to believe the evidence that surrounds you, my words won't help. But to the one who is willing to consider the existence of One unseen, One greater than himself, words are unnecessary (Psalm 19.3).

Allotment

The population of the entire world would fit comfortably in an area the size of Texas. Admittedly, that's not leaving room for Dairy Queen or Walmart, but still, a thousand square feet of space per person is nothing to sneeze at.

I think about that when I travel by car to other parts of the state. For every square mile covered in concrete there are dozens, if not hundreds, covered in grass and trees. Now, for the city-dweller tired of trading elbows with his neighbors, the allotment of space may seem unfair. But in reality, it's just space utilized differently. A cotton farmer or cattle rancher requires more land to provide for his family than a stock broker or policeman. And we should be glad for them to have it; they will use the extra space to help put food on our plates and clothes on our backs. Which brings us back to Dairy Queen and Walmart.

Unequal allotment does not necessarily equate to unfair allotment. The Lord, in His wisdom, has showered His blessings upon us in different measures. Some may take issue with that, thinking "stuff" is a measure of God's love. In reality, God may simply think some are in position to accomplish more in His name with extra resources as illustrated in the parable of the talents (Matthew 25.14-30). Or He may be testing us to see if we will, like Job, serve Him "for nothing" (Job 1.9).

In any case, God owes us no explanation. He has given the most poverty-stricken of us far more than we deserved. Instead of fretting about the blessings He has not given, we should try to handle better the ones he has.

Fantasy

My wife thinks I fantasize about retiring, buying a few hundred acres and raising cattle. She couldn't be more wrong. In my real fantasy, I buy a few thousand acres and raise exotic game. I'd import sable antelope, zebras, maybe a cheetah or two (if they would promise to play nice with others). I would have a whole crossword puzzle section—gnu, ibex, oryx, emu, all the Sunday crossword favorites. I say if you're fantasizing, go big.

I'd plan the whole thing out carefully, get just the right property, build shelters and tall fences, consult with experts as to what species would coexist and prosper in the local climate, buy the animals, let them loose, and ...

That's where the fantasy breaks down. What would I do then? Drive through the range every day trying to get a glimpse of something? Sit in a 50-foot watchtower all day? Install cameras so I could watch from my living room? Wouldn't it be easier just to watch Animal Planet?

It would be just like any number of other fantasies I've had—albeit on a much grander scale. I get excited at the prospect of getting something, it finally arrives and, lo and behold, the perfect accessory to my life has not made my life perfect. And as such, it's really almost depressing.

That's why we are to pursue contentment, not happiness. Paul writes, "I have learned to be content in whatever circumstances I am" (Philippians 4.11). If we can learn to appreciate the blessings we already have, we will find our "wish list" will get a lot shorter. And the happiness will take care of itself.

Word for Word

Bulletproof

Mitchell Siegel died as a result of an armed robbery of his second-hand clothing store. His son, Jerry, was traumatized by the event. Only 17 at the time, Jerry soon immersed himself in a world of imagination where the inequities of life could be handled more simply, more effectively. And soon he conceived of a character who was invulnerable—literally bulletproof—who would use his strength to protect those who were less strong.

He called the character "Superman." And the combination of Jerry's writing and his friend Joe Shuster's art eventually made the character an iconic part of American culture. People were drawn to the idea of a hero from another world, better than the rest of us, capable of spectacular things, sent by his father to serve the interests of humanity at great sacrifice to himself.

But then, why shouldn›t that story appeal to us? It's the same story we've heard told since we were children. It's the story of power, of service, of love.

It's the story of Jesus.

Of course, Jesus wasn't bulletproof in the normal sense of the word while here in the flesh. But "the flaming arrows of the evil one" (Ephesians 6.16) could not touch Him. Because of this, Paul can write, "I will rather boast about my weaknesses, that the power of Christ may dwell in me" (2 Corinthians 12.9). That power, available to us through the gospel, is all the protection we need.

We are not spiritual Supermen, and never will be. But He is. By His grace, that is enough.

Soccer

I gave it a shot. I really did. After all, the World Cup is the biggest sporting event in the world. If I'm ever going to "get" soccer, it will be now. So I did. And I don't. I really don't. A perfectly good cow pasture gets mowed down and marked up so grown men can run around bouncing balls off their faces and complain about imaginary injuries. *Oooooh*.

(By the way, if you feel like I'm being unduly disrespectful to "the world's game," feel free to shove a yellow card in my face. I think I'll be able to take it.)

And don't tell me how it's the world's most popular sport, how billions and billions of people can't be wrong. Of course they can be wrong. For crying out loud, a whole continent of them won't wear deodorant. Trust me, being wrong is considerably more than a possibility.

Majority doesn't rule in the truly important things in this world. Right rules. Dogs are man's best friend; cats are furniture's worst nightmare. "Sunday dinner" is served in the afternoon and features a large piece of mammal. And a "football" always, *always* has pointed ends.

I'm not really concerned about how many people agree or do not agree with these opinions and a few thousand others I could list. And if I can be confident in my opinions against broad opposition, I ought to be able to do the same in regard to God's revealed will. Jesus warned us that the approved path for our life is unpopular; "there are few who find it" (Matthew 7.14). So if my neighbors are completely at ease with my understanding of the Scriptures, that's not good news for me. That's bad news.

Word for Word

Vuvuzelas

Just when you thought you had run out of reasons to hate soccer—just when you thought you might get used to scoreless ties, hooligans, goalies with wrong-color uniforms and Mickey Mouse gloves, clocks that count up instead of down, time running out and the referees saying to keep playing anyway, flopping, yellow cards, red cards, ...

Sorry, I lost my train of thought. Where was I?

Oh, that's right. Vuvuzelas. The bizarre high-decibel horns that have taken the World Cup hostage. The TV audience hates them. The announcers hate them. The players hate them. Every fan you talk to hates them. And yet they continue to burst eardrums by the thousands.

It would seem a few fans are so determined to impact the game, they are willing to subject other fans to the threat of permanent hearing damage, and the TV audience to concerns that their sets have been infested by hornets.

Some people cannot be content with being observers. They must be involved directly. No, they must make an *impact*. They want to be able to tell their buddies at the bar that their efforts were the key to their team's success.

Tragically, some Christians are like that. They don't think they are serious Bible students unless they uncover some hidden meaning or textual nuance that no one before was smart enough to find. It's arrogance in the extreme.

To the proud, God says, "you boast in your arrogance; all such boasting is evil" (James 4.16). If you are looking to make a name for yourself, serving Jesus is not for you. Go blow your horn somewhere else.

Marjoram

When the gardening season began, I decided it might be interesting to try growing marjoram. It was different, it was cheap, we had some space, and I know it's used a lot in cooking. So why not?

But I didn't really know much about marjoram. So when the weeding season arrived (way too late, as it typically does at my house), I had trouble identifying it. Two different plants were in the right general area and had the long branches and small, round leaves I remembered. After a minute or two, I had an idea. I broke branches off both of them, crushed one in my left hand and the other in my right, and tried to imagine each one on a pot roast. It wasn't too difficult to pick a winner.

It reminds me a bit of Jesus' parable of the tares in Matthew 13.24-30. The Lord sows His field (the world, according to His explanation in verse 38) with good seed, and the devil clutters it with weeds. And it's not always easy for us to tell the difference. But, "The Lord knows those who are His" (2 Timothy 2.19). And He can tell the difference between a plant that smells like a Christian and one that just, well, smells.

We forget sometimes that we are planted in His field for His purposes, not our own. We may see tremendous progress in our own lives (as we define progress) and assume the Lord blesses our actions. But we are not the judges of what is a fragrant aroma of worship. And if we continue to focus on our agenda instead of His, we may find ourselves on the wrong end of His sickle in judgment.

Word for Word

Daddy

I don't hear the word "Daddy" as much in my house these days as I used to. I miss that. There is little in the world more delightful than the voice of a child saying, "Daddy." (Then again, there's little in the world more annoying than the same voice saying, "Daddydaddydaddydaddydaddy." So it's a trade-off.)

Many of my favorite memories about the girls involve them speaking in childish ways. Like Taylor toddling to the door with her purse, saying, *"I go choppin Mommy"* on grocery day, or *"I checka may-il"* when the mailman is thought to have come. Or Kylie handing her grandfather an M&M, watching him eat it, then cackling, *"I wikked it, Papa!"* They were all potential and no vice. (I admit, there may be rose-colored lenses on my rearview mirror.)

But I think I love being "Dad" even more than being "Daddy." Sure, they disappoint and anger me more now. But that's because I expect more now. The pride I feel now is not based just on future potential, but also in large part on present accomplishments. And as pleased as I was to get hugs from my toddlers when I was their whole world, it means even more now when I am not my big girls' whole world and they hug me anyway.

I imagine God is the same with His children. He rejoices when we first cry out, "Abba! Father!" (Romans 8.15). But I think He's even happier when we "grow up" (Ephesians 4.15). Adult Christians with "senses trained to discern good and evil" (Hebrews 5.14) glorify Him better than babes—or at least, they should.

I hope I make Him as proud as my girls make me.

Rentals

Every comedian has a routine about rental cars. The prevailing thought seems to be that they are trashed-out, beat-up breakdowns waiting to happen. They appear to have come to that conclusion by assuming that everyone treats rentals the same way they do—that is, drive it like you're in last place at the demolition derby. After all, it isn't theirs. They will just give it back in a few days. Might as well get the extra insurance and have as much fun as possible.

My own experience with rentals has been very much the opposite. I've always found them to be clean, well-maintained, low-mileage, relatively comfortable vehicles—not usually the flashiest things on the road, but then, neither am I. I am mortified at the idea of mistreating someone else's property, and therefore I actually take far better care of the rental than I do of my own car.

I have the same philosophy with regard to the body I'm renting from God. A lot of people just use their bodies as mechanisms for maximizing short-term pleasure—eat, drink, and be merry. But I look at it as a loaner that God has given me to get me through until I get my real body, the one waiting for me in heaven. Corruptible will one day put on incorruptible (1 Corinthians 15.53). And as Jesus Himself argues in Luke 16.11-12, why would God give us something transcendent in heaven when we couldn't properly take care of the mundane here on earth?

Plus, I figure it's good practice. I'll be spending eternity glorifying God with my next body. It just makes sense to do the same now, as best I can, with this one.

Word for Word

Ladders

The warning label read, and I quote, "Failure to read and follow instructions on this ladder may result in injuries or death." So naturally I read and followed the instructions, right?

Are you kidding? I didn't even *look for* the instructions. It's a *ladder*, for crying out loud. I've been using ladders all my life, and so far without inflicting harm on myself or others. But it did make me stop and think. It would be pretty silly if my family were to hear at my funeral, "He died from using the top of a ladder for a step, even though the directions right there on the ladder specifically told him not to."

Warnings do us no good if we pay them no heed. This is especially the case with Biblical warnings. Repeatedly God tells us about sin. He gives us lists of specific sins to avoid (1 Corinthians 6.9-10, Galatians 5.19-21, Romans 1.28-31, etc.). He tells us stories about disobedient people "as an example, and they were written for our instruction" (1 Corinthians 10.5-11). He gives us graphic depictions of the penalty waiting for sinners (Matthew 18.8-9, Revelation 21.8, etc.).

And yet people ignore the warnings—even people who claim to love God and respect His word. I suspect the problem is the same as with the ladders. We have declared ourselves competent on the subject. We are in no further need of instruction.

But I would really, *really* hate to be wrong on this point. Perhaps rereading God's warnings a few hundred more times isn't such a hardship after all.

Lost

I was a big *Lost* fan. I know, lots of preachers think any TV show produced after *The Andy Griffith Show* went off the air is, by definition, of the devil. And I am not offering a blanket recommendation to all readers. (We didn't let our 13-year-old watch it.) But I was fascinated by the concept. Various people, strangers, are living their lives in various degrees of dissatisfaction—"lost souls" in a very real sense. And they are brought together by forces beyond their imagining, where they realize they are part of a bigger picture, a bigger plan, that they do not and perhaps never will understand, but that lends purpose and dignity to their existence.

Plus I thought the smoke monster was cool.

The idea of being lost, of course, is a prominent Bible theme. We go our own way, follow our hearts and instincts, and we wind up at a funeral, or divorce court, or the doctor's office. And we wonder whether any of it has meaning, whether life is worth the oxygen. Solomon was lost in the most opulent palace of his day when he asked in Ecclesiastes 1.3, "What advantage does man have in all his work which he does under the sun?" Simon was lost as the most popular man in town (Acts 8.9-13), Zaccheus as the least (Luke 19.1-10). It's not about our circumstances. It's about whether we will satisfy ourselves with an unsatisfactory life, or whether we will take a chance and listen to One who promises something better.

Jesus says, "Come to Me" (Matthew 11.28). So come. Come in the midst of your despair. Let Him find you. And in Him, find yourself.

Walk

The coolest thing happened to me today. I took Max out for his walk, and I noticed a front moving in. First, it started getting darker. Then I felt the temperature drop suddenly. Then I felt the breeze from the south pick up, bringing moisture from the coast. Then I literally heard the rain in the leaves of the tree on the other side of the street. And finally, it started to rain on us.

Now, I'm no Gene Kelly. Whatever singing I do in the rain is typically done from the security of a roof and four walls. But today's rain was different. I just smiled and kept walking at the same pace. I can't remember when Max and I ever had a more pleasant walk.

I suppose if you had asked me yesterday what my ideal walk would be like, I would have imagined a sunny day, or a starry night, or perhaps a snowy afternoon. But God has delights for us in every facet of life, not just the ones found on picture postcards and in photo albums.

Our relationship with Jesus is often described in travel terms. He leads us in "paths of righteousness" (Psalm 23.3). Paul called his life in Christ a "course"—one he had almost completed (2 Timothy 4.7). The early saints called their movement "the Way" (Acts 9.2). Jesus is our walking companion, providing a shower of blessings (pardon the metaphor) as we go. We "rejoice always" (1 Thessalonians 5.16) because we are always with Him.

Genesis 5.24 reads, "Enoch walked with God; and he was not, for God took him." I hope and pray my walk ends like that.

Waves

In Texas, we wave. Especially while driving. All waves look the same, but not all waves are equal. A wave from a fellow driver can mean, "Hi, Hal!" (a friend), "I'm a generally friendly person" (a total stranger), "Thank you" (a person I let through the intersection in front of me), or, "Be careful next time!" (a police officer who saw me put on the brakes right before hitting his speed trap).

Most of the time, I don't have much trouble telling the difference between waves. It's all about context. If I get the wave after I blow my horn at the guy who cut me off in traffic, it's probably the "I'm sorry" wave. If I'm the one honked at and the waver is in my rear view mirror, it's probably the "You're an idiot" wave. Context.

My whole preaching career I have told people that the same word means different things, sometimes even unrelated things, in different contexts. That's not preacher double-speak. That's common sense. How many words in English do you know that have multiple meanings?

Take "faith," for instance. Its root meaning is simply belief, especially belief in spiritual things—"the conviction of things not seen" (Hebrews 11.1). But sometimes it's a saving faith (Ephesians 2.8), sometimes it's a dead faith (James 2.26). Sometimes it represents everything we do to please God (Romans 5.1), sometimes it is paired with concrete action (Mark 16.16). Sometimes it even stands for God's entire plan of salvation (Jude 3).

Take the time to examine the context. God will explain His "waves" to you if you give Him half a chance.

Field

Trees make for great scenery, but I have a special place in my heart for wide-open fields of green. God told us to subdue the earth (Genesis 1.28), and cleared land is a sign that someone has taken God's admonition to heart.

I love pastureland. I enjoy the tranquil sight of cattle grazing or parading in unison toward a well-placed water tank. I can't help but grin at the sight of a newborn foal frolicking in the thick, short grass. And I love farmland. I enjoy watching rows of crops whiz by, giving me a quick glance of the care the farmer took in plowing his fields just so, with furrows as straight as a string.

But I get aggravated when I see a field going to no apparent use. The richness of the soil is wasted, supporting nothing but weeds. And yes, land needs rest just like people do; that's why the Lord required the Israelites to allow their land to lie fallow one year out of seven (Exodus 23.11). But modern science has taught us how to use even fallow time for a short-term purpose—growing hay, for instance. There's simply no excuse for idle land. Build a house. Put up a billboard. Do *something*.

The world is God's field (Matthew 13.38). Some sow it, some water it (1 Corinthians 3.5-9). But everyone does something. Pleading ignorance, incompetence or fear won't work for us any more than similar pleadings did for the "one-talent man" of Matthew 25.24-28.

Failures focus on what they could do with what they are missing. Successes focus on what they can do with what they have. Which are you?

Ants

Far be it from a Texan to admit defeat, but there's no point in denying the obvious: Texas has lost the war with fire ants. It's over. Sure, I'll still spread enough toxic chemicals to chase them away for a season. But they'll just infest my neighbor's yard instead. And next season, they'll be back.

And there's bad news for our friends in Oklahoma: Apparently the ants have learned to swim.

Sometimes I wonder how a species with a brain the size of a pinpoint could defeat one that split the atom and went to the moon. And then I remember Proverbs 30.25—"The ants are not a strong people, but they prepare their food in the summer." In short, they are workers. They work when food is abundant. They work when food is scarce. They always find something to do in the service of their queen and their colony.

And strength is a relative thing. An ant can lift twenty times his body weight. Granted, that's not much. But proportionally, it's a considerably better effort than I can make. For me, that would be like lifting … well, never mind. A lot, anyway.

Solomon urges the sluggard to learn from the ant—"observe her ways and be wise" (Proverbs 6.6). Instead of finding excuses to rest, we need to find excuses to work for our King and His body (Colossians 1.24). It may feel like we're carrying twenty people on our backs when we "bear one another's burdens" (Galatians 6.2). But if ants can do it, we can. And if we set a good example for our brethren, we may find more help than we expected.

Word for Word

Napkin

A feudal lord went to dinner with two items—a knife to cut meat, and a cloth napkin to wipe himself. As trade grew, materials improved, and Mrs. Feudal Lord got more control of the castle budget, the napkin was tied around the lord's neck to protect his shirt. The napkin grew to be a status symbol; the classier the napkin, the classier the lord. Eventually, the napkin became of better stuff than the shirt it was intended to protect. So now the mistress of Hammons Manor prefers I take my "napkin" off at our Sunday feast lest I besmirch it with the drippings of my joint of beef. (Sorry, make that low-fat salad dressing.)

Time changes our view of things. They may become less valuable—like a favorite shirt that becomes, in turn, a workout shirt, a shoeshine rag, a carwash rag, and (if the wife lets it get that far) lint. But some things, like napkins, acquire value instead; by lingering, they acquire significance that may be completely unconnected to their original purpose.

Such was the case in Numbers 21. The people were infested with poisonous snakes because of their complaining, and God healed them when they looked in faith on the bronze serpent Moses made. The people saved the bronze serpent, no doubt to remember God's salvation. But eventually it became an idol (2 Kings 18.4). It lasted too long.

If we are not careful, we can make idols out of the things of God as well. Simply having something that earlier Christians had does not mean we are honoring God as they did. If I forget the reason for God's tradition, it may be my own tradition I am actually honoring. That's one of the many reasons we must immerse ourselves in the Bible—so we can tell the difference (Matthew 15.9).

Revolution

John Adams, American founding father and our second president, is quoted as saying, "The Revolution was effected before the war commenced. The Revolution was in the hearts and minds of the people." I don't doubt that he was correct. That is the way of all revolutions. Whether in nations or individuals, revolt is initially and primarily a state of mind.

Obviously Mr. Adams felt revolution was good—or least necessary. But spiritual revolution against the King of Kings is the worst thing imaginable. And it too begins in the mind. That is the point made in James 2.10-11—"For whoever keeps the whole law and yet stumbles in one point, he has become guilty of all. For He who said, 'Do not commit adultery,' also said, 'Do not commit murder.' Now if you do not commit adultery, but do commit murder, you have become a transgressor of the law."

James' point, applicable as much under Christ's law as Moses', is that violating God's commandment is a demonstration of willfulness—an implicit statement of rebellion, tantamount to saying, "In this particular point of consideration, I don't care what you want, God; I am going to do what I want." And it doesn't matter which point of consideration it is, or how many of them there are. Adulterers are not better than murderers, nor is a liar better than either or both. Sin is sin. Revolution is revolution.

We need to declare defeat in our revolution. Immediately. Find the necessary humility to accept His path. His entire path. And beg His forgiveness for the times that we start acting and thinking like revolutionaries.

Word for Word

Tutoring

My daughter Taylor needs a little help on her math these days. And since Tracie is handling the household tutoring in every other discipline, it falls to me to handle the math. And I'm glad to do it—at least, I am until she gets to second-year algebra. Then, I fear, we may be in need of something more serious. Like matches.

At any rate, that's a problem for another year. For now, I'm glad to do my part. And as aggravating as the tutoring process can be, it is even more gratifying when little eyes light up with discovery.

My temptation is always to do too much. I want her to succeed. But too much hand-holding will keep her from finding her own way. The whole point of the tutoring process is to not just get her to the end of the road, but to teach her how to get there on her own.

Similar imagery is used in Galatians 3.23-24 with regard to the law of Moses. God was trying to prepare His people for the coming of the Messiah. He could have just announced it with a voice from the sky—He did it for some (Matthew 3.17); surely He could have done it for everyone. But He wanted them to get there on their own, to show their own desire to learn.

That's one of the reasons why we should continue to read the Old Testament. True, we are no longer under our tutor; we are under the law of Christ now (1 Corinthians 9.21). But the more we listen to the tutor, the more we come to know the One of whom it speaks, and the more gratifying the feeling when we finally find Him.

Encounter

I wasn't even supposed to be at the store. I was supposed to have gone on the way home from an earlier trip to town. If I had, I probably never would have encountered the woman in the orange shirt.

She was middle-aged, chatty, wore a big smile. She had no trouble striking up a conversation at the register as her payment was processed. So far, so good.

But then she decided to tell a joke. It was crude, lewd, and, technically, at my expense (although I didn't take it that way, and I'm sure she didn't mean it that way). She was out the door before I fully processed what had happened, before I even had a chance to lodge a complaint or suggest a less objectionable form of humor.

That's exactly the type of chance encounter I will remember for the next 40 years. I may never see her again, but I will never forget the woman in the orange shirt who seemed so friendly and turned out to be so vulgar.

It made me think about the hundreds of chance encounters I have with others every day, and the impression I leave with them. Is it for good? Is it for Christ? Or am I taking the one opportunity I may have to shine my light to someone and showing them my "dark side" instead?

Light doesn't take days off. Light stays lit permanently, else it ceases to be light. Jesus puts us on permanent display, like a lamp on a stand (Matthew 5.15). If I choose to be dark for just a moment, that may be the moment someone desperately needed the light. It would be tragic for them, and for me, if I were to miss the only opportunity I ever have to show them the light of the Lord.

Word for Word

Achieve

Every time I watch *Lawrence of Arabia* I get something new out of it. I guess that's what makes for great films. This last time I was impressed by how much more Lawrence wanted democracy for the Arabs than they wanted it for themselves. The squabbling tribes of Arabia ultimately were more interested in settling old blood feuds and achieving honor in the way of their ancestors than in bringing long-term stability and strength to their region.

That's the way I feel as a preacher sometimes. I stand in the pulpit, bellowing and begging, prodding and pleading, trying to get the people in the audience to try to achieve greatness in their relationship with Jesus Christ. I see the unrealized potential within them, I see the missed opportunities, I see the mediocre to poor examples they are leaving with their children, and it makes me want to cry. But instead of growing in the Lord (2 Peter 3.18), they are more interested in making excuses for apathy, laziness and worldliness.

I just think that's tragic. Not only are they missing out on much of the joy of service here, but they are imperiling their eternal salvation. Jesus warns the Ephesians, "Remember therefore from where you have fallen, and repent and do the deeds you did at first; or else I am coming to you and will remove your lampstand out of its place—unless you repent" (Revelation 2.5).

Don't quit trying to achieve. Jesus has tremendous things in store for us. But first, we must want tremendous things for ourselves.

Lukewarm

I thought I had a relatively good understanding of Revelation 3.16, and what it means to be "lukewarm." Then I had lukewarm seafood gumbo off a salad bar for dinner one night. Now I *really* understand it.

Now, if I'd been served a bowl of cold seafood gumbo, it wouldn't have been a problem. I would have just rejected it. Had the tomato basil instead. But no, I was served *lukewarm* seafood gumbo. And sending food back is a hassle. I hate to inconvenience anyone. And it's not like it wouldn't have cooled off anyway. So I ate it.

Well, to make a long and disgusting story short, I got a lot of exercise and not a lot of sleep that night. And I learned a lesson the hard way: Just say "no" to lukewarm.

Revelation 3.16 reads, "So because you are lukewarm, and neither hot nor cold, I will spit you out of My mouth." Jesus wants hot disciples, those burning with the fire of the gospel—people like Jeremiah, who wrote, "But if I say, 'I will not remember Him or speak anymore in His name,' then in my heart it becomes like a burning fire shut up in my bones; and I am weary of holding it in, and I cannot endure it" (Jeremiah 20.9).

Being cold for Jesus is bad, but at least there's no confusion on the matter. No one is going to get the wrong idea about Jesus from someone who makes no pretense of following Him. The lukewarm Christian can do far more damage. Clearly, judging from Jesus' own language, it sickens Him. We do Him no favor when we give Him half our heart, half our energy, half our love.

Word for Word

Character

My Bible study approach when I don't have a particular topic or text in mind is often to simply open it randomly and see what the Lord has in store for me. So far He hasn't told me to go out and hang myself or that I will be given a donkey's burial. Keep those fingers crossed!

Today I woke up early to go play golf—a strangely frustrating, maddening and fascinating game. And before we left, I opened to Deuteronomy 8 and read how God led the people through the wilderness for forty years, how He tested, disciplined and humbled them, how He led them through fiery serpents and scorpions. And I found myself thinking, "You know, maybe I need to take up tennis."

No doubt about it, golf is a test of character. A test of whether you are willing and able to keep your composure under duress, whether you will adjust to adverse circumstances or merely curse them, whether you are concerned about the speck in your playing partner's swing instead of the beam in your own (to borrow an image from the Lord in Matthew 7.3).

The trials of life (and golf) are not pointless burdens from a spiteful God, but rather tools given to us to help us develop Jesus' attitude of humility and gentleness. We read in Romans 5.3-4, "tribulation brings about perseverance; and perseverance, proven character; and proven character, hope." It may be more appealing today to ask God for fewer troubles, but in the long term it is better to ask Him for help in learning the lessons that come with them—and for a stronger hope in something better.

Tone

Not so long ago, "chat" meant to speak. Now it is an alternative to speaking. And it has advantages, as do its cousins texting, e-mail and online networking. Our world values speed and convenience, and the new modes of written communication are all about speed and convenience.

But written correspondence has no tone. Oh, sure, you can use the symbol keys to type in little smiley-faces. But that's hardly the same as listening to the inflection in a speaker's voice for signs of irony, humor or sarcasm. And if you don't know me that well, believe me—those are some popular tools of my trade.

Paul addresses this subject (voice tone, not texting) in Galatians 4.20. After describing his consternation at their rejection of his inspired message in favor of a stranger's false doctrine, he wrote, "but I could wish to be present with you now and to change my tone, for I am perplexed about you." Had he been there, he could have tailored his approach more specifically—get kinder, get tougher, get louder, whatever it would take to get the message across.

And although it isn't really his point, it does remind us of the different ways we can express the same sentiment, even the same words, to achieve different results—including results counter to those we had intended.

More than ever it is vital that we send all communication through the love filter. A message to us may not have had the innuendo we inferred. One from us may not have conveyed the innuendo we implied. A little benefit of the doubt goes a long way.

Word for Word

Youth

The more I read Job, the more confused I am that someone could take the position that Elihu is a wise advisor for Job. As you may recall, Elihu appears in chapter 32 after Job and his three "friends" have an extended exchange. Job does not challenge or refute the young Elihu's rebuke, giving some readers the impression that he could not.

I have a tough time with that interpretation. Look at what Elihu actually says. He spends a chapter and a half just talking about how important he is. He calls himself "perfect in knowledge" (36.4). He says a test of wisdom is whether the listener is willing to listen to him talk (34.16). The whole speech reeks of youthful arrogance.

Actually, he reminds me a lot of a young me. I was well nigh intolerable in my youth. I remember trying to lecture my dad on everything from movies to building a proper hamburger—and this was in my preteen years. I got worse when I got to college. Frankly, it's amazing in retrospect that I never got shot.

I very well may not be cured yet (arrogance is tough to self-diagnose), but I know I've made progress. It's embarrassing to think back to times when I acted like I had all the answers—even on the rare occasion when I did. I needed to spend a lot less time trying to get people to not look down on my youthfulness (1 Timothy 4.12) and more looking for hoary heads to honor (Proverbs 16.31).

The exuberance of youth has a place. But so does being sensible (Titus 2.6). And although the first is natural, the second usually takes work. In my case, lots of work.

Native

Sometimes a preacher will go into a foreign land and stay for several years, trying to get the locals to accept Jesus Christ and submit to His will. After a few years, an old friend from home may visit to encourage the preacher. And he is astonished at the difference in his friend's life. The preacher now wears different clothes, eats different food, enjoys different entertainment, speaks a different language. And he tells the preacher, not unkindly, "You've gone native!"

Well, that's probably a good thing. It's appropriate for a preacher to "connect" with his neighbors socially, and that's tough to do when he's wearing a three-piece suit and they're wearing burlap. Then again, it can become easy to defend any custom, including those the gospel condemns, by saying, "That's how they do it here." Sin doesn't become less sinful simply because everyone in the room is doing it. Imagine Lot trying to defend the native customs of Sodom. "Yes, Lord, I know that old-fashioned morality may have worked out in the sheep pasture with Abraham. But they look at things differently here in the city. I'm just trying to go with the flow."

I think the best way to avoid this mentality is to consider ourselves not, for instance, a native American in a foreign land, but rather a native "Heavenite" in the foreign land called earth. If the local customs call into question where our true citizenship lies (Philippians 3.20), we have to remember home and where we truly long to be—and remember that acting like a native of the world is a sign we are making ourselves too much at home here.

Word for Word

Service

I am old enough to remember "service stations." My dad would pull the Chevy Impala up to the gas pump, and a young man would come to the window. "Fill it with regular," Dad would say, and the young man would. And he would also clean the windshield and check the oil, tire pressure and wipers. No extra charge. Think of Goober on *The Andy Griffith Show*. (I've seen it in reruns; I'm not quite that old.)

Now, most gas stations are "self-service." (Unless you live in Oregon. Apparently Oregon doesn't trust common people like me with highly combustible materials. Whatever.) Self-service means they provide you the tools to do all the checks yourself. And they charge you a buck for air. For *air*. That kills me.

Believe it or not, I'm not looking to return to the ways of a bygone era—or to move to Oregon, much as I love the state of my birth. If adding a nickel to the price would provide a living wage for Goober today, I'd be all for it. But it wouldn't. I would rather pump my own gas than pay what it would cost to have someone do it for me. Service is not worth the price.

But service is not optional in the Lord's church. It is absolutely central. Galatians 5.13 reads, "through love serve one another." Paul considered himself "a slave to all" (1 Corinthians 9.19). And this service is *really* free. No strings. No *quid pro quo*. Just the natural response of people who have been given the greatest service of all by the greatest Servant of all (Matthew 20.28), and who are eager to follow in His footsteps.

Running

In *Chariots of Fire* (in my mind one of the few Academy Award-winning films in my lifetime that really deserved the honor—an absolutely magnificent movie), English sprinter Harold Abrahams is devastated after having lost for the first time in his career. After failing to console him, his exasperated girlfriend says to him, "If you can't take a beating, perhaps it's for the best." Abrahams literally shouts in reply, "I don't run to take beatings! I run to win. If I can't win, I won't run."

Well, we can discuss sportsmanship another time. Here I would like to actually commend Abrahams for the single-mindedness that prompted his petulant and somewhat childish response. Running was everything to him. It was his way of showing the elites of his society that he was just as good as any of them. Better. He absolutely refused to accept anything other than excellence from himself. Second place was not a "good show," as the Brits would say. Second place was a miserable, embarrassing failure that could not and would not be tolerated.

He reminds me of the apostle Paul, who himself evidently was an athletics fan. "Run in such a way that you may win," he wrote in 1 Corinthians 9.24. Running to win is tough. Challenging. Painful. But for the competitor who truly wants to win, there is no alternative.

But don't let this calling deter you from running. As Abrahams' girlfriend said, "You can't win if you don't run." Failing to try is the one way to absolutely guarantee your absence at God's medal ceremony. Run the race. Finish the course. Claim the prize.

Word for Word

Thanks

So I'm in a restaurant and my ice tea glass is empty (a phenomenon that occurs four or five times in an evening—good thing I don't drink alcohol). I attract the waiter's attention, he comes to the table with a pitcher and refills my glass, and I say, "Thank you."

Apparently, that's not SOP in all parts of the country. I have always been under the impression that you thank people who act on your behalf. But it seems some feel that when a person is "just doing his job," verbal appreciation is not only unnecessary but even inappropriate.

If any such ones are reading this column, do me a favor: Take off any eyewear you may be wearing, and smack yourself on the cheek. Hard. I'm serious. And then say, "Thanks, Hal, wherever you are. I needed that."

I do not know why people think that they are entitled to take a service for granted simply because it is someone else's job to provide it. Since when do we need a *reason* to be civil to one another? Or do we think that waiters, doormen and mailmen are somehow offended when we express appreciation? Just because someone has a thankless job, that doesn't mean it has to stay that way.

I fear that attitude bleeds over into our dealings with God. We become so accustomed to His blessings, we forget to be grateful. Yes, it's His "job" to bless us. It's a job He chooses, out of love for us (Matthew 5.45). And what does He ask in return? "In everything give thanks, for this is God's will for you in Christ Jesus" (1 Thessalonians 5.18). That's not too much for Him to ask, is it?

Tradition

I was a dyed-in-the-wool traditionalist as a young adult. If we've done it the same way for years, there's probably a good reason. If it ain't broke, don't fix it. And there's definitely a broad streak of that in me still. But I have also come to realize that the world changes. Society changes. Pretending otherwise doesn't make it so. And an approach that may have been adequate in earlier times may not be so now.

If your cultural inertia locks you into wide ties and (yikes!) polyester suits, I don't know if that will hold back the cause of Christ. But clinging to teaching methods that are not tailored to the modern mind, or to spiritual songs with language so antiquated as to become meaningless to most singers—these and similar behaviors can become serious problems, well-intentioned though they may be.

Jesus criticized those who considered the gospel a mere patch for an old garment, or new wine to be poured into old wineskins (Luke 5.36-39). The gospel was new. It changed almost everything the Jews thought they knew about serving God, and they were unwilling to change. In the words of the text, "the old is good enough."

We absolutely must uphold the traditions of God preserved through inspiration (2 Thessalonians 2.15). But when we elevate man's tradition to the level of law, *"teaching as doctrines the precepts of men"* (Matthew 15.9), we elevate man to the level of God. We should not be afraid to change the package in which we present Jesus to the world—provided, naturally, that Jesus Himself and His gospel remain as they were when we received them.

Word for Word

Reading

I sunk a 30-foot putt for birdie the other day. Really. I have witnesses. I understand how any of you who have seen me play golf might doubt me on this point, but it is absolutely true.

I got a good "read" on how the putt would move on the green. I could even see the faint trail my approach shot made when it rolled past the hole. (Almost hit the pin, by the way. Not that I'm bragging.) I knew the ball would travel the same line going back the other way if I hit it right. And, wonder of wonders, I did. And it did.

Reading a putt is tricky. It will almost always move left or right, sometimes both. It will lose speed quickly or slowly, depending on the terrain; it may even gain speed. But there is one correct "read" on the putt, and only one. A golfer who says his putt broke "the wrong way" is self-deluded. The green wasn't wrong. He was wrong.

Reading the Bible is the same way. Ten different people can line up to the same passage and read it ten different ways. That doesn't make each one valid. It just means nine (or even ten) of them aren't as good at reading as they think. And when they act on their "read" and wind up in the wrong place, they have only themselves to blame. Scriptures are hard to understand only when "the untaught and unstable" distort them (2 Peter 3.16).

God wants us to succeed—to know the truth that sets us free (John 8.32). As obvious as that point is, we sometimes overlook that. He will guide us. He will forgive our errors. But we have to forget what we think we know and find the one true "read" that is there waiting for us.

Early

Some people are "morning people." They pop out of bed at the crack of dawn (or before) with a song in their heart and a spring in their step, like they're auditioning to play Snow White in local dinner theater or something.

I am not one of those people.

However, I am not opposed to early mornings. I am willing—in fact, downright eager—to get up at virtually any hour. I just need a compelling reason. An out-of-town trip. An early tee time. A breakfast Bible study. I can remember getting up at 3.30 to have a truck stop breakfast and go deer hunting with my dad when I was about 12. It was one of the best mornings of my life.

If I have a big day planned, I want it to start early. The earlier the better. Why wait? The sooner the day starts, the more of it I will have to enjoy.

Even more so in regard to my life with Christ. He says in John 9.4, "We must work the works of Him who sent Me, as long as it is day; night is coming, when no man can work." It's time to wake up (Romans 13.11). Duties await that will enrich our lives, bring us closer to our Lord and our brethren, and help salt the earth (Matthew 5.13). What better time to start than early?

The one who hesitates in committing his life to Jesus not only imperils his soul; he robs himself of hour upon hour of the life he was born to live. Truly, as Ananias told Saul of Tarsus, "And now why do you delay? Arise, and be baptized, and wash away your sins, calling on His name" (Acts 22.16).

Word for Word

Sunrise

If I lived on the Texas gulf coast—I mean, right there on the water—I would wake up before dawn just to watch the sunrise. Sunrises in town aren't the same. The buildings clutter the horizon; you are never sure when the day has actually begun. I can see myself cooking up my oatmeal, taking it out to the porch overlooking the water, and reading Psalm 113.1-3—"Praise the Lord! Praise, O servants of the Lord, praise the name of the Lord. Blessed be the name of the Lord from this time forth and forever. From the rising of the sun to its setting, the name of the Lord is to be praised." That would be a great way to start any day. Every day.

The sunrise is a reminder that every day is a gift from God, and to be used for His purposes. Yesterday's failures are gone; by His grace, we have a chance to do better. And with His help, we will.

When Isaiah looked ahead not just to his nation's captivity but to its eventual restoration, he saw it as a fresh opportunity for his people to serve God as they should—serve Him as they had neglected to do for centuries. He wrote that the nation would find purpose, success and hope if it would take advantage of the new day God would grant them. "Then your light will break out like the dawn, and your recovery will speedily spring forth; and your righteousness will go before you; the glory of the Lord will be your rear guard" (Isaiah 58.8).

God has blessed us with a new day in Jesus. May He give us the courage and wisdom to live it in a way that brings Him honor.

Compassion

My dog Max's favorite time of day is not his mealtime. It's my mealtime. If I'm sitting in my chair eating a sandwich, invariably he'll be at my feet, staring me in the eye, like he's hypnotizing me with his cute little black eyes. *Your dog is adorable. Your dog is hungry. You want to give your dog a bite of your sandwich.*

Generally I find it in my heart to give him something—pieces of crust, a small nibble of chicken, the last bite of my banana. But I don't give him much. He has food that is made for him, suited to his dietary needs. Dogs eat dog food, people eat people food. Not a tough concept.

I stick with this plan for two very good reasons. One, it's not good for him to eat too much people food—in fact, it can be downright dangerous. Two, it's not good for me to clean up after him when he's been in the people food. One time he became violently ill just from eating a small piece of an onion ring. Lesson learned there.

Compassion is concern for another's well-being. But to some, compassion is a justification for keeping their light under a basket (Matthew 5.15). They say it's to spare others' feelings; in truth, it may be a way of avoiding an uncomfortable situation. That's not compassion; that's cowardice. And selfishness. And faithlessness.

True compassion gives what is needed, not what feels best. And the best way to be compassionate "in the midst of a crooked and perverse generation" is by shining as a light (Philippians 2.15). It may not be the most comfortable thing to do. But then, that's not our priority, is it?

Deer

My girls love to visit my parents and watch the deer. My parents live in the Texas Hill Country, and everyone in their neighborhood puts out spoiled lettuce, cantaloupe rinds, rotten tomatoes, basically any kind of non-meat food that's not fit for humans to eat. Then they sit back and watch the deer come and get it.

But the deer aren't pets. My parents don't want them to be pets. They even put up automatic sprinklers to keep the deer off the porch. (Evidently the deer like Mom's shrubbery as much as cantaloupe rinds.) And the girls don't want them as pets, either. They may sit on the back steps with corn in their hands and *think* they want to feed the deer by hand, but we all know they would drop the food and run for the door if the deer ever got too close.

Apparently that's not always the case. I recently saw two video clips on YouTube with deer actually playing with dogs. Now, I know a Labrador retriever is a long way removed from wolves and jackals, but still, he's got to smell a little bit scary to a deer, right?

But that's what happens when habitats collide. And Christians are a bit like deer. We watch our enemies making inroads into our world through materialism and carnality, and before long they're just part of the landscape.

But the devil's henchmen aren't Labradors. They are wolves. They may look cute and cuddly, but it's sheep's clothing (Matthew 7.15). They will devour us eventually. We must remain "wise in what is good, and innocent in what is evil" (Romans 16.19) if we are to survive.

Creation

My television provider just added The Travel Channel in high definition, and I'm telling you, I may never change the channel again. I will never see all of the "must-see" locations I see featured there—even just the ones in the United States. But in lieu of retiring, buying a travel trailer, and embarking on a tour of national parks, I will be satisfied with staying in my living room and sitting agape at the wonder and majesty of God's creation.

It gives fresh meaning to the apostle's words in Romans 1.20—"For since the creation of the world His invisible attributes, His eternal power and divine nature, have been clearly seen, being understood through what has been made, so that they are without excuse." I do not understand how people can look at Monument Valley, or the Grand Canyon, or Glacier Bay, or any of a thousand other sites around the country or around the world and deny the existence of an all-powerful Creator.

But forget about around the world; how about around the block? From starry skies to majestic trees to intricate spider webs, evidence abounds in the most mundane of life's details. Every piece of God's mosaic is that much more astonishing than the next.

If someone wants to make a "pilgrimage" to a volcano or desert or rain forest to encounter God, I wouldn't discourage it. I may do it myself one day. But God isn't hiding. As the prophet told King Asa in 2 Chronicles 15.2, "if you seek Him, He will let you find Him." So open your eyes. Take a good look at your Creator.

Word for Word

Waters

If you want to see something amazing, do an internet image search for "Meeting of the Waters." You will find something absolutely astonishing.

The two main tributaries of the Amazon River are the Rio Negro and the Rio Solimoes. The Negro, as its name would indicate, is extremely dark, almost black. The Solimoes is sandy brown. The waters meet to form the main body of the Amazon. But because of differences of temperature, speed and density, they literally flow side by side for six miles without mixing. Imagine putting creamer in a cup of coffee and watching only half the cup change color. That's what the river looks like.

It made me think of the separation that has been the status quo among the people of God (at least in my own experience). God makes us all "one in Christ Jesus" (Galatians 3.28). But that makes some brethren (on both sides of the river) uncomfortable. So we erect barriers to keep us separated. I wonder if people think God will have separate neighborhoods for "our kind" and "their kind" in heaven. Somehow I doubt it.

Of course, we are not talking here about barriers built by God. He has very definitely distinguished between those who do and do not "abide in the teaching of Christ" (2 John 9). But having churches defined by demographics instead of doctrine is the antithesis of the gospel message. If we are creating environments where we (implicitly or explicitly) welcome only "brethren like us," shame on us.

All those who serve Jesus are going to heaven (John 14.3). We might as well carpool.

Negotiation

I noticed that Anne Rice, of *Interview with a Vampire* fame, has renounced Christianity. Rice, who was raised Catholic but hasn't been involved in organized religion in decades, refuses to be anti-gay, anti-feminist and anti-artificial birth control—positions traditionally associated with mainstream Catholicism.

I'd say, "Don't let the door hit you on the way out, Ms. Rice," but that would accept the premise that she was "in" in the first place. And I don't. That's not because I oppose homosexuality (although I do) or women (I don't). It's because I oppose the idea of negotiating with God.

Honestly, it's like some people think God is the president of Christianity, Ltd., and they're union organizers. *"Now look here, God, we're trying to be reasonable. But You've got to give us something. If you don't try to make Your workers happy, we may have to go on strike. But if You give a little in, say, the extramarital sex thing, and the foul language thing, and the worship thing, You might be able to keep Your workers on board."*

Well, this is not a negotiation. We can't bargain for adjustments to His spiritual law any more than we can with His natural law. Not that people haven't tried over the years. People like Adam (Genesis 3.11-12). And Nadab and Abihu (Leviticus 10.1-2). And Ananias and Sapphira (Acts 5.1-11). One-sided "negotiations" all.

As Christians, we follow Christ—always, not just when He agrees with us. The day we disagree is when we show whether we are truly following Him, or just going where we like and asking Him to come along for the ride.

Word for Word

Legends

Jesse James is a fascination for me. Not the former Mr. Sandra Bullock, the guy with the motorcycles and tattoos. He's more of a conundrum. I mean, have we gotten where absolutely *anybody* can get his own cable TV show? Don't get me started.

No, I mean Jesse James, the bank robber. Gunman. Killer. All-around bad guy. All the evidence paints him with the blackest of tones. And yet, Jesse James has acquired a weird aura of heroism— a modern-day Robin Hood, bucking the establishment on behalf of the little guy. It probably began as a result of his absolute commitment to the Confederate cause, which endeared him to most of his fellow Missourians, as well as many others in the South and West. And his manner of death probably is a factor—shot in the back of the head by a trusted friend while standing on a chair, unarmed, dusting a picture. You tend to get the sympathy vote with a story like that.

But whatever the reason, people often prefer legends to facts. With time, brand new storylines borne of supposition become preferable to boring, staid explanation that has been accepted (with good reason) for generations.

People do the same thing with the Bible. Paul warned us that people "wanting to have their ears tickled" would reject sound doctrine and "turn aside to myths" (2 Timothy 4.3-4). Everyone loves a good conspiracy.

It's unfortunate that people can't be satisfied with the most amazing tale of all as originally penned—epic saga, thrill ride, love story, tragedy and triumph all in one. No story concocted by men could possibly compete with that.

Fuse

I changed a fuse in my car the other day. The power outlet (known in pre-PC days as a "cigarette lighter") didn't work. I went to a parts store. I looked for and found a particular type of fuse. I installed it properly. And the outlet started working.

That may not impress you if you're a car guy—if you know how to overhaul a carburetor (I do well to spell it), or how to get 200 horses underneath a hood the size of a large coffee table, or basically how to do anything more complicated than changing a tire. But I wasn't even aware that my car *had* fuses until recently. So I was impressed. And more importantly, so was my daughter Taylor, who was there to witness the whole thing.

It's easy to define yourself based on inadequacies. We come to think of ourselves as flawed beings, incapable of anything beyond our current circumstances. And certainly we are flawed in the sense that we all sin (Romans 3.23). But that isn't because God's design is faulty; it's because we have not yet learned how to read the manual properly.

I may never be a fully functional auto mechanic. (I "may" never be an astronaut or professional basketball player, either.) But I'm confident that I can probably pick up another trick or two if I put forth a proper effort.

And more importantly, I can grow in my efforts to serve Jesus Christ. If I'm falling short in one area, I can work on it—and with His help, succeed. Paul's prayer should be ours, both for ourselves and for others—that God would "comfort and strengthen your hearts in every good work and word" (2 Thessalonians 2.17).

Saved

The report said the family, which wished to remain anonymous, was on the verge of bankruptcy. The bank was about to foreclose on their house. All hope appeared lost. But then, while rummaging through the basement for packing boxes, they stumbled onto a cache of old comic books. And one of them was the Holy Grail of comics—*Action Comics* #1, dated June 1938. The first appearance of Superman. The magazine is expected to bring around a quarter million dollars at auction.

Superman saves the day again.

We've all been there, to one degree or another. I have been homeless a couple of times (never roofless, thanks to my gracious and exceedingly patient family), jobless numerous times, dateless on far more Friday nights in my youth than I care to remember. And then, often from out of nowhere, I was saved. Despair gave way to hope, sorrow to joy, stress to peace.

Often the biggest problems in our lives are the ones over which we have the least control. Economic downturns. Crime. Cultural depravity. We find ourselves wondering how we can possibly survive.

And then we remember our Savior. And we know He will not permit us to stay here. He promises a life uncluttered by death, or mourning, or pain (Revelation 21.4). And knowing He remains faithful (2 Timothy 2.13), we wait for Him in faith.

He already saved us once. And He's coming back to save us again. Maranatha!

Superheroes

My daughter Taylor was recently texting back and forth with one of her friends on the critically relevant topic of whether or not Batman qualifies as a superhero. (That's unlimited texting for you.) Her friend argued that having a bunch of fancy gadgets isn't the same as having an actual "power." Taylor said the willingness to risk life and limb to fight crime was "power" enough.

And since you asked, I'm siding with Taylor on this one. Being a hero, or being super, is not about having abilities others don't have; it's about being willing to use whatever you do have—however common it may be.

That's what I love about Hebrews 11, and about the Bible in general. It reminds us that ordinary people can and do make a difference every day—in life, yes, but especially in the Lord. Abel was a shepherd. Sarah was a housewife. Gideon was a farmer. Joseph was a teen-ager. Rahab was … well, we all know what Rahab was.

They weren't superheroes. They were just people. People who had faith. People who were willing to put themselves in God's hands and allow Him to accomplish His will through them.

Mordecai told his cousin in Esther 4.14, "And who knows whether you have not attained royalty for such a time as this?" The same could be said for us: Who knows whether God has put us in a particular place at a particular time to accomplish a particular purpose for Him? You may not have super-strength. But with God's help, you can find enough of the regular kind to get the job done.

Word for Word

Wait

There are two kinds of people in the world: people who make other people wait, and the people who wait for them. Which one are you?

The first group comprises self-centered egocentrics. They are concerned only with their own priorities, their own schedule. Often they are conceited enough to assume everyone else will accommodate them, and selfish enough to be angry when and if they don't. But many of them simply don't think about it. It never occurs to them to consider how their actions impact others.

The second group comprises selfless givers. They are just as busy as the first group, with issues just as pressing. But they do not presume to impose their own will on others. They know the inconvenience they suffer by waiting is no greater than what others would suffer if they did not. Certainly the time will come when waiting becomes unproductive. But they are willing to put their lives on hold until that time comes. After all, it is what they would want others to do for them (Matthew 7.12).

Many in the second group derive strength from the example of Jesus, the perfect Example of selflessness. He did not concern Himself with the motives and failings of others; He simply served. It's why Paul writes, "Have this attitude in yourselves which was also in Christ Jesus" (Philippians 2.5).

There are two kinds of people in the world: people who make other people wait, and the people who wait for them. Which one are you?

Directions

Let's just say someone is on an out-of-town trip. Let's say he is so determined to get there in timely fashion that he brings directions with him. But then, let's say the directions take him in a direction contrary to his instincts. And let's say he goes with his gut, gets it wrong, and almost ruins a beautiful evening for him and his daughter.

Let's just say.

What's the point in having directions if we aren't going to follow them? If we're ultimately going to trust our hunches, why bother with directions at all? Or do we look at directions as starting points from which we are free to deviate? Or last-ditch options in case we don't have any ideas of our own?

A lot of people look at God's directions like that. They are perfectly willing and eager to read the Bible, believing that it contains God's will for their lives. But they have a will of their own. And when push comes to shove, they will choose to follow their instincts rather than God's word. That's not the way they will usually phrase it, but that is what they are doing.

But God's directions are not a mere supplement to our own instincts. In fact, they are often a recipe for overcoming instincts. Following our "nature," is what caused us to be "children of wrath" in the first place (Ephesians 2.3).

Anyone can do what comes naturally. Animals do that. Only a devoted follower of Jesus can accept the inherent flaws of his "best guess" and agree to follow His directions, no matter where they may lead.

Word for Word

Whiners

Everyone hates a whiner. You know the kind. He is required to do something unpleasant or inconvenient, and he proceeds to tell us how miserable he is in his unfortunate state. *"This is too hard. I'm tired. Isn't it someone else's turn? I'm never going to be finished. Are we going to stop soon?"* On and on it goes.

I think I've figured whiners out. Some are egotists who think the world owes them a good time; the rest of us have failed in allowing them to be in a less-than-adequate circumstance, and it's their duty to tell us about it. But most, I think, are simply trying to lighten their own load, and they think the best way to do it is by making everyone around them irritated. If they can be obnoxious enough, someone will let them quit the job just so they'll shut up.

Either way, it's a demonstration of self-centeredness. Whining does nothing to help anyone else. It does nothing to accomplish the task. It only gives a voice to the whiners' discontent. And a very annoying voice, at that.

I wonder if people think whining is going to work with God. After all, it works pretty well with brethren. We're pretty quick to lighten the load of whiners in the church; after all, we want the job done, and we don't like the noise. It's easier all the way around to do it for them.

But God expects us all to work. He gives us duties, and He expects us to carry out the work—one-talent and five-talent men alike. "For each one shall bear his own load" (Galatians 6.5). Whining doesn't make it lighter.

But a good attitude might. It's worth a shot, at least.

Pools

I'm not a big swimming pool guy. I don't like water in my face. I hate water in my ears. I don't like the atmosphere of public pools. I don't like the expense of private pools. Plus, I'm not that great a swimmer. Deep water makes me nervous. It's a control thing. I'd rather stay in the shallow end where I have less to worry about. As a result, I'll never enjoy pools as much as some others. I won't give myself the chance.

I've known Christians my whole life who have the same attitude about Bible study. Certain texts are comfortable, familiar, easy to grasp. Most of Genesis. The gospels. Psalms and Proverbs. Maybe an epistle or two. That's their wheelhouse. They can handle that. But announce a six-month study of Isaiah, or the minor prophets, or Hebrews, and they get very nervous. They haven't studied those books much. They don't have any songs set to the tune of the alphabet song to assist them. It becomes a vicious circle. They aren't comfortable with the material, so they avoid it, so they get even less comfortable.

The only way to break the cycle is to let yourself be uncomfortable. Get out of the shallow end. Don't be afraid to get in over your head. If you're nervous, swim with a buddy—a brother or sister in Christ who can give you some tips until you can go solo.

It's vital that we try. We will be challenged eventually by "the error of unprincipled men," and if we don't "grow in the grace and knowledge of our Lord and Savior Jesus Christ," we may not be able to swim to safety (2 Peter 3.17-18).

Word for Word

Numbers

I have been privileged to work and worship with churches of all different sizes in my life. I have been one of 600 brethren in a local church, and I have been one of less than a dozen. I have been a part of a gathering of thousands, and I have directed a worship service with just myself and an 8-year-old boy in attendance. And at no point did I assume that the number of people in the room had anything to do with my proximity to God at that moment. Nor should I have.

And yet sometimes I find myself measuring the quality of my work in numbers. A "good" worship service is one that is well attended. A "good" Bible class curriculum is one that gets families to show up regularly. A "good" year is one that saw plenty of baptisms. I know better than that. Of course, there's nothing wrong with any of those things. But proximity to God is what makes something good, not an arbitrary number we might assign.

In Luke 21.1-4, Jesus saw one rich man after another pour money into the temple coffers; He singled out a widow who gave virtually nothing. He called the richest church in Asia "lukewarm," the one with the best reputation "dead," and the most established one "fallen," and He lauded the poorest and smallest (Revelation 3.16, 3.1, 2.5, 2.9, 3.8). Clearly He has a different yardstick than we do.

We should not obsess on things the church could do with bigger numbers—as if we do not have enough to do with our situation as it is. We would do well to focus less on what we don't have, and more on what we are doing (or not doing) with what we *do* have.

Education

Our girls attend public school. We're not opposed conceptually to homeschooling, and we know many people who do it, and do it well. We just prefer to let the professionals do their job (as we watch carefully).

But that doesn't mean we aren't taking a lead role in their education. Not only are we aware of their progress in school, we are constantly instructing them in subjects that, for whatever reason, are not covered within the confines of the big building with the flagpole in front. Tracie is a highly qualified instructor in home economics and rhetoric. I teach music appreciation and the history of film. (Kylie struggles mightily with Johnny Cash, and Taylor barely passed the Charlie Chaplin section. Clearly I still have work to do.)

Ultimately it is my responsibility to see that my children are properly educated. Not the teacher's, not the school board's, not the president's. Mine. I am glad for the help others offer. But I chose to bring them into the world; I must make sure, to the best of my ability, that they are responsible and productive while they are here.

It is even more important for me to "bring them up in the discipline and instruction of the Lord" (Ephesians 6.4). I am glad the local church provides Bible classes for them. But I would be negligent if I let a couple of hours of group study comprise their entire spiritual education. I need to be nurturing good study and prayer habits, leading spiritual discussions, and finding good outlets for spiritual expression and exercise. That's my job. No one else's.

Word for Word

Thou

I am of two minds when it comes to some of our classic hymns. The sentiment and instruction behind works such as "How Great Thou Art" and "O Thou Fount of Every Blessing" are indisputable. My heart is lifted at the thought of their words even as I write. It's what I grew up thinking worship sounded like.

But when the songs we sing are admired for their art instead of their content, the purpose for singing them can be lost. We do not sing songs of praise to *feel* worshipful, but rather to *be* worshipful. "Thou" isn't a religious word; it's a King James Bible word. That doesn't make it bad. But it does make it old—and to an extent, antiquated.

That's one of the reasons I lean more toward more modern hymns, personally. I still sing the old ones, and occasionally I will lead or request them. But I like the thought of praising God in my own words instead of my great-great-great-great-grandfather's. It's certainly possible to sing "I Need Thee Every Hour" and mean it. But I worry that eventually we will wake up with a generation that knew not Fanny J. Crosby. And these young people will look at their hymnals full of wouldsts and whithers, and decide that worship is irrelevant to their lives.

Worship is intended to tug at the heart. But more than that, it is meant to tug at the mind. We are to be "speaking to one another in psalms and hymns and spiritual songs" (Ephesians 5.19), and we must understand and appreciate the words to do so. Whether our songs are of this century or another, let us sing them as true worship and not just "meaningless repetition" (Matthew 6.7).

Chairs

My wife and I have different philosophies regarding chairs. She sees chairs as a part of a decorating scheme. A chair needs to match the room, both in color and style. It should show minimal wear and discoloration. It should make a statement about who we are as individuals, as a family, and as a microcosm of society. (Okay, I made the last one up.)

I think a chair should be comfortable. Period. No complications. After all, that's why we call them "easy chairs." (Yes, I made that up, too. But it could be true.)

It reminds me of an old episode of "All in the Family." A museum curator wants to buy Archie Bunker's chair and put it on display (which, ironically, is exactly where Archie Bunker's chair is now, in the Smithsonian Institute). Archie ultimately rejects the offer. Chairs are, after all, meant to be sat upon, not looked at.

I know some people who take Tracie's approach, except with the Bible. Bibles are often heirlooms, storage for birth and marriage certificates, or simply decorations. Using the Bible as a family centerpiece tells visitors that God's word is a focal point for the family.

I have no problem with that, necessarily. But may I suggest a better way of accomplishing the same thing?

Read it. Study it. Talk about it frequently, with family and visitors alike. If you want to use it as a decoration, fine. But leave it open, maybe to Joshua 24.15—"as for me and my house, we will serve the Lord." Keep using it, and you'll be surprised how comfortable it becomes.

Lawnmowers

I saw something interesting coming home from the office today. A man was going down a street in our neighborhood on a riding lawnmower. Well, that's fine. Maybe he was cutting his neighbor's lawn. Maybe his car was in the shop. Whatever. The point is, there were two cars behind him, unable to pass.

Now, lawnmower man was legally entitled to keep poking along at minimum speed—as long as he had his driver's license with him, that is. But he also could have pulled over and driven on the grass, allowing vehicles with more horsepower to move along. And he didn't.

That does about as good a job as anything of describing the sort of people I call "rights-claimers." You've seen them. Been inconvenienced by them, I'll wager. You politely suggest they move their car out of the street to talk to their neighbor, or not play their stereo so loud, or shower more frequently, and the answer is the same. *"Who are you to tell me what to do? I have a right!"*

And maybe they do. But then again, maybe constantly asserting our rights is not the best way to co-exist in a society. After all, what kind of world would it be if everyone honked his horn simply because it wasn't against the law to do so? It would be utter chaos.

God's way works better. (No surprise there.) By not taking advantage of every available liberty, making myself "a slave to all" (1 Corinthians 9.19), I pursue the common good. That helps everybody, which in turn comes back to help me. It's a win-win. Of course, it works best when everyone participates. But it starts with me.

Jerks

Did you hear this one? A male flight attendant, angry with an irate passenger (and no doubt a few hundred others he'd served over the years), screamed at the passenger, grabbed a beer from the drink cart, blew the inflatable emergency door, and slid out into the unemployment line.

The flight attendant's mommy gave an interview later in the day explaining how *mean* and *unfair* the passenger in question was. Well, I don't doubt that flight attendants (and waiters, cabbies, teachers, etc.—whoever deals with masses of humanity) see their patience pushed to the max. There are a lot of jerks out there, and people like this fellow run into more than their fair share.

Having said that, I have a message for the angry flight attendant, the cook who spits in customers' food, and every other person in the service industry who is having a bad day and is tempted to take it out on the rest of us:

Grow up.

So people take you for granted. So people don't appreciate your work. So people don't treat you with basic human dignity. Get over it. You think you're the first to suffer the slings and arrows of outrageous fortune? Give me a break. Talk to the apostle Paul about his problems (2 Corinthians 11.23-28) and get back to me.

Turning the other cheek (Matthew 5.39) is not about curing jerks of their jerkiness. It's about teaching us to deal with the jerks of the world without becoming jerks ourselves. I know we'd like Jesus to fix the world. But we're going to have to settle for Him fixing us.

Word for Word

Hats

In the early days of westerns—Roy Rogers, Gene Autry, Tom Mix—you could always tell the heroes from the villains by their hats. White hat dies, everybody boos. Black hat dies, everybody cheers. Simple. The same concept applies today. If, say, one group of scuba divers attacks another, the groups wear different color wetsuits. That, and the choice of music, tells us how the good guys are doing.

I think we set children up to think real life will be like that. A choir will sing when they meet the boy/girl of their dreams. Ominous music will build when they enter dangerous situations. And they will be able to tell at a glance whether someone is a "white hat" or a "black hat."

Unfortunately, it's more complicated. "Satan disguises himself as an angel of light" (2 Corinthians 11.14). The "false prophet" in Revelation 13 looks a lot like the "lamb of God" in Revelation 5. Wolves wear sheep's clothing (Matthew 7.15). How can you identify them?

Not by numbers; many will deny the Lord by following false words (2 Peter 2.1-3). Not by personal preference; Paul condemned those who reject "sound doctrine" for that which tickled their ears (2 Timothy 4.3). And not by the speaker's enthusiasm; "zeal for God, but not in accordance with knowledge" (Romans 10.2) is not enough.

No, we must judge them the same way we will be judged: the words of Jesus (John 12.48). If the Bereans were commended for examining the words of Paul himself (Acts 17.11), we should be equally cautious about examining preachers today. Including this one.

Hoaxes

Maybe you saw the series of pictures floating around the internet recently of "Jenny" and her whiteboard. She said she put up with her obnoxious boss for a long time, until she heard him call her a name that was highly complimentary, but not in reference to her work performance (if you know what I mean). So she quit, and in the process skewered her boss, his breath, and his propensity for playing Farmville on company time.

Turns out, it was all a hoax. "Jenny" (not her real name) is an actress. The job, the boss, the resignation—all fake. And yet you can Google "Jenny whiteboard boss" and find more than a million references to the stunt, thousands of links to the photos in question, even a Facebook group encouraging "Jenny Whiteboard" to pose in Playboy. (I didn›t join.) There aren't nearly as many links to the truth of the matter. That's the nature of hoaxes. It's a lot easier to start a fire than put one out.

This particular hoax was all in fun. I object to some of the language used, but in the end no one was really hurt (unless "Jenny" really *does* pose in Playboy). Not every trick is like that. Solomon writes in Proverbs 26.18-19, "Like a madman who throws firebrands, arrows and death, so is the man who deceives his neighbor, and says, 'Was I not joking?'" We have to take responsibility for the things we say, as well as the consequences that result.

Apologizing doesn't reverse time. The damage done by loose tongues is often irreversible. Better we learn to bridle them sooner than later (James 3.2-3).

Word for Word

Duplicate

I write just about one article like this per day. I publish some on Facebook. I publish others in our church's weekly bulletin. Some I just archive. I try not to use an article more than once, and I have measures in place to help with that. Still, despite my best efforts, occasionally one gets published more than once. (Sorry.) And when I do, I've noticed, I lose readers.

That used to bother me. Well, it still bothers me. I am sharing God's word, and for me it doesn't get more important. But I've come to grips with the fact that not everyone who receives my messages actually reads them. In fact, they may have dismissed them already, only they haven't found a good excuse for cutting them off. And when I duplicate myself, I give them one. *I get too much clutter in my inbox anyway. Now Hal wants me to read the same article twice? Forget it. I'll just unsubscribe.*

I'd be lying if I said I didn't care. But I'm not going to let it ruin my day. And I'm certainly not going to let it dissuade me from my efforts to reach others. Jesus told His disciples to just shake the dust off their feet and move on when they found an unreceptive audience (Matthew 10.13-14). To do otherwise, He said, would be casting pearls before swine (Matthew 7.6). That's not to say people are pigs; it just means His gospel and our time are too valuable to be squandered in pointless, fruitless ventures.

I would love to touch the heart of every person within my reach with the gospel of Jesus Christ. But I won't. So I'll keep sharing with those who read, and keep praying for the ones who don't.

Jigsaw

I am back in jigsaw puzzle mode. Every few months or so, I feel the urge to take little pieces of pressed paper and piece them together just so, forming out of a couple thousand pieces of nonsense a complete, unified whole. It's like solving a mystery in reverse. I know whodunit. The box top tells me whodunit. I just have to figure out a way to get there.

Sometimes a piece and an opening seem absolutely perfect for one another. Like Cinderella trying on the glass slipper. The color is right. The shape is right. The size is right. I just know that I've found the happy ending.

And it doesn't fit.

It's actually quite disturbing. I've been known to talk to the puzzle piece. *"How can you just sit there and not fit?"* (So far they haven't talked back, so I figure I'm not insane. Yet.) But I've learned no amount of yelling, begging, pushing, prodding or ignoring will change the facts. And the quicker I come to grips with that, the better.

My life is sort of like a big jigsaw. I know what the end product is supposed to look like; God's making me over in Jesus' image (Romans 8.29), and I have four detailed descriptions of Him. But sometimes I convince myself that a particular event in my life should have gone differently—that God's plan would work better if, in fact, things had gone differently. Quite disturbing.

I try to lean on my faith on those days. He knows best how to accomplish good through me (Romans 8.28). If a piece doesn't fit where I think it should, I can have confidence another will fit far better. I just have to find it.

Word for Word *223*

Sharks

I love salmon, make no mistake. But I have nothing on salmon sharks. Salmon sharks travel thousands of miles up the American west coast to Prince William Sound in Alaska to get their fill. No guide, no compass, no GPS. And countless numbers of them do it every year, many for the first time. Me, I'm Mapquesting any destination beyond the county line.

Such a trip is unthinkable for any other shark. But the salmon shark is warm-blooded, giving it remarkable stamina in extreme situations as well as the ability to survive in the frigid waters near the Arctic Circle. Me, I'm warm-blooded too. But if my survival depended on a swim more than a few hundred yards, well, glug glug.

They complete their three-month journey just in time to catch the salmon returning to their spawning ground. For a few days out of the year, salmon absolutely pour into the Gulf of Alaska on their way to their birthplace. At that precise time, the sharks position themselves between the salmon and their destination and absolutely gorge themselves. Me, I am at my limit trying to arrive at school in time to pick up the girls.

Watching a show on the National Geographic Channel about these sharks, I was peppered with terms such as "brilliant," "hardwired," "programmed," "somehow," "instinctive," even "miraculous." But instead of allowing the sea monsters to praise their Creator as intended (Psalm 148.7), they are called "one of evolution's greatest success stories" by the naturalistic, atheistic TV producers.

No wonder atheists don't listen to my feeble efforts.

Death

If you've never seen *Butch Cassidy and the Sundance Kid,* forgive me, but I'm about to do something I absolutely hate for people to do. I'm going to reveal the ending. Are you ready?

They die.

I am willing to break my own rule in this instance because most people figure out early into their first viewing of the film that it's not about two outlaws, but rather about the death of two outlaws. They chose a path for their life, they passed on plenty of opportunities to change, and eventually they wound up where the path leads—the only destination they could possibly hope to find.

In a sense, that's the way it is with life "under the sun," as Solomon phrased it in Ecclesiastes. We can take steps to delay it, we can grouse about it, but death will find us all. Maybe it won't find us with a hail of bullets in a backwater town in Bolivia, but it will find us.

The Christian should not feel embarrassed about delaying the process a bit. Self-preservation is an instinct given to us by God. He put us here for a reason, and there's no reason to shorten our days spent in His service. But the Christian should not fear death. Death is a rest from our labors (Revelation 14.13). Death is the end of a painful life (Romans 8.22-23) and the beginning of a blissful one (Revelation 21.4). Most of all, death initiates the full fellowship that is only hinted at in this life; truly, we have "the desire to depart and be with Christ, for that is very much better" (Philippians 1.23). And thus prepared for death, we are better equipped to face life.

Word for Word

Tirades

Service is big with me. Always has been. I remember in college eating lunch at a local eatery several times per week just because of the waitresses. Sure, they were pretty. But that's not the point. They offered good service. Yeah, that was it.

Poor service is likely to send me into a funk for hours. Take last week, for instance. I went to a local establishment to have a computer part ordered. On the day it was to arrive, I was told over the phone that not only had they not ordered it, but that they would not order it. Sorry we wasted a week of your life. And have a nice day.

I had my tirade all ready to go. I practiced it with my wife a couple of times. Rehearsed it in the car. Got it just the way I wanted it—a tight 45 seconds of cool, collected venom ready to be unleashed on whatever unfortunate company representative might be in the room.

And I didn't do it. I folded. The receptionist seemed genuinely sorry for my hardship and her minor part in it. She repeatedly apologized for herself and the company. And suddenly my tirade didn't seem as vital to the success of the free-market economy as I had previously thought.

That's the way it usually works with me. And that's a good thing. Venting my spleen rarely accomplishes anything more than making someone else feel bad.

Instead of choosing words that give me satisfaction, I should choose "a word as is good for edification according to the need of the moment, so that it will give grace to those who hear" (Ephesians 4.29). I'm not as good at it as I ought to be. But I'm working on it.

Elementary

This week my older daughter entered high school and my younger daughter entered junior high. I have no more elementary school students in the house. And I'm not quite sure how I feel about that.

Part of me is nostalgic, and perhaps a bit sad. I enjoyed the days when I taught my girls to walk, watched cartoons with them, be-bopped around the house with them to the tunes of my favorite musicians. And now they want to go places I don't like, watch shows I don't like, listen to music that barely merits the term.

But Tracie and I always knew it would be like this. And we wouldn't have it any other way. (Well, we might change their music.) We don't want them to remain children. As much as it pains us, we want them to grow up.

The whole point of going to elementary school is to move on to higher levels of education. We get the basic principles down, then we use them in other, more challenging applications.

Or not. That's why the author of Hebrews was so frustrated with his readers; they had not moved beyond the "elementary principles of the oracles of God" (Hebrews 5.12). They should have been teaching classes for novices; instead they were struggling to pass the classes themselves.

We should not be satisfied with merely doing well (as we define "well") at our current spiritual level. We must develop. We must graduate. We owe it to ourselves, to the Lord, and to the next generation of students.

Word for Word

Intentions

Agatha Christie once penned a story that included a nightclub called Hell. Low lighting, lots of red, weird characters. You get the idea. I especially remember the stairs leading down to the front door. (Naturally it was located in a basement.) The steps were individually inscribed with good intentions. "I meant well." "I thought it would work." "It seemed like a good idea at the time." Get it? *"The road to hell ..."*

Good intentions are used to justify virtually anything these days. Who cares whether a plan works, or even if it makes the problem worse? If the planners had "good intentions," that's supposed to make everything okay.

Uzzah is the poster boy for good intentions. I'm sure he meant well when he reached up to steady the ark of the covenant (2 Samuel 6.6-8). But God struck him dead anyway. God said don't touch. He didn't say don't touch unless you mean well. Motives aren't necessarily irrelevant, but they don't excuse rebellious behavior.

I think a lot of people prefer to be judged by their intentions instead of their actions because it helps them avoid accountability. After all, who's to say I *didn't* mean well? No one can read my mind.

But the thing is, God can. And God knows the difference between a person who is genuinely trying to serve Him and making a mess of things, and a person who is making his own judgments instead of accepting God's.

Convincing others of our good intentions is one thing; convincing God is quite another.

Panic

It is getting down to crunch time at the time of this writing. I am scheduled to leave town in (let me check my watch) sixteen hours. That's about one hour for every vital task I have yet to accomplish before I leave. One of those tasks (get in some quality family time) will take a couple of hours, another (get a good night's sleep) will take seven or eight, and a third (finish this article) is looking like it may take even longer.

I am rapidly approaching panic mode.

I have found that the best way to deal with panic is to breathe. Seriously. Go back to basics. In and out, slow and regular. If you can regain control over your mind at the most fundamental of levels, then you can move ahead to step two: think. Line up the stressors that are shaking your world, and evaluate them calmly. Formulate a strategy. Then you are ready for step three: act. Do your best. Enlist help if necessary. Do like you learned in Little League—keep your eye on the ball, focus, swing level, and follow through.

Really, the Christian has no excuse for panicking. That's the advantage he gets from turning his life over to God. When he breathes, it is to lift his voice in prayer. When he thinks, it is about God's will in his life. When he acts, it is based on His infallible word.

That's how Paul can write, "Be anxious for nothing, but in everything by prayer and supplication with thanksgiving let your requests be made known to God" (Philippians 4.6). God doesn't have a panic mode. That means we don't have to have one either.

Word for Word

Sloth

I've never seen a sloth. Well, maybe that's not entirely accurate. I've never *noticed* a sloth. Once I was in an exhibit that allegedly held a sloth. But sloths do a great job of blending in with their environment. And they hardly ever move. And when they do move, they move … v e r y … v e r y … s l o w l y. So it's entirely possible that he was there all the time.

Now if you want to talk about the Lord's sloths, I've seen plenty of them. Stealth Christians, you might call them, determined to blend in, a nameless face in a sea of worshipers, never taking any duty that can be passed to another. It's like they say in the old Monty Python skit—the first rule of blending in is, learn not to stand up.

Standing up for Jesus is a good way to get noticed. It's also a good way to get shot at. Outsiders will see you as a threat. Fellow Christians may take umbrage at your activity, feeling that it reflects poorly on them. It's much easier, much more comfortable, to be a sloth. And an excuse for sluggishness is always readily available. There's always a lion in the street, or its equivalent, that will make work seem inconvenient (Proverbs 22.13). And usually we can convince ourselves that "a little sleep, a little slumber" (Proverbs 24.33-34) won't do any harm, that the tasks assigned to us can wait another day. Or week.

The sloth seems to have the best of all possible worlds—rest, relaxation, safety. But I doubt any of us, given the choice of being any animal in God's creation, would pick a sloth. No activity. No thrills. Not much of a life.

So why would we choose to be a sloth for the Lord?

Clarinet

My daughter Taylor took up the clarinet in sixth grade. Tracie and I knew what we were getting into. Tracie played clarinet herself in school, so she knew full well what the first few years would sound like. And she gave me fair warning: Expect some serious squeaking.

And Taylor delivered on those expectations. If you haven't ever heard a clarinet squeak, you probably can't appreciate how wonderful your life is. Try imagining fingernails against a chalkboard, except much, much louder. It's sort of like that.

But thankfully, Taylor has gotten much better over the years. Squeaking is now the exception rather than the rule. So does she get to take it easy, now that she is starting to get good? No. Now her director wants her to play while marching in a precise pattern while wearing a heavy, cumbersome, and (she says) horribly ugly uniform.

Our Divine Director asks similar things from us. He gives us the "pure milk of the word" (1 Peter 2.2) until we acquire a real taste for it. Then, just as we're getting comfortable, He gives us "solid food" (Hebrews 5.14), pushing us to get stronger in the faith, capable of accomplishing bigger and more significant things in His service.

There's always another level of mastery, another stage of development. He does not allow us to plateau. And every time we try to take a step forward, it feels like we're taking a step back. But God continues to be patient with us. With His help, we grew out of our early awkward phases; He will help us grow out of our later ones as well.

Word for Word   *231*

Analogies

You may have noticed my fondness for analogies by now. I am constantly on the lookout for a great illustration from nature, or history, or my personal life, which will help me illustrate Biblical truth. Just the other day someone sent me a forwarded e-mail message about how an old eagle, unable to hunt as it did in its youth, breaks off its own beak and talons by pounding them into a rock. It's extremely painful, but the old, worn parts are soon replaced by newer, stronger ones. And the rejuvenated eagle goes on to live another twenty years.

It's a great story. A lesson in perseverance and dedication. A perfect starter for an article like this one.

Too bad it isn't true.

It's tempting to take a story from a trusted source at face value—especially when it serves my immediate purposes (like helping me catch up on my writing, for instance). But convenience and utility are not substitutes for accuracy. We can't afford to pretend otherwise.

Over the years I have heard preachers repeat the most outlandish of tales without a scintilla of corroboration, simply because they made for good analogies. But God's word doesn't need the support of lies. And when the lies are found out, it gives the appearance of fakery to the message. God's word deserves better treatment than that.

Jesus wants us building on the rock-solid foundation of His words (Matthew 7.24-27), not the shifting sands of human wisdom. If my point requires a lie to prop it up, it probably isn't a point worth making in the first place.

Commingling

Tracie and I agreed to be the treasurers for the high school band boosters this year. (I plead temporary insanity.) On my first trip to the bank I needed quarters. The teller gave me a $50 bill and told me to get the coins from the drive-through window. I started to put the money in my pocket for safekeeping (the same pocket where I keep my own money), and quickly decided to put it in the cash box instead. Keep it honest by keeping it simple, I told myself. If it's in my pocket, it's mine. If it's in the box, it's the band's. No commingling, no confusion, no exceptions.

It's the same attitude I take toward my spiritual responsibilities. God gives me certain jobs as a Christian, and He gives the church certain jobs as the body of Christ. The jobs may look similar, but they are not identical. For instance, Paul states specifically that certain widows were to be cared for by their own families; *"the church must not be burdened"* (1 Timothy 5.8,16). The church has a job, as does the individual. Respect God's boundaries.

We greatly err by taking the shortcut of putting all spiritual responsibilities into a pile and distributing as we see fit. God kept them separate for a reason. I can't honor my responsibility to care for the needy (Matthew 25.34-46) simply by writing a check on Sunday and trusting the church to do it for me; God gave that job to me. And I can't solicit funds from Christians to hire preachers and send them out to spread the gospel; God gave that job to the church (Acts 13.1-3).

No commingling, no confusion, no exceptions.

Word for Word

Tests

Everybody in the class has an A while the teacher is still lecturing. Every ship floats before it's put in the water. Every play works on the chalkboard. But with everything in life, eventually there comes a test. And in that day it doesn't matter how theoretically valid the schematics were, or how effective similar approaches were in the past, or even how noble the intentions of the participants were. All that matters is the test. Pass or fail.

It's the same with faith. It's easy to be a good Christian when it doesn't cost us anything, when we have plenty of support, when Satan is tempting us with things that we don't find appealing. But life isn't like that every day. Life comes with tests. Real tests. Challenging tests. Tests that truly examine the depths of our commitment.

Adults looking back at their school years don't tend to remember and admire the teachers who gave simple tests. We remember and admire the teachers who made tests simple. They made them simple by giving us information they knew we could process, drilling it into our heads until we had it down cold, and then giving us an opportunity to display our progress. We didn't always appreciate the process fully at the time. But we appreciate it now.

God is trying to teach us the same way. He is preparing us for the ultimate final exam. He tells us, "My righteous one shall live by faith" (Hebrews 10.38), but only if it's a faith that works (James 2.17). So He helps us examine ourselves now (2 Corinthians 13.5) so we will be ready then. With His help, and with a lot of effort, we'll pass.

Helipad

Taylor's high school is next to a hospital. I saw the helipad this morning and thought, "That would be a great way to get to school." Can you imagine? I suspect the average geeky freshman wouldn't have any trouble getting the homecoming queen to accept a ride home if it were in a *helicopter* (assuming the freshman in question wasn't *quite* as geeky as I was).

But I started thinking about it. The helipad is a good 200 yards from the school. I guarantee you, if somehow one of Taylor's classmates were to score a helicopter ride to school, he'd say, "Hey, this is cool and all, but could you drop me off a little closer?"

The gift isn't ever good enough. And that doesn't just go for teenagers. God blesses us in this life with comfort, and joy, and companionship, and peace. We are flooded daily with the rain of blessings He pours out on the righteous and the unrighteous (Matthew 5.45)—and especially on Christians as His special spiritual creation. And even so, we find ourselves in "need" of something else.

But you know what? Maybe that's part of the plan. Instead of looking at ourselves as ungrateful wretches, maybe we should look at ourselves as people who are incapable of finding pure, complete contentment with anything this world has to offer. We are constantly, instinctively desirous of something bigger and better.

And one day we will get it. One day we will receive a gift that is absolutely impossible to improve upon. Contentment won't be a problem on that day, I assure you.

Word for Word

Cereal

Do you ever feel cheated when you open up a box of cereal and find two inches of air at the top of the box? I do. I'm the type that has to finish his iced tea before leaving the restaurant. I paid for it, after all. And if I pay for a full box of cereal, I expect a full box of cereal.

The problem is, the contents have settled. It was corn flakes all the way to the top on the assembly line. But with all the shaking between the factory and my pantry, the flakes work their way to the bottom, and the air works its way to the top. Blame Isaac Newton. Still, I wonder why they can't just shake the boxes really well at the factory, get the settling over with, and then *really* fill the box.

Of course, the box is full one way or the other. It's just that I want it to be full of cereal, and the factory send it to me full of cereal and air. Well, I already have air. I don't need air. Send the air to some guys in a submarine somewhere. Or Los Angeles.

We were full before we found Christ. We were just full of the wrong thing. And when we put Him into our lives—"Him who fills all in all" (Ephesians 1.23)—it pushes all the evil out. That's why we must remove "all that remains of wickedness" (James 1.21); we need all the room we can find for more Jesus.

Jesus warns us about banishing our demons and not replacing them with goodness (Matthew 12.43-45). Getting rid of sin doesn't save us any more than getting rid of air fills my breakfast bowl. Nature and the soul both abhor a vacuum. We will be full of something; let's make it Him.

Adequate

It's funny how words will acquire certain connotations. Take the word "adequate," for instance. It simply means, "good enough." But that's not "good enough" for most people. They bristle at the idea of being adequate. No, make that *merely* adequate. "I want to be *excellent*," they say. "I want to be *outstanding*. I don't want to be *merely adequate*."

Well, that's fine, I guess—as long as they cover themselves on the adequacy front. The trouble is, in their strivings for higher accolades, often they don't do the things necessary to be "merely" adequate. It's like the batter who swings for the fences and strikes out, when all he needed to do to win the game was simply put the ball in play.

I wish more Christians would try to be outstanding in their service to God. But I cringe to see the efforts of some overachievers who, in their quest for greatness, abandon the thing that would make them adequate.

Paul writes in 2 Timothy 3.16-17, "All Scripture is inspired by God and profitable for teaching, for reproof, for correction, for training in righteousness; that the man of God may be adequate, equipped for every good work." Clearly, the inspired apostle believed that the Bible is all a Christian needs to be what God wants him to be. So then, how can we do things in Jesus' name for which we have no authorization in the text? The plans may seem grand, and the results may seem spectacular. But if they are not grounded in His word, they are not even "adequate." And that's not good enough.

Word for Word

Markers

If you drive down Texas highways very long at all, you will find historical markers. We Texans are very proud of our heritage (maybe you've heard about that), and we are quick to point them out to anyone who can bear listening to us—whether it's the battlefield at San Jacinto where we won our independence, or the first stump Jim Bowie ever threw a knife at. (I made the second one up. I think.)

The idea behind historical markers is not just to remind us who did what when to whom and why. By reminding us where we came from, we grow in appreciation for where we are—and perhaps gain some wisdom in regard to getting where we eventually want to go.

The ancient Israelites believed in markers. Joshua set one up where the people crossed the Jordan River, and a matching one in the middle of the river itself (Joshua 4.1-9). He wanted every generation of children to become curious, and every generation of parents to tell the story of God's power and grace.

I suppose that's why so many people travel to the Bible lands. It is an unspeakable thrill, so I am told, to stand in the ruins of the Acropolis, where Paul preached. Or swim in the water Jesus walked on. Or read Peter's Pentecost sermon where it was actually preached.

But truth be told, I have all the markers I need here at home. I have a starry sky. I have a baby's laugh. I have a sinner's repentance.

God's power and grace are everywhere. It's my job to tell my children. It's your job to tell yours.

Swarms

I love watching swarms of birds in a field of freshly cut grass. Hundreds of them will sit together, eating. Then as one, they rise up in flight and move a few yards to a new location. They are not following a leader. They just decide collectively when to move, and then they move. It has nothing to do with individual intelligence. (Most birds are pretty stupid, to put it bluntly.) It's simply an example of the whole being greater than the sum of its parts.

Humans swarm, too. The best example I can think of is a group of cyclists on a road race. If one stumbles, dozens simultaneously move out of the way. If only one rider dodged the wreck, he would make another, larger wreck. But they all move simultaneously. And they all benefit.

God tells Christians to form swarms as well. He calls them churches. And He doesn't mean denominations, which are basically groups of groups—a concept foreign to the New Testament. His plan is simpler. Put Christians in a location, have them meet regularly and worship collectively, and let them help one another through this life on the way to the next. Don't make them dependent on other groups; make them dependent on their Savior—and to a lesser extent, on each other.

By gathering together regularly, all are encouraged (Hebrews 10.25). By collectively pursuing God's truth, all are strengthened (1 Corinthians 14.26). Being a part of the swarm benefits the individual. Including the individual benefits the swarm.

God's plan works. Go figure.

Word for Word

Dancing

Yes, I am part of the small (and getting smaller) group of Christians that still oppose dancing. Call me Ward Cleaver. I just believe certain gestures, movements and hand placements should be reserved for husbands and wives. And I don't mean *other people's* husbands and wives.

Which brings me to *Dancing with the Stars*, the best illustration I have ever seen for the perils of close, intimate contact. Just when it seemed like the world was rejecting the idea of "look but don't touch," they go and televise a running documentary on fornication (disguised as a reality show) and convince millions of Americans to watch. It's an old-school preacher's dream.

Now, before you say it, I'll admit it: Not every contestant on *DWTS* winds up having actual sexual relations with his or her partner. At least, we're pretty sure not. But to my completely disinterested eyes (I've seen maybe ten minutes of the show in as many seasons), it seems every year I hear about a couple from the show doing the tango off screen, if you catch my meaning. And a fair number of them were already married to other people.

Solomon wrote long ago, "Can a man take fire in his bosom and his clothes not be burned? Or can a man walk on hot coals and his feet not be scorched? So is the one who goes in to his neighbor's wife; whoever touches her will not go unpunished" (Proverbs 6.27-29). Simply put, I should avoid any activity with other women that is specifically designed to arouse the senses. I respect my wife and marriage too much to do otherwise.

Flying

If I had my choice of superpowers, I would want to be able to fly. In fact, I remember having very realistic flying dreams when I was young. I loved, and still love, the idea of stepping off planet earth and soaring above all the filth, clutter and hardships of this life, just looking out in amazement at the wonder of God's creation, unencumbered by earthly things.

You would think that a person like me would be trying to get his pilot's license, or at least be out there skydiving or chartering hot-air balloons occasionally. But I'm not. I don't even get on airplanes very often. And the reason is simple: It costs too much. I'm not willing to pay the price for flight. And so here I stay, earthbound, jealous, wishing things were different but not trying to make them so.

Most Christians are like that. They know a greater relationship with Jesus is available. They see others enjoying it. They wish they had it. But they're like the rich young ruler in Mark 10.17-22—desirous of walking with Christ in close fellowship, regretful that such is not the case, but ultimately unwilling to do what it takes.

Flying with Jesus is the most expensive activity you will ever contemplate. It cost at least five apostles their jobs (Mark 1.16-20, 2.14). It cost Epaphroditus his health (Philippians 2.25-30). But if you truly want the feeling of true freedom, true bliss, you will do whatever it takes. Anything less is unsatisfactory.

Count the cost that comes with carrying the entire cross of Christ (Luke 14.27-28). Then, when you're ready, sign up with Jesus for flying lessons. It's worth it.

Word for Word

Mirage

We've all seen movies, TV shows or cartoons (especially cartoons) where a person is crawling through the desert, literally dying for a drink of water, and he sees an oasis on the horizon. Exhilarated, he gets up and runs toward his salvation, only to realize it was only an illusion, a mirage. I could explain the physics of the phenomenon (actually, I couldn't), but it wouldn't make the sand any wetter for that poor slob in the desert.

I do know this much: The oasis is real. It's just not where the poor slob thinks it is. The curvature of the earth is playing tricks on his eyes. And with more effort, more courage, he can get to the real oasis.

Happiness in this life is kind of like that. People see something on the horizon that appears to offer them everything they are looking for. Maybe a marriage. Maybe a degree. Maybe a higher salary. In any event, they get to the desired destination, but the anticipated satisfaction is not there. Now it appears to loom over the next horizon. The next raise, the next degree, the next marriage.

The satisfaction is there to be found. But it isn't where they think. The joys of this world are only intended to be foretastes of the pleasures awaiting us in the next. And the more we insist upon drinking the mirage, as it were, the more frustrated we will become.

Christians should be blind to these illusions; Jesus tells us to look to the future reality, not the present illusion. As Paul writes, "If we have hoped in Christ in this life only, we are of all men most to be pitied" (1 Corinthians 15.19).

Lunch

My lunch habits confuse my wife. Well, lots of things about me confuse my wife, but let's not get into that. Anyway, I will crack open jars of natural peanut butter and blackberry jam and eat PB&J until the jars are empty. Then I'll move on to, say, ramen noodles. Again, I'll stick with that until they're gone. Then it might be non-stop ham sandwiches with mustard and pickle relish. Then low-fat tuna salad. Honestly, if I had a grocery store in my garage, I might eat the same lunch every day for a month and not get burned out.

She calls that boring. I call it sticking with what works. The way I see it, I'm the same, the sandwich is the same, the gnawing feeling in my gut is the same; why shouldn't my lunch plan be the same?

I suspect my listeners and readers feel a bit saturated with the "bread of life" at every spiritual meal. But that's because it's the best meal—really, the only meal—that can truly satisfy, regardless of the issue. Moral failings? Read your Bible. Doctrinal questions? Read your Bible. Problems in the family? Read your Bible. Battling depression? Read your Bible. Sure, it gets repetitive. But that doesn't make it any less nutritious or filling.

After all, "His divine power has granted to us everything pertaining to life and godliness, through the true knowledge of Him who called us by His own glory and excellence" (2 Peter 1.3). Getting to know Jesus better will fix any and all spiritual cravings. And reading your Bible is the only way to get to know Jesus.

Word for Word

Created

I am a stickler for terminology. I'll give you an example from a typical summer family dinner in the Hammons house. I might *cook* (or *fix*, or *do*) pork chops on the grill. The girls might *heat* some vegetables in the microwave. Tracie might *make* a salad. You only *make* something that did not exist before in the same state. The girls didn't *make* the vegetables; God *made* the vegetables.

Yeah, and I wonder why I don't get invited over to people's houses for dinner very often.

The point is, the proper choice of terminology makes sure that the appropriate degree of credit goes where it is due. Tracie gets more credit (and she should) for putting various elements together into a cohesive, delicious whole than I get for just making sure the meat is cooked to a safe temperature without it getting to resemble shoe leather.

That, to me, is the true impact of Genesis 1.1—"In the beginning, God created the heavens and the earth." He didn't just *make* the world, like you might make a sandcastle or an automobile. He didn't take existing elements and arrange them in a new and special way. He *created*. From nothing, He made something.

Humans don't truly create. We use that word for things like art and music. But even those don't really come from nothing. The arrangement of colors or notes may be different, but no human can claim credit for coming up with blue. Or B-flat.

God created blue. And B-flat. And absolutely everything else. Wow.

Warm

Every autumn comes a very special day—a day that "warm" becomes a good thing. In Texas, we spend nine or ten months out of the year running away from "warm." But no matter how blistering the summer, eventually a dreary day will come when a blast of heated air is actually welcome.

Today was that day for this year. It was a good day.

Now, don't get me wrong. I'm not looking to add a couple more weeks to our Texas summers. I love the chill of autumn and the bite of winter. (Well, it's Texas—make that the moderation of autumn and the occasional chill of winter.) But it's easy to forget how wonderful it is to be warm, and it's great to be reminded.

And speaking of being reminded, being warm makes me think of James 2.15-16—"If a brother or sister is without clothing and in need of daily food, and one of you says to them, 'Go in peace, be warmed and be filled,' and yet you do not give them what is necessary for their body, what use is that?" I enjoy feeling a chill in the air because I know a fire, a sweater, or a blast of breath on my hands can banish that chill. But mere "warm regards," as welcome as they may be, do little real good. If I appreciate warmth, I should be eager to share it with others.

It is easy to turn a blind eye toward those who are in need. But Jesus asks us to use such ones as opportunities to serve Him; "With good will render service, as to the Lord, and not to men" (Ephesians 6.7). James says failing to do so when we have opportunity is not just cold; it is sin (James 4.17).

Word for Word

Cauliflower

My older daughter, Taylor, doesn't like vegetables. Go figure. Her mother and I, on the other hand, enjoy vegetables. And more to the point, we are convinced it is in the girls' best interest to eat them—partly because they are part of a healthy diet, partly because we enjoy inflicting misery on our children. Just kidding. Sort of.

Recently Tracie, tired of the old-fashioned "clean your plate or it's back to the waterboard" approach, decided to make mashed cauliflower. Now cauliflower (for the benefit of the unfortunate uninitiated) is white. Mashed potatoes, a favorite of the above-mentioned older daughter, are also white. Do you get where I'm going with this?

Tracie wants me to emphasize at this point in our story that at no time did she or any of her representatives actually say we were eating mashed potatoes. We merely left it to the girls to assume as they liked. And Taylor, assuming she would enjoy the creamy white stuff on the side of the plate, did. At least, she did until The Great Reveal, at which time she began insisting she knew the difference all along and really didn't enjoy it after all. Whatever.

Two applications. Firstly, playing mind games with your children is highly entertaining. Secondly, and more importantly, parents can find ways to give their children what they need in a way they will accept, and even appreciate. This is especially true for spiritual training (Proverbs 22.6). Sure, you might have to get a bit creative. But it's worth it. And at some, perhaps distant, point in their lives, they might even thank you for it.

Cicadas

Late summer is cicada season in my region of Texas. If you don't have cicadas, it's difficult to explain what you're missing. It's like having ringing in the ears. Or an alarm clock that won't shut off. Or an mp3 player endlessly repeating the latest inanity from the soundtrack of *High School Musical 6. When Zits Attack*. Either filter it out, or go insane.

Every once in a while I actually see one. (They're kind of like big, bright green cockroaches.) But most of the time they just sit up in the trees and sing their song.

They remind me a bit of gossips. Gossips don't like to do their thing on center stage; they'd get squashed if they tried that. So they hover in the background, singing their song, getting as many of their compatriots to join in with them (and usually succeeding). It gets to where society just accepts gossip as part of the natural order of things.

And that's a shame. Because God roundly and repeatedly condemns it (1 Timothy 5.13, Romans 1.29, 2 Corinthians 12.20, etc.). Idle negative chatter does serious damage to human societies. Including the church.

I love the layered logic of Proverbs 20.19—"He who goes about as a slanderer reveals secrets, therefore do not associate with a gossip." First, we are known by our associations; if we hang around with gossips, people will assume we are gossips too. Second, listening to a gossip empowers him; "for lack of wood the fire goes out" (Proverbs 26.20). Third, if you are close to a gossip, whose "secrets" do you think he is revealing?

Think about it.

Word for Word

Sandwiches

As Bill Cosby once said, "An American can eat anything on the face of the earth, as long as he has two pieces of bread." Sandwiches are what we Americans do—our fallback approach to lunch, entertaining, and leftover disposal.

Interestingly (to me, anyway), sandwiches were being invented in England at about the same time that sushi was being invented in Japan, and for the same reason. Gamblers were too engrossed to leave the gaming table for the dinner table—not quite "too busy to eat," but pretty close. So they had someone prepare "finger food" they could eat with minimum mess and effort. If necessity is the mother of invention, I guess addiction is the father.

I worry that some Christians look at their service to Jesus kind of like a sandwich—no fuss, not too complicated, and over with quickly, freeing them up to get back to their life. Of course, Jesus Himself is supposed to *be* our life. But our priorities would seem to argue differently at times. We act like we're too busy to eat.

The Bible constantly uses food to tell us how vital the gospel should be. We are to "hunger and thirst for righteousness" (Matthew 5.6). Jesus is "the bread of life" (John 6.35). He said, "My food is to do the will of Him who sent Me, and to accomplish His work" (John 4.34).

The question is, are we too busy to eat? Are we so addicted to the pleasures of this life that we can only squeeze Jesus in between appointments, if then? Jesus said it is God's word, not bread, that sustains us (Matthew 4.4). Our lifestyle will show whether we believe Him.

Like

So, like, I have two daughters, right? And, like, I take them to, like, school, and then, like, pick them up. And, like, I'll ask them how their day was, and, like, what they, like, did, and do they have any, like, homework, and, like, ...

Sorry, that's going to have to do it. I only have 300 words to play with. If you don't get where I'm going with this by now, clearly you have children of your own and you have become, like, immune.

It's especially grating to me because I was trained as a journalist, where absolutely every word counts. Don't use six words when three will do. Listening to the girls tell a story sometimes makes me want to scream, grab a red marker, and start editing the daylights out of their copy. If I could just get them to eliminate the words that don't, like, *mean anything*, I could get an hour of my life back every week. Instead, I find myself, like, *doing it myself!*

The problem, though, is not just wasted time and aggravated dads. It's the devaluation of the spoken word. It's just like in economics: More dollars chasing the same number of goods makes the dollars less valuable. And when we start tuning out our neighbors' drivel, we run the risk of missing some actually important information.

Jesus tells us our words are important. All of them. "Every careless word that men shall speak, they shall give an accounting for it in the day of judgment" (Matthew 12.36). If you catch yourself in gossip, boasting, dissembling or vulgarity, remember this: "I didn't mean anything by it" isn't an excuse; it's a condemnation.

Word for Word

Following

Do you remember the valedictory address at your high school graduation? Me neither. I was busy worrying about whether I would trip on stage, having lost one of my brand-new contact lenses. But that's a story for another day.

Anyway, I suspect it was pretty much like every other valedictory address I've heard over the years. *"Graduates, we are the future leaders of this nation. It is our responsibility to take the skills we have learned here and take them into the world to blah blah blah blah blah."*

(If Jenny McDowell is out there somewhere, no offense intended. I'm sure you were brilliant.)

Personally, I think leading is overrated. Really, what's the likelihood of you ever becoming a CEO? Running for Congress? Getting marooned on a desert island with Gilligan and a cast of nitwits? Not many, I'll wager.

What we really need to teach the younger generation (and the older ones too, while we're at it) is how to *follow*. Everyone has to be a follower. We follow government (Romans 13.1), employers (Ephesians 6.7), church leaders (Hebrews 13.17), and particularly Jesus Christ (Luke 6.46). It's part and parcel of life here on earth.

And following is not as easy as it sounds. We seem to have an innate wanderlust, always trying to blaze our own trail. But when we rebel against the authority instituted by God, we rebel against God Himself. We implicitly argue we know how to run our lives better than He does.

Submitting to God is mandatory (James 4.7). If you don't know how to follow yet, learn. Quickly.

Burning

A Florida pastor has been in the news recently for his plans (now, evidently, canceled) to burn Qur'ans at his church. Everyone begged him not to. The military. The government. Political groups. They said it would inflame anti-American sentiment overseas, rejuvenate our military's enemies, and widen the rift between faiths.

I don't buy any of that. Seems to me, radical Islam's opinion of the USA is pretty locked in already. I oppose the Qur'an-burning too, but because it's a naked attempt to energize people with hate for Islam instead of love for the Lord. I'm insulted as an American and as a preacher.

I suppose someone might argue that the event is in keeping with Acts 19.19, where books of magic worth 50,000 drachmas (about 160 years worth of wages for the average man of the day) were burned publicly to show the Christians' opposition to the occult. But those books were the personal property of the Christians themselves; destroying them was their way of turning away from their own sinful past. And the books were practical; destroying them would actually keep the books' next readers from sin. Burning a Qur'an won't convert a Muslim. It won't prevent sinful behavior. It might even stir more up.

A better way of combating false religion is standing loud and proud for the true one—to say with Peter, "there is no other name under heaven that has been given among men by which we must be saved" (Acts 4.12).

It may look brave to stand on a street corner and burn a book. But it may be more effective to preach out of one.

Word for Word

Band

We are a band family. Taylor plays clarinet in the high school marching band. Kylie is just learning the flute. Tracie is a band alumna. And Tracie and I serve on the band counsel.

I actually was in the orchestra in my youth. (Band wasn't quite geeky enough for me.) But even back then, I loved the idea of the band. Different people all wearing the same clothes, sitting in the same place, playing the same song (more or less)—it's a unifying experience unlike any other. *E Pluribus Unum*. From many, one.

A band unifies. Just like a wire band turns strands of hay into a bale, so human beings become more than just the sum of each part when tied together. And the differences between members in instrument tone and harmonic pitch only make the union that much more marvelous.

All of this presupposes, of course that the members of the band work in harmony. If the brass plays one song and the percussion another, chaos ensues. That was the problem with the church in Corinth. Various factions had formed, making unity impossible and hindering the growth of everyone involved.

If we are to make a "joyful noise" (Psalm 100.1, KJV) as a band of brothers, we must play the song given us by Jesus, our Head (1 Corinthians 11.3). We must play properly; vocalizations with no intelligible meaning are worse than useless (1 Corinthians 14.7-9). And we must be united in love; otherwise we're just a motley crew of gongs and cymbals, making noise (1 Corinthians 13.1).

Birthday

I had a tremendous birthday yesterday. I reveled in the love of my family. I shared a nice lunch on the town with my wife, who that night cooked chicken Kiev and peach cobbler. The rain kept me out of the office, but I got some quality work done at home. I had a relaxing evening with my jigsaw puzzle and Alfred Hitchcock's *Young and Innocent*. And scattered throughout the day, I wrote thank-you notes to everyone who dropped me a "Happy Birthday" line on Facebook.

That last one was a bigger chore, and a bigger joy, than I had anticipated. I was genuinely touched at the number of people who took the time to tell me they were thinking of me on my special day—which, of course, made it that much more special.

It brings to mind Proverbs 15.30—"Bright eyes gladden the heart; good news puts fat on the bones." I wish I had seen the eyes of everyone who wished me well. But imagining them smiling at me was almost as good. Their kind wishes were like the ice cream on my cobbler—perhaps not totally necessary, but a true blessing nonetheless.

Of course, the "good news" from Jesus is even more heartwarming. His message includes the greatest gift of all—"The time is fulfilled, and the kingdom of God is at hand; repent and believe in the gospel" (Mark 1.15). And I don't have to wait for September 7 to receive it.

"Like cold water to a weary soul, so is good news from a distant land" (Proverbs 25.25). Whether the land is the Philippines, Nigeria, or heaven itself, I am truly blessed to have the blessing of fellowship. Thank you.

Football

Andy Griffith has an old radio comedy routine in which he plays the part of a country bumpkin who stumbles upon a football game. He expresses a great deal of confusion over why two groups of men would go to such extremes to get a "pumpkin," only then to kick it away again. To him, the uninitiated, it made no sense at all.

Of course, it's different for me. I grew up in Texas watching Roger Staubach and Calvin Hill every week. I was quoting completion percentages and reading blitz schemes before I could tell Richard Nixon from Richard Simmons. (Hey, a boy has to have priorities.) But if you were to drop me into a cricket match, or a rugby scrum, or a jai alai ... whatever it is they call a jai alai competition, I'd be as lost as Kanye West at a Taylor Swift concert.

I try to keep this in mind when I am talking about the Bible to people who don't read the Bible. Their confusion has nothing to do with their intelligence (or lack thereof), or even necessarily their interest. It's not time for me to show how smart I am (yeah, right) or how dumb they are. It's time for me to play the part of Philip to their Ethiopian nobleman. *Well, how could I [understand], unless someone guides me?*" he asked Philip on the road to Gaza (Acts 8.31). And Philip guided him, right into the water to be baptized, right into a relationship with the Lamb of God who takes away the sins of the world.

Being a Christian isn't about looking down at people. It's about looking up at the Lord, and then looking out for someone to help.

Emotions

We football fans are nuts. We spend six months poring over our team, eagerly anticipating the first kickoff in the fall. We have plenty of time to convince ourselves that new players will plug last year's holes, new lessons have been learned from last year's mistakes, new strategies have been implemented to correct last year's shortcomings. And by August, we've worked ourselves into a bit of a frenzy. "*They're great!*"

And then the first actual game is played. And things don't go the way we expect. And immediately we jettison six months of analysis and develop a new assessment on the spot. "*They stink!*"

How did we flip so quickly? Well, we probably made mistakes in both cases. The team is probably not as good as the starry-eyed optimist in us thought before the season. And it probably is not as bad as the doom-and-gloom pessimist in us thought in the heat of the ugly, ugly moment.

Emotions are not much of an asset when we are trying to judge a thing's merits. We can get carried away with enthusiasm in the absence of real knowledge. And we can get despondent at the first negative turn. Neither overreaction is likely to help us find the truth.

That's why God says, "prepare your minds for action, keep sober in spirit" (1 Peter 1.13). Being sober, keeping an even keel, will keep us from the devil's despair, which can easily devour us (1 Peter 5.8). Prepared minds are able to recognize God's truth, apply it, and abide in it—even when emotions threaten to get the better of them.

Word for Word

Drunk

I heard this morning that an airplane pilot from New Jersey was pulled over for drunk driving in Amsterdam. Driving a *plane*, that is. The Dutch police literally pulled over the 767 on the runway, escorted the pilot off and made him submit to a breathalyzer test, which he failed. This is the city famous worldwide for its legalized narcotics, by the way.

Interestingly, the report says he blew a .023, which is well below American standards. American drivers typically are not ticketed with blood alcohol concentration lower than .08. A .023 BAC means, for the average person, a single drink sometime in the previous eight hours.

Now, you might argue that a pilot endangers the lives of hundreds of passengers, by operating an airplane in an impaired state, whereas a drunk driver only imperils himself and perhaps a few riders. But there's a lot more traffic down here than up there. I'm not too concerned about crossing paths with drunk pilots on my way home tonight.

Those who are paid to know such things say big things with motors are unsafe in the hands of people who have been drinking. In any amount. That's one reason why I take such an extreme position on alcohol. The Bible requires us to exercise self-control (2 Peter 1.6); alcohol forces us to lose self-control. Any step away from God's will, however small, is a step in the wrong direction.

How much of my mind and body are enough to give the Lord at any given time? Most? Nearly all? If even a fraction of me is given to alcohol, that's a fraction that I'm keeping from God. And that's a fraction too much.

Parents

Children grow up too fast. And I don't mean that in the typical father-of-a-teenager way. I mean it in more of a "What's the world coming to?" kind of way.

I'll give you an example. Recently the parents of a young cheerleader raised an objection to one of the squad's chants—*"Our backs ache, our skirts are too tight, we shake our booties from left to right."* The other parents disagreed, and voted to kick the girl off the squad.

The cheerleader in question is six years old. *Six.*

And it gives me a good opportunity to share one of my favorite rants. I call this one "Lazy Parents." (It's in my files between "Latecomers" and "Leaning Pictures.") My generation has by and large surrendered its parenting responsibilities to MTV, XBox and Hollywood. As a result, the kids dress like vampires, talk like rappers, and act like the cast from *Jersey Shore.* Yuck.

Does a six-year-old girl have any concept of the sexual connotations of tight skirts and "bootie-shaking"? Almost certainly not. But she will eventually. And by that time she may have already developed the wrong habits. Sensuality is among the deeds of the flesh that will keep practitioners from the kingdom of God (Galatians 5.19-21).

Of course, alert, proactive parents could protect her. But that would require them to be in the same room. And if they let her hole up in her room with the internet and Taylor Lautner, they can watch their own shows in peace.

Kids grow up fast enough as it is. Let's keep them innocent as long as we can, okay? It's worth the effort.

Word for Word

Harassment

I am completely and totally opposed to sexual harassment. It is absolutely wrong for members of one sex to view members of the other sex as playthings in a mental game, assuming that every interaction is a sexual one, every thought is a sexual one.

And I am tired of being sexually harassed. Seriously.

I was thinking about it while watching Ines Sainz, sports reporter for TV Azteca, explain her innocence in the dust-up between her and the New York Jets. Apparently some of the players saw her skin-tight jeans and made some observations about ... well, you get the drift. She insisted she did not do anything to bring it on herself.

"They are my size," she said of the jeans in question. Of course, she was wearing a shirt cut halfway down to her navel while doing the interview.

Now, I do not watch TV Azteca sports. But those who do say the sexy look of its reporters (who make Erin Andrews look like a frumpy old maid) is very much part of the network's appeal. Turns out, male sports fans like shapely women in tight, revealing clothing. Who knew?

I'll keep watch over my own eyes and heart. And I'll answer for my thoughts, regardless of what brought them on. But women who put their ... attributes on display for all and complain when men have the nerve to look will answer for that as well. There's nothing modest and discreet (1 Timothy 2.9) about tight and revealing clothes.

We're being victimized here too, ladies. You know it's true. Please, take responsibility for your choices. Be part of the solution, not part of the problem.

T-shirts

As I type, I am wearing a t-shirt that reads, "Will Golf For Food." It was a gift a few years ago, and I've worn it any number of times. I like it. But at some point, it occurred to me—"That's a pretty stupid saying."

Of course, I *would* golf for food. But then, I would golf for money as well. Or for free, as far as that goes. Why wouldn't I? After all, in most instances you have to actually *pay* to golf. (That's one of the reasons I golf so seldom—that and my palpable lack of skill.) So why wouldn't I golf for food?

So I started wondering. All this time I thought wearing this shirt was telling people I enjoy golf. But maybe it was just telling them I'm an idiot.

Either way, I guess, people are getting an impression of me from the t-shirts I wear. Maybe where I or a loved one spent a vacation. Or my favorite eatery. Or my favorite college football team. I certainly wouldn't want to advertise (and that's basically what I'd be doing) for a product, service or organization I didn't support.

That's why I hate seeing Christians advertise for the devil. The shirt may not read, *"Lose your soul in three easy steps: go to www.eternaldamnation.com."* But it may support a beer joint, or an outfitter famous for vulgarity. Or it may just show an appreciation for a carnal lifestyle—lewdness, vulgarity, violence, sensuality, etc.

Paul says, "do not touch what is unclean" (2 Corinthians 6.17). Can we do that when we're tacitly encouraging our friends and neighbors to get down and dirty?

Word for Word

Sandpaper

I have a lot of rough edges. For instance, I tend to insert myself in situations that don't concern me. I often jump to premature conclusions. I can be pretty stubborn. I don't always follow through. I'm an awful procrastinator.

Okay, Tracie, that's enough. They get the idea.

I'm working on them. God is helping me. By submitting to Him, I am surrendering my life—all of it—to His will. Whatever part does not conform to His word gets changed. In that sense, the Bible is like divine sandpaper. God smoothes out the rough spots in our character and behavior by showing me the life of Jesus and holding my life up to His mirror (James 1.23-25).

But sandpaper is coarse. It works by means of friction. And friction causes heat. If having God scrub you head to toe with sandpaper sounds uncomfortable, well, sometimes it is. And the rougher the surface, the bigger the grain of sandpaper God has to use. Bigger grain, more friction, more heat. That's why most hardened sinners would rather just skip the process. They decide they like the rough look and figure God will get used to it.

They're wrong. Jesus didn't die on the cross so you could stay the way you were. God's will is for you to be "transformed by the renewing of your mind" (Romans 12.2). You can't do that and stay in your rough state.

And the process never ends. He just moves to smaller grains of sandpaper. But the more He works on us, and the closer we get to His will, the more we love Him for the marvelous things He is accomplishing in us.

Scenic

I took the scenic route on my last out-of-town trip. It wasn't entirely by choice. I couldn't locate our GPS device. (It's kind of pathetic how dependent we are on technology these days, isn't it? That's a subject for another day.) And my map gave the highway numbers and town names in tiny, tiny type that refused to come into focus no matter how much trombone-playing I did. (Young people, if you don't understand that particular idiom, trust me—you will one day.)

Long story short, my trip look longer than necessary. And it reminded me that the phrase "scenic route" is not just a figure of speech for driving around in circles without a clue. The fact is, interstate highways don't tend to be very attractive. In Texas, it's pretty much billboards and blacktop as far as the eye can see.

The roundabout route, though, offers a closer look at the world— its people, its sights, its smells. It's really a far more enjoyable way to get from here to there. I was reminded how much I miss by obsessing over timetables and destinations. I kept hearing Yoda talk about Luke Skywalker like he was talking to me. "Always looking to the future. Never thinking about *Where He Was*. Mmm. *What He was Doing*. Mmm."

When we obsess over the future, it's easy to miss out on the wonders of now. Solomon writes that when we contemplate the joys of now, it's tougher to obsess on potential problems of later; "God keeps him occupied with the gladness of his heart" (Ecclesiastes 5.20).

Take the scenic route next time. I plan to.

Turtles

My favorite traveling game is called "Roadkill." The rules are simple. Everyone in the car makes a guess as to what dead critter we will come across next. On the rural Texas roads we frequent, there's no telling what you will find—armadillo, raccoon, possum, squirrel, deer, buzzard, a veritable cornucopia of protein.

Unfortunately, for reasons I've never fully understood, the rest of the family never wants to play. Bummer.

Had we been playing on our last family outing, though, I doubt anyone would have picked "turtle." Yet, "turtle" it was. And it struck me as strange. Turtles, after all, are as slow as my daughter Kylie in the morning. Almost. And they're dark and relatively small, making them tough to pick out from a moving car. Basically they are roadkill waiting to happen. But until the other day, I don't think I'd ever seen one that had been Michelinized.

And the explanation is pretty obvious. Turtles don't get out on the highway very often. No road, no roadkill.

This is one of my favorite lessons for Christians—especially young Christians. You'd be amazed how much trouble you avoid simply by not being in the wrong place at the wrong time. Hang out with troublemakers, you get in trouble (Proverbs 1.10-19). Date a troublemaker, you get in trouble (Proverbs 9.13-18). But "abstain from every form of evil" (1 Thessalonians 5.22), and you give yourself a good chance of staying pure.

Sin is right at the door for us, just as it was for Cain (Genesis 4.7). Keep the door closed. Stay off the road.

Ready

As the father of two daughters, I have come to realize that "ready" is a vague concept. As in, "I'm ready! Just let me put on my shoes. And grab a bite. And find my homework."

But then, I'm one to talk. I'm well known in the house for letting little things go until the absolute last minute. And of course, if the checkbook or cell phone is not where I expected it to be, then we're automatically an extra minute or two behind schedule. And as hot and bothered as I get over being late, you'd think I would do something about that. But it's just too easy to take "readiness" for granted.

I'm trying not to be like that in regard to my date with God at the judgment seat (2 Corinthians 5.10). I know it's coming. And I'm ready. At least, I think I'm ready.

Then again, my life is not entirely what I would like it to be. Jesus wants to "present to Himself the church in all her glory, having no spot or wrinkle or any such thing" (Ephesians 5.27). And the part of the church for which I am accountable (myself) is not there yet. I know I will need to leave room for God's grace no matter how righteous my behavior (Ephesians 2.8-9). But still, that's no excuse for a lack of growth on my part. I was really hoping I would be further along than this by now.

Plus I have a lot of work to do on my girls. They're great girls, mind you, but still … a lot. I'm not the husband I ought to be, either. And lots of my friends and neighbors still need the gospel.

Maybe I'm not as ready as I could be. Or should be.

Word for Word

Teachers

I love teachers. I always have. From Mrs. Bennett (who taught me to raise my hand) to Professor Johnson (who taught me to get to the point quickly) to Mrs. DuBose (who gave birth to a girl who would later become my wife), teachers have worked hard to provide what I needed to become the man I am today.

Then again, some people become teachers just to get their summers off. And I'm not saying that is such an ignoble aspiration in and of itself. But if any young readers out there are considering going into teaching to avoid work days, please let me save you from yourself. Teachers work constantly. Workshops (usually in the summer, by the way), classroom maintenance, grading papers at night and over weekends—I even heard this week about teachers being "asked" to participate in "Saturday school." I don't know what that might be, but I doubt it includes wings and college football. And that leaves me out.

Of course, some teachers get by with minimal effort, as with any other profession. But the ones who are in it for the students and not just themselves embrace the work, and find joy in the impact for good they are having.

Teaching God's word for a living, as I do, is much the same. The great ones, the ones who truly make a difference, are doing it for others. The word "minister" itself means "servant." If I can learn to first be "a good servant of Christ Jesus" (1 Timothy 4.6), then a minister of the Christ to others (Romans 15.16), then maybe I can make a difference, too. It's a lot of work, granted. But the rest waiting afterward (Hebrews 4.1) makes it all worthwhile.

Questions

There are no stupid questions. That's what I have been told all my life by people trying to instill learning in others, particularly children. The idea is, if you are confused about something extraordinarily basic, better to go ahead and ask and look foolish than to persist in ignorance and actually *be* foolish. It doesn't mean you are excused for being ignorant in the first place. That's why I prefer my corollary to the rule: "There are no stupid questions, but there are stupid people."

People don't like asking questions because doing so displays their own inadequacy. After all, if they knew what they were doing, they wouldn't need to ask questions, would they? And no one likes to appear foolish. "A babbling fool will be ruined" (Proverbs 10.8); surely the less babbling, the better.

Then again, coming to the Lord is all about our own inadequacy. We tried life our own way, and we made a mess of it. "A man's way is not in himself" (Jeremiah 10.23), and the discerning man eventually realizes that.

To find the right way, he is going to have to ask some good questions—like, "Why am I here?" "Who can I trust?" "What shall I do?" And God's inspired word answers back. "Fear God and keep His commandments" (Ecclesiastes 12.13). "Every word of God is tested" (Proverbs 30.5). "Repent, and let each of you be baptized … for the forgiveness of your sins" (Acts 2.38).

It may seem foolish at first to broadcast our ignorance. But we won't get the answers until we ask the questions.

Word for Word   265

Photographs

I really hate my driver's license photograph. Honestly, it looks like a mug shot—like I just got busted at 3 a.m. for dealing drugs after having used too much of my own product.

(As it happens, I'm not a drug dealer. Or any other sort of person who would get his picture posted on the post office wall. Just wanted to clear that up.)

Most people seem to feel the same way about their own DMV photographs. And it's strange because we've all had our pictures taken before. We've all had relatively flattering photos made—at least, for me, as flattering as they could be, given the subject matter. And the one that will be seen the most looks like something off a milk carton.

Clearly, professional photographers earn their keep. In this day of digital cameras, virtually anyone can point and shoot. But it takes skill (and, in some cases, stuffed animals) to get a subject to appear in a favorable light. "Good" pictures are no less accurate than "bad" ones, and they are a lot more likely to be framed and mounted. And what's wrong with that?

I wish we could all work on our spiritual photography skills a bit. I don't mean we should do some spiritual Photoshop just to make people feel good about themselves. But "speaking the truth in love" (Ephesians 4.15) means telling the truth in a palatable way. If a friend is lost in sin, I don't want to just highlight his shortcomings; I want him to see what I see—a success story, waiting to surface. That's a photo he might be willing to look at.

Orange

I am a big supporter of Texas A&M University. (This is where my 300-word limit comes in handy.) And we Aggies wear maroon. Also in our fair state there is a school identified with the color orange. Orange is, let's just say, not a popular color in Aggieland. In fact, it is actually against city ordinances to build an orange and white building in College Station, Texas. Not that Aggies are fanatics or anything.

Myself, I have several orange articles of clothing. And I am going to keep them. And wear them. Why not? I like the color. (Gasp!) And I refuse to surrender an entire swath of the spectrum simply because of an association some people may make. If people confuse me for a fan of some other school because of the color of my shirt, I must not be much of a fan of my school.

Loyalty is more than just skin deep. It emanates from deep within the heart. And it finds expression in innumerable ways—most often and most easily, our words. Jesus says, "For the mouth speaks out of that which fills the heart. The good man brings out of his good treasure what is good; and the evil man brings out of his evil treasure what is evil" (Matthew 12.34-35). If we are truly devoted to Christ, we are going to sound like it—starting with our confession of Him as Lord (Romans 10.10), continuing with our constant affirmation of His lordship (Matthew 10.32), and encompassing absolutely every word that comes out of our mouths. No exceptions.

Just wearing the right shirt, or avoiding the wrong shirt, won't get it done.

Word for Word

Notebook

If you see me around town, you may notice that I usually carry a notebook with me. It was a present from my daughter, Taylor, a couple of years ago. She gave me the book to help me take notes for my sermons and articles. She decorated the cover to remind me how much she loves me. Both plans work.

At any point in the day I may stumble across an idea—surfing the Internet, listening to another preacher, driving, whatever. And I'm not in position to develop the idea fully. So I'll jot a few notes down in the notebook and come back to them later. (I usually wait for a red light when I'm driving, just in case you were concerned.)

I picture Solomon doing much the same thing with his notebook, going through his daily affairs, collecting snippets of wisdom along the way and putting them down in his book of Proverbs. He passes by the field of a sluggard, and he takes some notes (Proverbs 24.30-34). He watches a young man give his heart to the wrong woman, and he takes some notes (Proverbs 7.6-23). He even solicits and records the wisdom of others (Proverbs 30, 31).

That's what I'm trying to do. Of course, I don't have God's inspiration guiding me as he did, but it's the same principle. God is trying to impart wisdom with every step I take—wisdom for me to use to enhance my life, and then to share with others. And if I can first pay attention, then make note of it (at least figuratively, preferably literally), then put the lesson to work in my life, I can use "the fear of the Lord" (Proverbs 1.7) as the basis of a lifetime of learning—and sharing that learning with others.

Fairness

I am sick and tired of intolerant people telling me I have to be tolerant of others. Honestly, I can't protest the construction of a mosque near Ground Zero (instead of one of a hundred equally adequate locations) because it might hurt the feelings of people who were dancing in the streets burning American flags on September 11, 2001. I can't protest illegal immigration because it would interfere with the dreams of thousands of "law-abiding citizens" (except they're not law-abiding, and they're not citizens). I can't protest "The Reverend" (yeah, right) Jeremiah Wright's grotesque, racist diatribes because that would somehow make me a racist. As Charlie Brown would have said, "*AAUUGH!*"

Thanks for listening. I feel better now.

Typically after such screeds, the answer comes back, "We hold ourselves to a higher standard. If other nations, or if some people in our nation, want to be insensitive to others, that doesn't mean we have to respond in kind."

And you know what? That's absolutely right. Not fair, mind you, but right. How many times did Jesus Himself tell us that very thing? He said turn the other cheek, go the extra mile, love our enemies (Matthew 5.39, 41, 44). It's not about being *fair*, it's about being *right*.

I'm not suggesting we muzzle ourselves in the face of injustice. Paul didn't (Acts 16.37; 24.10-12). But we have to disabuse ourselves of this notion that fairness is just a stump speech away. It's not—not as long as Satan is the ruler of this world (John 14.30).

I just have to make sure he isn't ruling me.

Word for Word

Pests

Say a mosquito is loose in your house. Maybe it has bitten you once or twice. (The mosquito is assumed not to be carrying West Nile virus, dengue fever, malaria, or any other potentially life-threatening illness by the way—regular, garden-variety mosquito.) Anyway, you become obsessed. You can't concentrate on your book or TV show. You go on a rampage. You wind up breaking a lamp and tearing a rotator cuff before finally making the desired red smear on the wall—which, of course, you must now wipe up.

Does that sound like a good way to spend a typical Tuesday evening? I didn't think so.

Now, I'll swat the 'skeeter on my arm as quick as the next guy. But I'm trying to be an example of patience and perspective for my girls. Pests only ruin your life when you allow them to do so. And I won't.

Satan pesters like that. He knows you are blissfully happy as a child of God. He knows every blessing in the heavenly places is yours (Ephesians 1.3). So he distracts you, annoys you, gets you thinking about life's problems instead of heaven's glories. And it works. It works well.

Thankfully, Jesus helps us keep our eyes on the prize. He says, "Set your mind on the things above" (Colossians 3.2). He teaches us life lessons during our trials, helping us become "perfect and complete, lacking in nothing" (James 1.2-4). And He promises, "momentary, light affliction is producing for us an eternal weight of glory far beyond all comparison" (2 Corinthians 4.17).

No mere pest is going to keep me out of heaven.

Loitering

After Kylie's middle school lets out, a teacher roams the grounds reminding students to leave school property. I find that interesting. We spend gobs of tax dollars and man hours getting children to go to school, and then as soon as the clock strikes 3:30 it's, "Okay, kid, beat it! And don't come back for at least 16 hours!"

Loitering is a moot point at other grade levels. An elementary-school student wouldn't stay an extra second on campus even if Selena Gomez were personally handing out chocolate-coated tickets to Disneyland. High-schoolers either have cars or friends with cars; they can buy drugs and plot the assassination of the principal from anywhere.

Middle-schoolers, though, are old enough to get into big trouble but not quite old enough to go and find it. So administrators assume any child hanging around school after the bell is up to no good. And they're probably right.

Being in the right place at the wrong time, or for the wrong reason, is merely loitering. And usually a loiterer is doing more harm, to himself and others, than good.

Church buildings have loiterers, too. And that's a shame. You don't benefit from sitting in the parking lot drinking beer (although it appears some do try). Nor does it help to have your body inside the building during worship while leaving your mind at the lake or ball field.

Isaiah wrote of the "worshipers" of his day (and of Jesus' day, according to Matthew 15.7-9), "they remove their hearts far from Me" (Isaiah 29.13). Did he write it of us as well? Are we worshiping, or merely loitering?

Word for Word

Fried

After years of indulgence, followed by more years of heartburn, I have learned that three is the magic number in regard to deep-fried food. Two pieces of fried chicken, or two Krispy Kreme doughnuts, I'm fine. But go back for a third, and I will soon pay the penalty. And the pleasure derived from a few minutes of wanton abandon (Okay, with the doughnuts, "a few seconds" would be more accurate) does not outweigh the consequences.

This is all Tracie's fault. In my wayward youth, I could eat anything I wanted. Then I got married. And her first task was to wean me off of whole milk and deep-fried food. And it worked. I got to where I didn't even miss all the fat that had absolutely characterized my diet before. After 17 years, my mom still stands agape in amazement.

The problem is, my body no longer knows how to tolerate fried food. So when I eat much of anything greasy, it starts complaining. A lot. The things that had brought me so much joy now bring me misery. Thanks, Trac.

The lesson is not that I should have stayed single. It's that Jesus changes the way we look at things that are contrary to our best interests. We don't especially enjoy giving them up, but we do. And the closer we draw to Him, the less we miss them. In fact, they begin to nauseate us.

Our new attitude confuses our friends back in the world (1 Peter 4.4), who still love to gorge on the spiritual equivalent of deep-fried Snickers bars. They don't get it. I don't want sin in my system. Sin is toxic. It was going to kill me. And now, thanks to Jesus, it won't.

Signs

A man walks down the street and sees a sign in a store window—"Pants pressed, 50 cents." (Clearly this is an old story.) He goes in and tells the man behind the counter, "I'd like my pants pressed for 50 cents." The man replies, "Oh, we don't press pants here; we paint signs."

If you've heard me preach for any length of time, you've probably heard me tell that story. It's one of my favorites—partly because it's a lot shorter than most of my stories (ask my wife about that), but mostly because it addresses what I consider a chronic problem in churches today: an obsession on externals.

Jesus gives a similar illustration in Matthew 23.25—"Woe to you, scribes and Pharisees, hypocrites! For you clean the outside of the cup and of the dish, but inside they are full of robbery and self-indulgence." A cup with a clean exterior looks nice on a shelf, but that is of little consequence if the inside is filthy.

I am blessed to have been associated with many churches over the years that were obsessive about presenting the proper front to the surrounding community. That's important. People get a lot of information from signs, and we need that information to be accurate. But if we don't have Christ on the inside, it really doesn't make much difference what we have on the outside.

Calling Jesus our Lord, either as individuals or as a group, does no good if we do not make it so through obedience (Matthew 7.21). I have no problem with painting signs. But let's press some pants, too.

Word for Word

Octopus

I eat octopus from time to time—mainly at Chinese buffets and sushi restaurants. It's not bad. Kind of chewy. Partly I do it because it's unusual, and I don't get the opportunity very often (like listening to Irish music, or watching a decent Tom Cruise movie). But mostly, I suspect, it's just to say I do it. "Yeah, I eat octopus. It's not bad. Kind of chewy."

I don't mind being different. I wear sweater vests. I won't eat ketchup, even on fries. Some march to the beat of a different drummer; I march against the beat. And this attitude serves me well in the kingdom of Jesus Christ, where I am expected to defy cultural norms on a regular basis—"'Come out from their midst and be separate,' says the Lord" (2 Corinthians 6.17).

But different is not always better. Feeling free to experiment is fine; valuing something based purely on its peculiarity is just … weird. I guarantee, if I ever get sick from octopus, my wife will never let me hear the end of it.

Some people are drawn to Jesus because of His unique take on life. They're bored with climbing mountains to converse with yogis, and with connecting with their "inner truth" through various exercise and pharmaceutical regimens. And the call to join "a peculiar people" (1 Peter 2.9, KJV) sounds intriguing. But like the similarly minded Athenians (Acts 17.21), their interest in the gospel is only skin deep. And when it gets challenging or distasteful, they'll move on to something else.

Don't come to Jesus because He's different. Come to Him because He is Lord.

Than

Is it, "He is taller than *me*"? *Or*, "He is taller than *I*"? Apparently among grammarians this is quite a controversial topic. Some claim "than" is a conjunction, joining two equal clauses. Thus, "I" is a shortened version of the clause, "I am tall" and therefore correct. However, others claim "than" is a preposition, requiring the objective case pronoun "me" to complete the prepositional phrase. Both groups make compelling cases. What to choose, what to choose ...

Well, after considerable research into the subject, I have come to a determination. And since I know you are all on pins and needles, I will share it. Are you ready?

I have determined that I am wasting my time.

Grammar is important. Proper usage of the language helps us communicate messages to one another accurately. And meticulous points can be important. "My wife loves Diet Dr Pepper more than *I*" means I, personally, prefer Pepsi Max; "My wife loves Diet Dr Pepper more than *me*" means I need to buy her flowers more often. That's a distinction worth noticing. But obsessing over minutia to no practical purpose is a waste of time and energy.

It's why Paul told Timothy, "instruct certain men not to teach strange doctrines, nor to pay attention to myths and endless genealogies, which give rise to mere speculation rather than furthering the administration of God which is by faith" (1 Timothy 1.3-4). We can get so bogged down in our ideas of what is important that we turn our backs on the actual gospel. Not only does that not bring us closer to God, it may drive us further away.

Word for Word

Wrinkles

My parents bought me a black dress shirt and matching tie for my birthday this year. (Thanks again, folks.) A few weeks later, they had occasion to hear me preach. So I bet you can guess which shirt I wore.

Unfortunately, it was a bit wrinkled when I unpacked. But no worries. I got out the iron and ironing board and took care of business. (Marriage hasn't sapped me of all of my self-sufficiency, it would seem.) Showing my appreciation for the gift was not enough; I wanted to make the best presentation possible.

I would have had the same diligence, and more besides, if I had been preparing for my wedding instead. (I probably wouldn't have worn a black shirt in that case, but you get my point.) I wanted to do everything I could, with the limited resources this homely fellow had, to be someone of whom my bride could be proud.

How eager are we to iron out the wrinkles in our character, though? After all, our "wedding day" is coming. The church is "the bride of Christ" (Revelation 19.7), and we eagerly await the day He will take us for His own. In that day, according to Ephesians 5.27, He will "present to Himself the church in all her glory, having no spot or wrinkle or any such thing." Whatever work remains to be done will be done then through His grace.

But what about now? If I truly love the Lord, can I just "continue in sin so that grace may increase" (Romans 6.1)? I need to be "applying all diligence" (2 Peter 1.5-7) to be as pure and wrinkle-free as possible today.

Purses

I was in a purse store today. Hooray. It reminded me of how thankful I am that my wife's tastes in such things are simpler than many. Say, around $300 simpler. I love you, sweetheart!

I saw a bright purple one that made me think of my older daughter, Taylor, who would gladly cast a vote to paint every tree in town purple if she were four years older. I could just imagine the conversation. *Can I, Daddy, please?* No. *Pleeeeeeeese?* No. *I'll love you forever!* Oh, in that case, no.

Maybe if I were a multi-zillionaire in Beverly Hills and all Taylor's friends had fancy purses, I would think differently. Maybe. Hey, Paris Hilton is on TV again. Maybe I wouldn't after all, now that I think about it.

Anyway, however poorly I understand it, purses are a silent form of communication between women. *I'm better than you. I'm richer than you. I have way too weird an attachment to my dog.* (Sorry, saw Paris Hilton again.)

But bragging is bragging, whether it's implicit or explicit. That's the point of 1 Peter 3.3-5; although we apply it appropriately to revealing clothes, Peter is really writing about flashy clothes, adorning oneself with "braiding the hair, and wearing gold jewelry, or putting on dresses" instead of "the hidden person of the heart." Nice clothes, hair and accoutrements go too far when they tell the world what we most want the world to know about ourselves. And that goes for men and women alike.

I'm not saying a $400 purse doesn't have its place. I'm saying its place isn't my 14-year-old daughter's arm.

Criticism

Preachers have to learn to deal with criticism. I guess everyone does. And it can be difficult, especially when we are not inclined to criticize ourselves. Ego can be a real bear.

I truly believe most critics are well-intentioned, giving with love from their experience and judgment. Others are talentless bystanders living vicariously. Some are theorists and academicians, having grand ideas of how the world ought to work but little practical knowledge of how it actually does. And some are just cranks, never feeling high unless bringing someone else low.

Occasionally I "answer a fool as his folly deserves" (Proverbs 26.5). But normally it's more productive to sit quietly and take my lumps. That doesn't come easily to most of us—certainly not to me. But no one said growing would be painless (Hebrews 12.7-13).

Galatians 1.10 reads, "For am I now seeking the favor of men, or of God? Or am I striving to please men? If I were still trying to please men, I would not be a bond-servant of Christ." Know your target audience. If you want to please yourself, don't resent those who do not appreciate your work. If you want to please others, be prepared for feelings of self-loathing and doubt. If you want to please God, don't squawk every time you get your feathers ruffled. In any case, you can't have it all.

Pleasing God means working through hurt feelings (and yes, sometimes bad motives) to find nuggets of character-honing truth. It's easy to lash out at the critic; it's tougher, but far more productive, to carefully weigh the criticism to see if it can actually be of use.

Sprinklers

Sprinklers that run while it's raining have to rate in my top ten pet peeves. That's elite company, by the way. Lots of things annoy me. Waiters who ignore me all evening and then ask if I will need change. Misspellings on billboards. Smart-alecks. (Other than me, naturally.)

I'm the kind of guy who carefully peels the last square of toilet paper off the roll. Letting something go to waste is like a cheese grater across my knuckles. And watching someone pay for water only to watch it literally go right down the drain, well, it's enough to drive me to the word processor. As you can tell.

At some point an act that may have the best of intentions, that may in different circumstances be exactly what the doctor (or gardener) ordered, may be completely wasted at best and counterproductive at worst. At that point we can either congratulate ourselves for the pig-headedness that we prefer to call "determination," or we can abandon an obviously flawed plan and move on.

This decision becomes even tougher when dealing with evangelism. Jesus Himself told us, "Do not give what is holy to dogs, and do not throw your pearls before swine" (Matthew 7.6). Jesus would never have left Nazareth if He had insisted on teaching people who would not be taught (Mark 6.1-6). And where would we be then?

We do not give up hope for such ones. But neither do we neglect potentially fertile fields to throw good effort after bad in a poor one. We cannot become so enamored of dust that we cannot shake it off (Matthew 10.14).

Word for Word

Lyrics

Recently I happened to hear "Beat It," one of the most popular songs of my high school days, for the first time in a long while. And it reminded me of a question that haunted me throughout the '80s: Does anyone actually know the lyrics to a Michael Jackson song? Any song? Really? Is it, *"Beat it! Beat it! Don't want to risk the bitter feeling"*? Or is it, *"Don't want to lose a thing, I mean it"*? *"Don't want to see 'E.T.', I've seen it"*? *"Don't want to eat a peach unseeded"*? *"Poland could never be defeated"*?

I'll admit, my ear for lyrics is worse than many. I can't make heads or tails out of my daughters' music. (Then again, I vacate the room as soon as I hear it.) But I know plenty of music aficionados who blissfully jam out to their favorite tune, *blah blah blah* their way through the confusing passages, and couldn't care less.

That's started to bother me more and more in recent years. If I crank the volume on Billy Joel's "Only the Good Die Young," am I telling my girls in the back seat that I approve of boys' efforts to get innocent Catholic girls to trade religious conviction for commitment-free sex? It's tough to answer that question in the negative.

Our tongues can't serve God's interests and Satan's simultaneously any more than a fountain can produce both fresh and bitter water (James 3.11). And if my musical interests interfere with my spiritual interests, I'm not seeking the kingdom first, as Jesus required (Matthew 6.33).

This barrier shouldn't be as tough to overcome as it is. But I'm sure I can "Beat It" with God's help.

Dragons

People think I'm joking when I tell them I believe in dragons. But I'm not. I don't believe they exist *now*, of course; I figure they'd be all over the Discovery Channel if they were still out there today. But with volumes of anecdotal evidence from all over the world, from St. George to Marco Polo (one I have read dates as recently as 1793), the burden of proof would seem to lie squarely with the naysayer.

The main reasons I have ever heard for not believing in dragons are (1) we've never seen one, and (2) it's crazy. But I've never seen a germ, or my tonsils, or a Frenchman who didn't stink; that doesn't relegate any of the above to the category of Bigfoot (on which I have no official position, by the way). And flying lizards might have seemed crazy until we found pterodactyl fossils; since we know better now, is it so unrealistic to imagine one of them breathing fire? And if you're not convinced yet, read Job 41, especially verses 18-21. Then get back to me.

I think the real reason people don't believe in dragons is that they cannot believe such creatures would not have destroyed mankind. They never consider that it could have been the other way around—that humans could have banded together for the common good, knowing that many or all of them would die, but determined to rid themselves of this monstrous, seemingly invincible threat.

Thank God for such ones who battled the greatest dragon of all (Revelation 20.2) and those who battle him still. They give us courage that we can successfully resist him as well (1 Peter 5.8).

Word for Word

Boundaries

Max is a bit of an amateur decorator, and he seems to think that shredded paper matches absolutely everything. So we usually keep our bedroom door closed. If Tracie or I are in the room with the door open, Max will park himself at the doorway, paws on the carpet, ever the optimist, thinking it might be one of those times when he is granted entrance. And if we don't specifically tell him otherwise, he will eventually assume silence is license and let himself in. But he knows better. And at the first snap of my fingers, he's back in the hallway, hoping his sad little face will change our minds. Keep dreaming, buddy.

Max knows his boundaries. He knows when he's reached them, and he knows when he has transgressed them. It's the same with humans. My girls' world is considerably more complicated than Max's, and my world more complicated still. Boundaries can be difficult to ascertain. Still, certain behaviors are required, others permitted, and others prohibited. The sooner we learn them, the more peaceful and free of conflict our lives will be.

It is strange that we think God's boundaries are some sort of exception to this rule—strange in that God invented boundaries, both for nature (Job 38.8-11) and for humanity (2 John 9). If He can command the sea to restrain itself, surely He can command us.

Unfortunately we, like Max, like to test our Master, doing as we like and hoping to weasel out of any consequent punishment. But grace is His job; obedience is ours. We would do well to not confuse the two.

Autumn

I suppose we get the word "fall" (referring to the time of year, not the career of Humpty Dumpty or O.J. Simpson) from the bevy of multicolored leaves that decorate so many yards and driveways this time of year. That term probably wouldn't have caught on in Texas; our pines, live oaks and mesquites have a different timetable than maples and chestnuts.

But even though the harbingers of autumn may look different in the mountains of Vermont than in the gulf coastal plains of Texas, still the message comes through loud and clear: God is closing the book on another year. Time for the squirrels to come and collect all the acorns out of my yard. Time for the Cowboys to invent a new way to lose football games. Time for me to see if, yet again, my sweaters have mysteriously shrunk while in storage.

Solomon wrote, "There is an appointed time for everything. And there is a time for every event under heaven" (Ecclesiastes 3.1). Maybe that's why I hesitate to call autumn my favorite time of year. I love the weather, the sports, the festive spirit. But then, the other seasons have their joys as well. Each is marvelous in its own special way, because each is a gift from God.

Rains come in their season (Leviticus 26.4), grain is harvested in its season (Job 5.26), trees produce fruit in their season (Psalm 1.3). Each is important. Each is different. And God sorts them all out for our benefit. No matter how short the days get, they all start with the sun in the east and end with it in the west (Psalm 19.6). And they all glorify God in so doing. As should we.

Word for Word

Concrete

What is it about wet concrete that makes us want to make impressions? Whether our initials, or our handprints or footprints, or even a nonsensical saying (who is "Kilroy," anyway?), we feel compelled to leave a mark. I suppose we like the idea of having "concrete" (sorry) evidence that the world is a different place because of us, that we will leave a legacy, however small and inconsequential it may seem. And concrete is only poured so often and only stays wet for so long; the opportunity must be seized while it is available.

Of course, we are all leaving a legacy—one that may not be as easy to identify and photograph as scrawl in a sidewalk, but that is ultimately far more significant and far more permanent. Our life leaves an indelible mark on those with whom we come in contact. Our friends, neighbors, and especially family members will be different, for good or for ill, because of our involvement.

We may make that impression accidentally, as though we were blindly and thoughtlessly walking along and happened to step in the wrong place. Or we may put great thought and preparation into it, meticulously planning and executing it as precisely as possible. It's our choice.

We will be remembered. Will it be for our faith—as with Abel, who still speaks to us long after his death (Hebrews 11.4)? Or for our doubt—as with Lot's wife (Luke 17.32), whose very name is forgotten but whose tragic hesitation will never be? The concrete is still wet; the choice is still ours.

Loneliness

There may be someone reading this article who is overcome with loneliness. Perhaps he feels friendless in the world. Perhaps she despairs of finding that special someone. This one may be sitting in an empty room, listening to someone singing the blues on the radio and envying the singer's life, desperate for someone to walk through the door and bring joy and meaning to a dreary, depressing life.

I have a message for that someone. Get over it.

That may sound harsh, and maybe it is. Putting limbs back in joint hurts, to paraphrase Hebrews 12.13. But it's better than being an emotional cripple for life.

"He who separates himself seeks his own desire, he quarrels against all sound wisdom" (Proverbs 18.1). Loneliness is selfish at its core. It presumes that it is others' responsibility to roust themselves from their (presumably) happy and satisfied existences and come to minister to the one who is lonely. It has absolutely no interest in anyone else's welfare. And, as the verse goes on to say, separating yourself doesn't fix loneliness. How could it? When was the last time you found a friend by sitting around and doing nothing? That's what I thought

God's solution to loneliness is tough, but it works. Get involved. Find someone to help. Paul writes, "do not merely look out for your own personal interests, but also for the interests of others. Have this mind in yourselves which was also in Christ Jesus" (Philippians 2.4-5). Does this guarantee you will find exactly what you seek? No. But it does guarantee you will find exactly what you need.

Word for Word

Plums

If the outside of a fruit can be eaten, I typically eat it. Usually that's because peeling fruit is messy, time-consuming and wasteful, and I hate all three of those qualities. So if I can bypass all the objectionable aspects and get right to the eating, why not?

Plums are different. I still eat the skin, but I do it by choice. I love how the sweetness of the interior of a plum is offset by the bitterness of the exterior—not too much of it, mind you, just enough to add a bit of a zip. I think it's a shame that people will go to such trouble to remove part of the experience in the pursuit of pure, unadulterated pleasure. To me, crunching through the barrier of the skin and encountering the initial tartness, only to quickly have it blend with, and ultimately yield to, the smooth, mellow flavor beneath—that's what eating a plum is all about.

It seems to me that a lot of my friends and neighbors want to peel the bitter skin off their own lives. They encounter hardships, challenges, setbacks, and they see them as barriers to happiness—things to be expunged, often at great effort and expense. Well, far be it from me to ask someone to suffer unnecessarily. But at the same time, I don't want to be constantly assessing my life's quality on the basis of how much negativity I can avoid. In the first place, it's a lot easier to peel the skin off a plum than peel the difficulties off a life. And secondly, the hardships can make life's successes seem that much sweeter.

Trials can be a joy (James 1.2). Persecution can be a joy (Matthew 5.10-12). Even suffering can be a joy (Acts 5.41). Why rob yourself of that?

Treats

My family doesn't do the whole "Trick or Treat" thing on Halloween. That's not because of implicit participation in Satanism (although more and more I'm questioning whether it is appropriate for Christians to masquerade as agents of the devil in the name of "having a good time"). Nor is it because I'm afraid my girls will come home with a bag full of cyanide and razor blades.

It's because I think the idea of getting dressed up and going door-to-door begging for goodies is, well, stupid.

Feel free to disagree with me here; I'm not passing moral judgment on the hardcore trick-or-treaters. But I fear we are creating for ourselves a society of people who think they *deserve* treats. And "treats" by their very nature are not *deserved*; they are *given*.

Similar, but far worse, is the attitude many take toward God's grace. Plenty of people will unashamedly live their life under God's sun exactly the way they want with no thought of God, confident they can knock on the pearly gates at the appropriate hour and collect.

The trumpet of God (1 Thessalonians 4.16) will be a rude awakening for them. Those who do not obey the gospel are specifically excluded from grace (2 Thessalonians 1.6-10). Even those who do accept Jesus as Lord, at least in word, do not get an automatic pass. Jesus Himself said, "Not everyone who says to Me, 'Lord, Lord,' will enter the kingdom of heaven, but he who does the will of My Father who is in heaven" (Matthew 7.21). Jesus will "treat" us when we treat Him as Lord. And only then.

Word for Word

Celebrity

I am constantly amazed at what people are willing to do to get attention—the more, the better. *"Humiliation? Fine. Eat cockroaches? Hand me a fork. Hit myself with a hammer? With which end? As long as people are watching, and I can maybe pay a couple of bills with the proceeds, sign me up."*

Used to be, a person like this was called the village idiot. Now he's called a reality television star. Entertainment has really progressed over the past thousand years, hasn't it? From biting heads off live chickens to biting heads off live chickens when an overpaid host says, "Go!"

I used to think people were that way because it was easier than getting a job. I've changed my mind on that. I think today celebrity is a goal unto itself. If it pays well, terrific. But that's not the main objective. No one is paying these knuckleheads on YouTube to swallow spoonfuls of cinnamon, or dive into a pool from a fourth-floor balcony, or French kiss a dog. (If I'm lying, I'm dying.)

Is it really so important that we be recognized? I say yes, but in a way far different from that of anyone who ever lived in the Big Brother house. I think of the attitude of Nehemiah—"Remember me, O my God, for good" (Nehemiah 13.31). And Nehemiah didn't mean "good" at dunking a basketball, or drinking beer, or juggling chainsaws. He meant good for others, for his nation, for the cause of his God.

The "tranquil and quiet life in all godliness and dignity" (1 Timothy 2.2) is no way to become famous, true. But it's a great way to get recognized by God.

Divas

A diva used to be the star of the opera—the infamous "fat lady" who would before its end, we were promised, sing. Her piercing contralto voice would resonate throughout the concert hall, thrilling and inspiring every audience member, making it impossible to look on anyone else.

Today's divas are somewhat different. Most of them still sing. And some of them are, shall we say, shopping in the "women's" department. (Sorry, Aretha, we love you, but the extra-long measuring tape doesn't lie.) But generally when we talk about the voice of a diva filling the room, it is not to proclaim the glories of Verdi, Puccini and Mozart. It's more likely to be screeching for a fresh coat of white paint in her dressing room, or for her Norwegian glacier water in a glass container to be 37 degrees and not 38, or for a perceived rival to be marginalized (or, if convenient, killed).

It appears that the average diva proves her (or his—yes, I'm looking at you, Sir Elton) importance in the world by watching people cater to her every whim. And the more ridiculous and insane the whim, the better. (If you don't know about the milkshake that helped break up J-Lo and Ben Affleck, Google it. It's worth the effort. I promise.)

Such an attitude has no place in the kingdom of Jesus Christ, who Himself came to serve, not to be served (Matthew 20.28). And as He said, "a slave is not greater than his master" (John 13.16).

Jesus invites everyone into His kingdom. But the inner diva in us all will have to drop the attitude first.

Word for Word

Seagulls

Don't feed the seagulls. Please. Do yourself a favor. Tracie tried to teach me this lesson on our first trip to the gulf coast as a married couple many years ago. I thought I knew better. One curly fry and one scene out of a Hitchcock movie later, I had learned that listening to my wife might come in handy from time to time.

I suppose we like to think we are giving back to the planet with these little gestures of generosity. But we're not. Have you ever taken a trip to the coast? Have you ever had to duck into the carwash after a trip to the coast? Trust me, the seagulls are doing fine.

Unfortunately, the suckers of the world (including my former self) have trained the gulls to look for a new source of food—food that flies up to meet them, rather than diving underwater to avoid them. And of course, they're just as competitive for the new food as for the old. (Have you seen *Finding Nemo*? Hearing the gulls screech, *"Mine! Mine!"* gave me flashbacks.)

I wonder if that's how Jesus felt the day after He fed 5,000 people with a handful of food. They found Him and asked how He had arrived, but all He heard was, *"Mine! Mine!"* They wanted more bread and fish. And instead of feeding them again, He told them, "Do not work for the food which perishes, but for the food which endures to eternal life" (John 6.27). No bait and switch for Jesus.

Gathering a crowd is no trick. The trick is gathering the *right* crowd, the crowd that wants to hear the gospel. And handing out bread and fish won't help.

Highlighter

Taylor has taken to reading her Bible with a highlighter. If she sees a passage that is particularly useful, or that she feels she should memorize, she colors it yellow. Maybe you do something similar in your Bible study.

I noticed this particularly the other day as I saw her turned to Matthew's account of the Sermon on the Mount. And virtually every line was highlighted. Did she do it all at once? Was this a result of repeated visits to the text? I didn't ask. But either way, obviously she thought the words of Jesus were important; and equally obviously, she had trouble picking out one verse that stood above another.

I can relate to that. I'm hard-pressed to single out one passage to lift above another in those marvelous three chapters. The Beatitudes? Instructions on prayer? The parable of the house on a rock? Depending on where I am in life at any given time, any of them or a few dozen others could qualify as my "favorite."

That's why I have trouble identifying a single "favorite" verse of the Bible. I mean no offense to you if you would quickly blurt out, "John 3.16!" or "Philippians 4.13!" or some other equally marvelous one. But I kind of feel like I am slighting every other text by elevating just one. I think my Bible might wind up looking like Taylor's if I went that way. All yellow.

Paul says all Scripture is profitable (2 Timothy 3.16), not just the "highlights." If you want to read one verse every day of your life, great. Just don't neglect the others.

Word for Word

Buffets

My girls love eating at Chinese restaurants. Well, that's not quite so. They love eating at Chinese *buffets*. Sometimes I think they are almost indifferent to Chinese food itself. They may get a piece or two of sweet and sour chicken or General Tso's chicken, maybe some chicken-on-a-stick. (Are you noticing a trend here?) But they'll make sure to save room for a slice of pizza that, sure as shooting, came straight out of Walmart's freezer.

I think they like the control that comes from eating at a buffet. Pick what you want. Eat as much of it as you want. Don't like it? Just leave it alone, and the nice lady with the water pitcher will come and take it away. As long as grumpy ol' Dad doesn't make you eat sushi or anything green, it's a wonderful world.

That desire for control works its way into our efforts to serve Jesus Christ. We may call Him Lord, but we're the ones deciding what goes on the plate. *"I'll have a big scoop of grace, and maybe a few pieces of worship (if they don't look too chewy), and maybe a smattering of gratitude. I'll definitely want to save room for heaven. And I'll skip the humility, service and self-denial (it's a buffet, after all).* And we wind up with a dinner that exactly suits our personal preferences and tastes. Perfect.

Except He really *is* Lord. And He *requires* us to study His word (John 8.31-32), to be baptized (Mark 16.16), to walk in good works (Ephesians 2.10), etc. As long as we maintain this illusion that we can pick and choose commands to follow, we show He is not really our Lord.

Gratitude

Pretty much every time I send an article out to the thousand or so members of my Facebook group, someone replies with a "thank you." I love that. I don't mean to suggest I'd quit writing if I quit getting acknowledgements; but it's nice to get them anyway. It reminds me how important it is to be grateful to the ones who make life a little easier, a little happier.

It also reminds me of the thousands of times I have received blessings from the hand of God without showing the proper gratitude. I can't tell you how many times I have given thanks for a meal, eaten, gone back for seconds, started to pray a second time, and then stopped myself. I hear myself saying, "It's okay, Hal, you already thanked God. You don't have to thank Him again."

And I don't "have to" thank Him again; I'm not suggesting otherwise. But since when did gratitude become an obligation? A box to check, like taking a vitamin or brushing your teeth? Should we not rather delight in every opportunity for thanksgiving? I don't believe "pray without ceasing" (1 Thessalonians 5.17) means that literally every second of every day should be spent on our knees. But I do think we should consider the next verse in a more literal sense—"in everything give thanks, for this is God's will for you in Christ Jesus."

There's nothing wrong, and everything right, about saying a quick "thank you" to God for a light snack, or a beautiful sunset, or a good night's sleep. That's the sort of thing I would appreciate hearing; why wouldn't He?

Word for Word

Stoned

Back in 1972, Johnny Cash had a big hit with Kris Kristofferson's classic song, "Sunday Morning Coming Down." Cash successfully fought to keep a controversial line in the chorus—*"On a Sunday morning sidewalk/I'm wishing Lord that I was stoned/'Cause there's something 'bout a Sunday/That makes a body feel alone."* Keep in mind, for what it's worth, that "stoned" in 1972 often referred to being drunk instead of being on drugs—although with Johnny and Kris, it could go either way.

Personally, I've always thought that if the person in the song had spent his Sundays honoring Jesus instead of taking His name in vain, he might have found himself in a better place, both emotionally and literally. For me, Sunday is the least lonely day of the week. It's the day I spend with my brethren—not that I don't associate with them on other days, but joining hearts and minds in spiritual fellowship is something special, unparalleled in any other human relationship.

In fact, forget about wishing; I *do* get stoned on Sundays. Ephesians 5.18-19 reads, "And do not get drunk with wine, for that is dissipation, but be filled with the Spirit, speaking to one another in psalms and hymns and spiritual songs, singing and making melody with your heart to the Lord." The world's idea of drunkenness ruins lives instead of repairing them. Getting "drunk" God's way provides a high that is spiritual, not chemical, and that leads to true joy, both here and in the greater fellowship to come. I'll take door number two, thank you.

Eating

The late great Luciano Pavarotti is quoted as saying, "One of the very nicest things about life is the way we must regularly stop whatever it is we are doing and devote our attention to eating." (If you've ever seen a picture of the famous opera singer, you might not be surprised at his feelings on the subject of food.) His point, of course, was that the need for physical sustenance forces its way to the forefront of our consciousness several times per day—and, if our head chef is talented, that can be a wonderful thing.

I guess this is where I'm supposed to talk about the dangers of an unhealthy diet—cut the fat, cut the salt, cut the carbs, all that business. And I'm not going to do that. Yes, I eat healthy for the most part. But occasionally I have been known to inhale a chicken fried steak with mashed potatoes and peach cobbler. I'm not apologizing, I'm not bragging. I'm just saying life is good, and sometimes it's even better when smothered in cream gravy.

What I am going to do is bemoan the way so many Christians have such trouble finding pleasure in their spiritual diet. Yes, it is necessary for us to eat from God's green pastures (Psalm 23.2). But that doesn't have to be a chore. In fact, it should be a source of true joy.

If you haven't read Psalm 119 recently, do so. God's word revives us (v.25). It lights our path (v.105). We open our mouths wide to receive it (v.131). The time we spend meditating on His word (v.97) should be the highlight of our day. Let us say with the Psalmist in verse 162—"I rejoice at Thy word, as one who finds great spoil."

Politicians

Harry S Truman said, "A politician is a man who understands government. A statesman is a politician who has been dead for 15 years."

I say, we need more statesmen.

This is not a political column, and so I will spare you all of my numerous political opinions. But it seems I share one opinion with almost all of my neighbors—that politicians rate as a life form somewhere between sea slugs and turkey buzzards. (And no offense intended if someone out there has turkey buzzards in the family.)

I'm sure there are exceptions out there. Somewhere. But by and large, politicians give the impression of being in permanent self-preservation mode. They will say or do anything to keep their careers afloat. No real convictions or allegiances—nothing worth taking a bullet for, anyway. And most of us take great offense at that.

Then again, do we do the same thing in our spiritual lives? Plenty of people are terrific at talking the talk; they say, "Lord, Lord," with the best of them. But when it's time to walk the walk, suddenly they develop bunions.

The Christian's first commitment must always be to God, not self. That goes against every impulse we have. But just as God gave us the instinct for survival, He also gave us the capacity to overcome that instinct for a greater good. It's how some people can run into burning buildings while others run out. It's how Christians "walk by faith" (2 Corinthians 5.7) in a world full of landmines. The cause is worth it. The Lord is worth it. Heaven is worth it.

Shirt

As I type, I am wearing my favorite shirt. It's yellow, my favorite color. It's silk, which makes it comfortable. It's washable, which appeals to my stingy side. (I'll dry-clean a casual shirt on the day Max meows.) It looks great with jeans, with nice shorts, or dressed up with a blazer. I put my shirt on in the morning, and I figure I'm setting myself up for a great day.

In reality, my choice of shirt has little or nothing to do with the weather, or the behavior (or misbehavior) of my children, or the current state of the housing market, stock market or supermarket. But none of that matters. I have decided I am going to have a good day. And far more often than not, I do.

I do not understand why people are so willing to surrender their quality of life to forces beyond their control. It's so ... *random* to wait for the stars to align themselves correctly. Why not instead just *choose?*

You say, "It's not that simple, Hal." I say, "Yes, it is!" You say, "You don't know my problems." I say, "I don't care about your problems!" (That came out wrong. Sorry. I do care. They just are not relevant, that's all.)

God says we should not kill ourselves trying to create joyful circumstances; instead, we should find joy where we are. If we are really clothed with Christ (Galatians 3.27), we have cause for joy every day we put Him on.

God promised "everlasting joy" (Isaiah 61.7) for those who would come to His Messiah. Who am I to make a liar of Him who cannot lie (Titus 1.2)?

Them

I'm going down kicking and screaming on the substitution of the word "them" for the word "him" when the antecedent of the pronoun is indeterminate. Sorry. A generation ago women got upset at the assumption that an undetermined person was male. So it became popular to say "him or her"—as in, "For that special someone in your life, consider getting him or her a toaster this holiday season." And I had no problem with that; frankly, in the example given above, I prefer it.

But now, it seems, "him or her" is too bulky. "Them" is concise and gender-neutral. So now, I am told, I have to consider getting "them" a toaster, which makes me feel like a polygamist. Or Charlie Sheen. Well, I'm all for being concise. But when it keeps someone from understanding what you mean, it's effort wasted, not saved.

A lot of people want a theology that fits on a matchbook cover—something quick, something pithy, something easy to remember. That's why John 3:16 is such a popular verse for T-shirt wearers and sign-carriers in sports venues across the country. The idea seems to be, just read John 3:16 and you'll find everything you need to know.

Well, that's just not true. I love John 3:16 as much as the next Christian, don't get me wrong. But if God had wanted John 3:16 to be the end-all be-all of salvation, He wouldn't have given us Philippians 2:12, or James 2:26, or 1 John 3:23, or Mark 16:16. All Scripture is profitable (2 Timothy 3:16), not just the verses that fit on the bill of a ball cap.

A little extra effort on our part is called for. But it's worth it. We have God's word—check that, His *words*—on that.

298   *Hal Hammons*

Endorse

Not that long ago, it was unheard of for a star from the world of entertainment to endorse a product. Appearing on commercials was for actors who weren't good enough to get real jobs. It was a taint. Once seen hawking a product, he or she could not be taken seriously.

That's all changed now. Gone are the days when we assumed a pitchman actually used the product he or she pitched. I remember when Whitney Houston, in the midst of her Diet Coke ad campaign (yes, having Whitney Houston on your side used to be a good thing), was pictured in a magazine with a Diet Pepsi. Oops.

Now it's just another job, and we all understand that. In fact, often television ads will identify Robert Wagner or Wilfred Brimley as a "paid spokesman." I used to think that was a legal maneuver to protect the company, to keep us from believing they were licensed to sell insurance or medical plans. Now I think it might be to protect the actor. *"Hey, I don't actually believe in this stuff I'm selling. I'm just here for the check."*

But I'm not a paid spokesman. Neither are you, I'll wager. And so when we say we endorse filth and vulgarity, people assume we approve of filth and vulgarity. Why wouldn't they?

God says, "Woe to those who call evil good, and good evil" (Isaiah 5.20). When a Christian endorses a film, book or TV show, he is doing so in Jesus' name. And if we're constantly qualifying our endorsement to placate our conscience, perhaps it wasn't worth endorsing at all.

Word for Word

Upright

I have rotten posture. I always have. I cannot sit up straight to save my life. When Tracie and I first started sitting together in church services, she started thinking I was not tall enough for her. And there were plenty of good reasons for her to cut and run; it didn't make much sense for me to give her an extra one.

So this week I've been having a lot of back pain. I suspect it's a result of years of poor posture and inadequate exercise, coupled with too many hours hunched over my jigsaw puzzle. And I've found that putting a pillow behind me in my chair forces me into a better sitting position, decreasing the strain on my spine. Less strain, less pain. It would have been better, looking back, to train myself to sit correctly. But since that ship has sailed, I'll just have to do the best with the situation I have.

I am not aware of any other consistently "upright" part of God's creation ("part-time" upright walkers like bears and chimpanzees notwithstanding). So it is fitting that being upright has come to represent moral character. God calls Job a "blameless and upright man" (Job 1.8). And sin causes spiritual slouching; "God made men upright, but they have sought out many devices" (Ecclesiastes 7.29).

We need to prop ourselves up while we can, before the consequences of our behavior become irreparable. Bad habits threaten our salvation. If artificial means must be employed to keep us away from sin, then employ away. "For the Lord is righteous; He loves righteousness; the upright will behold His face" (Psalm 11.7). That tells me I must do whatever necessary to be as upright as possible.

Love

What can move a husband to leave his warm chair at 11 p.m., get in the car, and drive to the grocery store to buy a candy bar?

What can move a mother to suddenly lose her appetite when dinner comes up one portion short?

What can move a parent to beam with pride as a young child makes the most beautiful screeching imaginable come from her musical instrument?

What can move a child to scrounge through the couch cushions for enough spare change to buy something special one Sunday every May and another every June?

What can move a dog-owner to clean up one mess after another? (Define "mess" as you like.)

What can move a young man to spend almost all of his savings on something smaller than a nickel and then give it away, hoping desperately it will not be returned?

What can move a young woman to see the potential for future greatness in a young man instead of the all-too-present reality of disorder and chaos?

What can move a God to sacrifice His only begotten Son to allow others to become His children as well?

What can move the only begotten Son to agree?

The same thing that can move a Christian to obey His Lord (John 14.15), to bear, believe, hope and endure all things for his brother (1 Corinthians 13.7), to actively seek the welfare of his enemies (Matthew 5.44).

The most powerful force in the universe.

How much is it moving you?

Zebras

An Irish filmmaker was recently reviewing the behind-the-scenes clips from Charlie Chaplin's classic film, *The Circus* (one of my favorites, by the way). He noticed a woman walking around the site of the film's premier holding something to her ear and, apparently, talking into it—in much the same way that you or I would talk into a cellular phone. The only possible conclusion, he says, is that the woman is a time traveler.

He is what I call a "zebra-hunter." He sees a U-shaped track in the dirt and starts rationalizing in his mind how it could be a zebra (instead of, say, a horse). Common sense and volumes of contrary evidence get jettisoned without a second thought to preserve the illusion of the bizarre theory. (The device was actually an ear-trumpet, by the way.)

Zebra-hunters abound in religious circles. Some see zebras because of a personal agenda—a job to protect, a book to sell, etc. Some are just attracted to the unusual; any obvious, uncluttered interpretation is obviously a plot fomented by the corrupt establishment. (Yes, Dan Brown, I'm talking about you.) And, as difficult as it may be to believe, some have been sheltered from horses; they literally may not know that a simpler, less problematical answer may exist.

I'm not suggesting that there are no complex truths in God's word. I'm emphasizing God's assertion that truth is accessible, that by abiding in His word we can know the truth that will set us free (John 8.31-32).

So, "buy truth, and do not sell it" (Proverbs 23.23).

Reality

There are two broad categories of what might be called "reality television." One kind might be called "Day in the Life"—we follow has-been celebrities (or, worse yet, complete nobodies) around all day, watching as they shop, ignore their children, and discuss the pros and cons of Botox. The other might be called "Chance of a Lifetime"—random people get an opportunity to compete for a big check, business opportunity, or marriage to a total stranger.

I can't help thinking we can come up with a better term for shows like these. "Reality" doesn't really seem to work. I mean, when was the last time you unwrapped a roll of toilet paper in a minute without using your hands? Or made a meal out of bison meat, bok choi and Frosted Flakes? Or went on a date in total darkness? (That last one might have helped me back in college. I was born in the wrong decade, I guess.)

Perhaps these shows appeal to so many because people are dissatisfied with their own "reality." They like the idea of thinking, "That could be me if I lived in Southern California, and had better teeth, and lost 30 pounds" (or gained 100 pounds, in the case of *The Biggest Loser*).

But instead of fantasizing about a different life, we would do better by trying to be more content in the life we already have. Solomon, whose life would have made for fantastic TV, finally decided that simply working hard and appreciating every day was the way to true satisfaction in this life (Ecclesiastes 8.15). We would save ourselves a lot of grief if we would take his message to heart.

Word for Word

Greatness

True greatness was described aptly once by Burt Reynolds. Speaking of his fellow football player and actor Jim Brown, he said, "For me, a lot of people want to talk about other actors. Nobody wants to talk to Jim Brown about other football players. They want to talk about Jim Brown."

Greatness does not inspire comparison; it inspires imitation. Greatness does not demand respect; it commands respect. A great person is not one who successfully gets the crowd to look at him; a great person is one who the crowd cannot help but look at.

We all aspire to greatness. But when we use the word "greatness" in reference to Jesus Christ, it sort of takes the wind out of our sails. I mean, how can we use the same word again for ... *us*? It's almost profane.

Isaac Newton helped us understand the rules of the universe. Jesus Christ *wrote* the rules. He created the universe itself (John 1.3) and maintains it even now (Colossians 1.17). Louis Pasteur helped us see the invisible forces that war against our bodies. Jesus Christ revealed the virus that kills the soul—and then offered a free cure (John 3.16). Christopher Columbus opened the door for much of mankind to travel to a new world. Jesus Christ opened the door to heaven for us all (John 14.1-3).

With all due respect to Newton and Pasteur and Columbus, you cannot compare their contributions to humankind to that of Jesus. We can argue over where they rate on a list of "greatest humans ever." But that argument has nothing to do with Jesus. Jesus is a list unto Himself.

Teeth

I went to the dentist this year. Finally. After 15 years of procrastination. I knew my girls really needed to go. And I figured setting a good example myself was a good way to ease into an experience that is at best uncomfortable, and at worst terrifying.

At no point did I think that I might actually have a *problem* with my teeth. After all, I've been completely problem-free for 44 years now. I had every confidence that it would be the same old boring good news yet again.

This is the point in our tale where I'm supposed to tell how years of neglect led to unseen problems, how regular maintenance could have avoided it, how I've learned my lesson and will never take my teeth for granted again.

Sorry. Clean bill of health. Again. The dentist actually pulled folks in from out in the hall to look at my teeth.

I wish I could give credit to regular brushing and flossing habits, staying away from sweets, all that stuff the dentist tells you to do in between check-ups. But the fact is, it's all genetic. I brush daily, but usually not more than once. I haven't flossed in, well, *ever.* Thanks again, Dad.

But how horrible would it be if I allowed my good fortune to become my daughters' bad fortune? It doesn't naturally follow that I will pass Dad's bulletproof teeth on to them. I, and they, need to be more proactive than that.

A legacy of good teeth cannot be taken for granted; so much the more for a legacy of faith. Yes, I can provide favorable circumstances. But that is not enough; ask Eli (1 Samuel 2.12-17). They need regular check-ups (2 Corinthians 13.5). And I need to set up the appointments.

Word for Word

Celebrations

ESPN is simultaneously the best thing and the worst thing that has ever happened to American sports. It's the best thing because it brings a wider variety of sports (although I'm still not sure poker and competitive eating count as "sports") and a larger number of events (yes, Random Directional Michigan University, even your games are televised) to a broader audience than was ever possible before.

It's the worst thing because of SportsCenter. *Nah nan nah, nah nah nah!* At first it was fine—a touchdown here, a home run there, no big deal. But eventually athletes realized they were a lot more likely to get on the highlight reel if they were outrageous. (The "E" did originally stand for "Entertainment," after all.) So after scoring a touchdown, the athlete now literally pushes away teammates coming to congratulate him, preferring to put on his little solo performance. Like no one else had anything to do with his success.

Celebrations in team settings should be about the team. It's selfish, arrogant and vain to strut around like a peacock instead of including one's teammates in the glory. That's why we are commanded to "rejoice with those who rejoice" (Romans 12.15)—because we Christians are in this battle together, and a triumph for one is a triumph for us all. Victory is an opportunity for us to connect with our brethren, not distance ourselves from them.

Christianity is a team sport. That's why we "put on" the same uniform (Romans 13.14). Let's act like a team.

Thanksgiving

America was founded upon religious principles. Anything you read that dates from 200 years or earlier will tell you that in no uncertain terms. Perhaps the most obvious example of this is the so-called "first Thanksgiving" in Plymouth, Massachusetts, in 1621. And since we've gone and set up a national holiday around that event, it's pretty tough to ignore—even for the most rabid of atheists. But they've figured out a way. Now, according to many textbooks, the Pilgrims were giving thanks to the Indians for teaching them how to survive, not to God for actually allowing them to survive. Who would have thought we could find ourselves taking God out of Thanksgiving?

But a hero arrives on the scene this time every year to remind us of the truth. And his name is Charlie Brown. And he will continue to call upon his friend Linus to recite his version of the prayer offered on that day long ago—"We thank God for our homes and our food and our safety in a new land. We thank God for the opportunity to create a new world for freedom and justice."

Perhaps one day the estate of Charles Schultz will sell the rights, and we will be treated to *Charlotte Brown's Politically Correct Vegan Tribute to Indigenous Cultures*. But until then, I guess we can settle for the truth. And God's people can echo the song from heaven given in Revelation 7.12, not just one day a week but every day He blesses us with life—"Amen, blessing and glory and wisdom and thanksgiving and honor and power and might, be to our God forever and ever. Amen."

Word for Word

307

Day

It is an absolutely glorious November day at the time of this writing—the very best Texas has to offer. It's a crisp 61 degrees outside, with a light north wind and low humidity. That makes it perfect for pulling a favorite sweater (finally) out of storage, or for stubbornly donning shorts and a T-shirt one more time before it becomes completely unreasonable. There's not a cloud in the entire state of Texas—and in case you haven't checked the map lately, it's a pretty big state.

On a day like this, it always seems like the world is in better focus. I don't know. Maybe my eyes respond better to my contact lenses. Maybe moisture in the air makes things look fuzzy. More likely, it's all in my imagination. In any case, as I was walking Max this morning, crunching acorns beneath my feet as I go (one of the best parts of November), the leaves on the live oaks seemed a bit more distinct, the shadows on the street a bit sharper, individual blades of green grass (still not needing a cut—have I mentioned how much I love November?) standing sharp and straight, reminding me why we call them "blades."

And I thought of Romans 1.20—"For since the creation of the world His invisible attributes, His eternal power and divine nature, have been clearly seen, being understood through what has been made, so that they are without excuse." Emphasis on "clearly." Barbra Streisand used to sing, "On a clear day, you can see forever." Indeed you can. You can see all the way to heaven.

You don't need a day like today to believe in a Creator. But it sure doesn't hurt.

Sandstone

Coasters have never been a big deal to me. In my single days, I didn't have any furniture that would be made appreciably worse by water stains. And if I was worried about water getting on my book or homework, I just used a piece of paper, cardboard, clothing, whatever was on the table.

So needless to say, I wasn't picky about the look of coasters in our (reasonably) tastefully furnished home once I dragged Tracie down the aisle. She, on the other hand, wanted coasters that looked nice. Whatever.

Enter sandstone. A rock that absorbs water. Wow.

Sandstone is a collection of sand that got trapped under tons of pressure and turned into rock over time. But ultimately, sandstone is still sand. And sand has grains. And grains leave gaps. And water finds gaps—at least, enough so the condensation from my cup will soak into the stone instead of spilling onto the tabletop and ruining my furniture. And, possibly, my marriage.

Hard finishes can still be permeable, whether in coasters or in character. Godly women may be married to men who care nothing for God. They may despair of ever teaching them. But, according to 1 Peter 3.1-2, the husbands "may be won without a word by the behavior of their wives, as they observe [their] chaste and respectful behavior." Simply by being excellent wives, they preach the best sermon their husbands could ever hope to hear.

Don't ever despair over a loved one who rejects the Lord. Even now your example may be soaking in more than you realize.

Word for Word

Lions

Male lions sleep 20 hours per day. They spend most of the rest of the day eating. "Work" basically consists of loud roars while the women-folk run around like crazy hunting for food, acquiring it, and getting it laid out for the family to eat—the male first, naturally.

On a related note, I love lions.

Seriously, some men appear to use the lion as their model of behavior. They think marriage is a way to get out of shopping and cooking. They think child-rearing is a way to get out of taking out trash and cutting the grass. And if they don't get exactly what they want exactly when they want it, they yell until they do.

It could not be more opposite of the Biblical model of husbands. God says husbands are supposed to act with love toward their wives, putting their needs first. We read in 1 Peter 3.7, "live with your wives in an understanding way, as with someone weaker." The point is not about which one can bench-press the most. Wives are sensitive to the most minute of gestures from their husbands—for good or ill. A husband cannot pursue his own will at the expense of his wife; he must act on her behalf, pursue her interests.

Yes, men, I'm afraid that will involve listening to them. Sorry.

Thank God we have the perfect Example: Jesus' behavior toward the church—moved by love, characterized by sacrifice (Ephesians 5.25). If we work more on our serving, and less on our roaring, we might just make it.

Crunching

I used to worry a bit about myself that I felt so compelled to crunch acorns beneath my feet at this time of year. I thought I might need to find a self-help group of some sort. "Crunchers Anonymous," or something like that.

But now I am satisfied the crunching compulsion is simply a part of human psychology—like rubbernecking, except much less dangerous. For crying out loud, my own mother pitched a fit on her last visit because her granddaughter crunched an acorn she wanted to crunch. And if Mom does it, that makes it downright American, right?

But why is crunching so appealing? I think it's because crunching is a way of utterly destroying something without consequences. It's why some cultures shatter glasses and plates as part of their celebrations. We just love breaking things—that is, as long as we don't need to use them later, and we don't have to clean up afterward.

Unfortunately, some people "crunch" their way through life, wreaking havoc everywhere they go, and then departing the scene of the crime without a thought of the mess they are leaving behind. The behavior ranges from missing the garbage can to failing to extinguish a camp fire to having an extramarital affair. And just as David had to suffer consequences for his sin with Bathsheba (2 Samuel 12.14), I often must "bear the penalty" (Ezekiel 23.49) in this life for ungodly behavior, even if, like David, I repent and God forgives.

God will clean up my acorn mess. But He leaves it to me to clean up my moral mess.

Word for Word

Stop

You know those octagonal signs by the side of the road? The red ones with the white border? They read "STOP" in big bold capital letters? Yeah, the Department of Public Safety calls those "stop signs." The rule is, when you see one of those signs, you are supposed to stop.

It may seem like the previous paragraph could have been handled in five words instead of five sentences. But as it turns out, stopping at stop signs is a bit more complicated. Some people think it's close enough to just slow down considerably. Or that the rule only applies when there's traffic, or when an officer of the law is watching.

Not that I'm speaking from personal experience.

The law is often a lot simpler than we make it out to be. To stop means not to go. If you are going, you are not stopping. To stop going, you must first start stopping.

Now, imagine a stop sign from God in front of your next sin opportunity. What do we do? We read in 1 Corinthians 15.34, "Become sober-minded as you ought, and stop sinning; for some have no knowledge of God. I speak this to your shame." If we think God will be satisfied with just sinning less, or less egregiously, or less publicly, we don't know God, and we ought to be ashamed.

God says stop. And stop means STOP.

Do not think this is too much for Him to ask. God will help us stop. He will even forgive us if we try to stop and fail. But if we just ignore His signs, we show ourselves to be rebels, not obedient citizens. And the Divine Policeman will not stand for that.

Prepositions

I want you to play a game with me. It won't take long, but it's educational, and you'll get a big kick out of it. It's called "Fun with Prepositions." (I know, you think I've finally lost my last marble. But stick with me. You'll thank me later.)

Imagine you are *in* a bathtub. Now, if you are *in* the bathtub, that means that at some point in the past you must have gotten *into* the bathtub, right? It can't work any other way. And the point at which you got *into* the bathtub was the point at which you began to be *in* the bathtub.

"Fun with Prepositions." See, I told you you'd like it!

Now, play "Fun with Prepositions" in Ephesians 1.3—"Blessed be the God and Father of our Lord Jesus Christ, who has blessed us with every spiritual blessing in the heavenly places in Christ." Clearly, "in Christ" is a place we want to be, since that is where spiritual blessings are found—forgiveness, grace, mercy, hope of heaven, right of prayer, etc. But I can't be "in Christ" until I get "into Christ." So I need God to tell me how to do that.

The Bible contains two, and only two, passages that tell us how to get "into Christ." The first is Romans 6.3—"Or do you not know that all of us who have been baptized into Christ Jesus have been baptized into His death?" The second is Galatians 3.27—"For all of you who were baptized into Christ have clothed yourselves with Christ." So I can't be saved unless I'm *in* Christ, I'm not in Christ until I get *into* Christ, and I get *into* Christ in baptism. I guess that settles the whole argument about whether baptism is necessary for salvation.

Word for Word

They

They say a bird in the hand is worth two in the bush. They say you shouldn't count your chickens before they hatch. They say you shouldn't put all of your eggs in one basket.

I say, who are "They," anyway? Is there a membership roster? Am I allowed to join? Is there a minimum IQ requirement? Because I wonder sometimes. Like when They say, "He who hesitates is lost," and then turn around and say, "Haste makes waste." Well, which is it?

To the best of my understanding, "They" refers to the collective as a whole. "Group Think," it's called. The idea is, if society as a whole agrees something is the case, it generally is. That's why contestants get to ask the audience for help on game shows—and why the audience's answers are so reliable. Two wrongs really do not make a right. A penny saved really is a penny earned. The Sundance Film Festival really was started by Robert Redford.

But They are not reliable regarding astrophysics, or differential calculus, or the history of Uruguay. Specialized topics require specialized knowledge. On issues like these, They tend to trust experts. As They should. And what knowledge could be more specialized than God's wish list for His people? As 1 Corinthians 2.11 states, "the thoughts of God no one knows except the Spirit of God." Yet They constantly weigh in with judgments, and then get offended if I ignore them.

If I wouldn't trust Them in picking a gift for my wife, why would I trust Them in choosing how to serve God? It serves no point to ask Them. I just ask her. And Him.

Land

For centuries, Texans were, by and large, poor. Settlers had no cash reserves, no established businesses. All they had was land. And often, that land wasn't much to brag about. And Texans brag about *everything*.

Then came Spindletop. Black gold. Texas tea. Overnight, Texans with 10,000 acres of worthless scrub brush became millionaires. It was the ultimate vindication of Texans' obsession with land: Buy a piece of Texas—the bigger, the better—and good things will happen.

Israelites of old had a similar attitude toward land. After centuries of wandering and servitude, they reveled in the prospect of owning land. Even generations after Joshua, to "inherit the land" (Psalm 37.11) meant to receive all of the blessings God had promised. And when Jesus referenced the passage (Matthew 5.5), He didn't mean some future generation would literally inherit a literal piece of literal real estate. He had far grander things in mind. The kingdom of promise would be absolutely everything God had promised. He would not be satisfied with simply giving them the land of Canaan this time; this time He would give them "the earth"—i.e., *everything*.

But, He said, the earth would go to "the gentle." Texans, and humans in general, are used to acquiring things through sheer force of will. That doesn't work in Jesus' kingdom. We receive our blessing when we allow Him to work for us, and then meekly and passively accept the role He gives us. Not the stuff of action movies, certainly. But the land He promises is well worth a little humility.

Word for Word

Versions

I bought a Bible in yet another version the other day. (How many is that for me now? Nine? Ten?) The New American Standard remains my translation of choice, though, for several reasons; at the top of the list is the fact that it is actually a *translation*. The scholars studied the original texts and worked to give the most accurate English equivalent. The King James, New King James, English Standard, and Holman Christian Standard (my new one) are that way. Works of man, including Bible versions, are flawed, but at least with these you can have assurance you're actually *reading the Bible*.

Other versions are *thought-for-thought* translations, as opposed to *word-for-word*. Those scholars decided what they thought the text meant, then sought to convey those thoughts in English. Such versions are only a step away from paraphrases, which I hesitate to even call Bibles. It's not God's word anymore; it's what some people think God's word is. That's a huge, vital difference.

We should choose a good version of the Bible. I refuse to study from (and I rarely even pick up) a non-literal one. But I have yet to find a version that was so mangled that the reader could not determine God's will for his life. Some interfere more than others, to be sure, but God's truth always worms its way to the surface. It is His power for salvation (Romans 1.16).

So read your Bible in faith. Know that God helps the motivated reader find what he needs (Philippians 3.15). But pick a good version; there's no point in making the search for truth tougher than it has to be.

Conflict

When I was younger, I was confused about the whole Memorial Day/Veterans Day thing. I mean, I'm as big a supporter of the military as you are likely to find. But I also appreciate the negative economic impact of sending a few million federal employees home for yet another paid holiday. Do we really need both?

I think we do. And the reason is, the two days really celebrate two entirely different groups of people. One reminds us of those who paid the ultimate price so the rest of us would not have to. The other celebrates those who emerged from conflict, perhaps a bit the worse for wear, to tell the tale. Both are vital. After all, if we didn't have veterans who survived the conflict, we wouldn't know what we were memorializing, now would we?

Conflict creates two breeds of heroes, each worthy of respect and remembrance, each with lessons for us all. Such is particularly the case in regard to our ongoing spiritual conflict. We read the story of Stephen (Acts 7), of John the Baptist (Matthew 14.3-12), of Antipas (Revelation 2.13), and we are reminded that faith sometimes requires us to pay a price—sometimes, the ultimate price. And we sit at the feet of older Christians to hear the stories of battles long before, learning how to be people of character (Titus 2.3-5), learning how to deny worldly impulses in our "good fight of faith" (1 Timothy 6.11-12).

Conflict comes in our lives as well. The more we remember and honor those who have gone before, the better chance we have for success in that day.

Elephants

Elephants have funerals. I've watched one. (Not in person, of course. I consider high-definition satellite TV to be an extremely low-cost alternative to world travel.)

Anyway, elephant funerals. It's really quite a touching scene. The mama elephant will nudge her dead calf with her trunk, pick it up, move it about a bit, then put it down and walk away as another adult will come and do the same. Genuine displays of emotion are rare in the animal kingdom, but it's difficult to see this any other way.

Why do they do it? No one knows for sure. Perhaps it's because elephants carry their unborn babies for almost two years. (Yes, ladies, you read right. *Two years.* So count your blessings.) Carry something around with you for that long, you tend to get attached (no pun intended).

The Bible calls this phenomenon "natural affection"—or just plain "love" in some versions. And it is hardwired into the psyche of humans—being, after all, made in the image of the One who is love incarnate (1 John 4.8). So it is no surprise when that love starts to disappear as the creation forgets its spiritual heritage. Being "unloving" is one of the traits of a culture that "did not see fit to acknowledge God any longer" (Romans 1.28).

It is no wonder that women have such emotional trauma, even to the point of suicide, after abortions. They are denying one of the most fundamental urges God has given them. They are denying their very identity.

It's said that elephants never forget. We would do well to remember our love as well as they do.

Carwash

In line at the automatic carwash today, a woman was spraying her truck's bumper and headlights with Windex before driving in. That struck me as odd. I mean, the whole point of driving through the carwash is that you avoid cleaning your car yourself. And if you don't have confidence in the carwash's ability to get the job done, why are you in line in the first place?

I object to helping someone (or some machine) do a job I am paying to have done for me. It's why I won't get up to pour my own iced tea at a restaurant. (If I did it anyway, would I have to tip myself? I lose sleep over this sort of thing.) It's an implicit acknowledgement that the service will be inadequate, even before you receive it.

Some people study the Bible like that. It's like they're saying, *"Lord, before we get started, I don't want to hear any of that business about loving your enemies, or turning the other cheek, or forgiving seventy times seven. I just want some practical advice on how to deal with people. Whatcha got?"*

Well, to be blunt, if you don't have confidence in the Lord's guidance, don't bother asking for it. James calls such a one a "double-minded man, unstable in all his ways" (James 1.8), and says the Lord's wisdom won't benefit him anyway. The person who has the solutions already figured out (allegedly) doesn't need Jesus.

We will look like He wants us to look at the end of His process. And it probably won't be a look we would have chosen on our own. We need to have enough faith to adjust our expectations instead of His requirements.

Pronounce

I about had a stroke the day Taylor came home and told us how she was going to compete in a speech *TORE*-nament. That is simply not something that Hammonses do. We compete in, and win, *TERR*-naments. (Did I just brag on my daughter there? Sorry.)

Call me provincial, but in my house I expect my girls to sound like me. Milk Duds have *CAR*-mel (like Elijah's mountain), not *CARE*-amel, no matter what the commercials say. And most importantly, we eat pe-*CAHN* pie, not *PEA*-can pie. Not even an Aggie would make a pie out of "pea cans." You'd break a tooth. (Ba-dum-bum.)

Yes, I know the song about to-*may*-toes and to-*mah*-toes. And if New Yorkers and Michiganders (honestly, how can you live in a state where you get called that?) want to pronounce words differently than Texans, that's perfectly fine. I cast no aspersions. But in Texas, you want to sound like a Texan. Got that, *y'all*?

And God wants Christians to sound like Christians. That doesn't mean going to war with every brother in Christ who literally can't pronounce "Shibboleth" properly. (Read Judges 12.1-6 if you don't get the reference.) But it definitely means not adopting crude and suggestive nomenclature, telling risqué jokes, and referring to our fellow humans with insulting terms simply because our worldly neighbors do it. As the Lord tells His people trapped in sinful Babylon, "Come out of her, my people, so that you will not participate in her sins and receive of her plagues" (Revelation 18.4).

We're Heavenites. Our language should give us away.

Immediately

I was in line at Walmart with Tracie. Our cart was full of Pepsi Max because they're selling two-liter bottles for $1. I found a refrigerated case by the register and grabbed a 20-ounce bottle of Pepsi Max for the drive home. A ten-minute drive, by the way. The small bottle, less than a third of the size of the two-liter, was $1.48. I drank maybe four ounces in the car, then poured the rest into a big cup for my day at the office—like I would have done from the bigger, cheaper bottle.

I did the math. The soda I poured into my cup was worth 24 cents at the $1-per-two-liter rate. So I spent $1.24 for what amounts to six cents worth of refreshment.

Why? Because I want it cold, and I want it now.

The craving for immediate, complete gratification permeates our society. We must be made to feel the way we want to feel *right now*. We recoil in horror at the idea of spending an extra second in an unsatisfactory status. (Okay, that's a bit of an exaggeration. But we don't like it.)

We would do well to have the same attitude toward the things of God. I love how Mark's gospel account uses the word "immediately" so frequently in regard to people's attitude toward the Lord. Peter and Andrew immediately left their nets to follow Him (1.18). The word immediately spread around Galilee about Him (1.28). Bartimaeus immediately became a follower after having his sight restored (10.52).

If Jesus isn't motivating us to act immediately, we haven't yet made Him Lord. He doesn't ask us to wait for forgiveness; we shouldn't ask Him to wait for obedience.

Hoarders

Have you seen these shows about hoarders? And I thought my garage was a mess. Seriously, some of these people don't throw anything away. Ever. They have newspapers dating back decades. (And there's nothing less valuable than a newspaper once the coupons expire.) Hundreds of empty Mason jars and cereal boxes. Papers of indeterminate purpose piled, literally, to the ceiling. One cluttered path connecting the bedroom, bathroom, kitchen and front door. Freddy Krueger was never this horrifying.

I realize we live in an uncertain world, and it makes sense to have contingency plans in place for worst-case scenarios. But this is not about preparing for nuclear holocaust or massive food shortages. This is about pathological insecurity. An absolute, will-crushing fear of being ill-equipped for the future.

Believe it or not, I get it. No one knows what the future holds. And our instinct is to hold on to a known quantity like grim death—"at least I have this," we tell ourselves, whether "this" is old tax returns, ketchup packets or a security blanket. The trouble is, even those things can and will be taken from us. No treasure, however valuable, is secure. The rich fool learned that the hard way (Luke 12.16-21).

It takes faith, more than the rich young ruler had (Luke 18.18-23), to put our faith in Jesus instead of ourselves. But ultimately, failing to do so makes us as "crazy" as any hoarder on any cable television show. Because hoarders are exactly what we are.

Border

Nations have borders. That's not just to create work for the people who draw maps. It's to let everyone (particularly the citizens of the nations on either side of the border) know where one nation begins and another ends. Laws, languages and customs may differ in the two places, and it is important to determine which ones apply in a given circumstance.

There is a border between the kingdom of Jesus Christ and the kingdom of the devil as well. We read in Colossians 1.13, "For He rescued us from the domain of darkness, and transferred us to the kingdom of His beloved Son." So we Christians crossed the border at some point (in the right direction, that is), and in so doing left behind the sinners with whom we once associated.

But where is the border? Clearly it is where the King says it is. I cannot remain in Satan's kingdom and claim citizenship in Jesus' any more than I could be born to English parents, live my whole life in England, and then claim to be an American. Jesus is an immigration office all unto Himself.

And He says we cross the border when we are baptized. That's where sins are washed away (Acts 22.16). That's where we have our conscience cleared (1 Peter 3.21). That's what true believers do (Acts 16.30-34).

That doesn't mean baptism saves us in and of itself any more than swimming from Vancouver, Canada, to Vancouver, Washington, makes you an American. But it does mean that at some point, you have to get wet.

Word for Word

Basil

Come over to my house if you need fresh basil. I'm serious. Tell your friends. The seedling we planted this spring is now nearly five feet high, with far more leaves than we can possibly use. It's something that might be under the big sheet at the beginning of "Iron Chef." I can hear the chairman now—*"Today's secret ingredient is … BASIL!"*

Tracie asked me to pick a few leaves for lunch today. (She was making me tortellini—have I mentioned lately how much I love my wife?) As soon as I started pinching off leaves, my fingertips started smelling of basil—a marvelously sweet, fragrant aroma. For the next hour or two, anyone who has ever worked with basil would have known exactly what I had been doing that morning.

Strong influences tend to rub off; the closer the contact, the bigger the impact. So it is not surprising that the apostles, after spending more than three years in the company of the Lord, began to take on His spiritual aroma. And as the Sanhedrin court brought them into the same trial chamber where they condemned Jesus, that aroma began to emerge. Acts 4.13 reads, "Now as they observed the confidence of Peter and John and understood that they were uneducated and untrained men, they were amazed, and began to recognize them as having been with Jesus."

How can regular people like Peter and John today show courage and faith in the face of adversity? By doing what they did: spending quality time with Jesus. The closer you get to Him, the more you start to smell like Him. And that's a very, very good thing.

Poems

My sister gave me a collection of poems for my birthday this year. And I'm reading them in much the same way I listen to music, or look at art. Sometimes I sit in awe, sometimes I admire the talent but miss the point, and sometimes I think, "Don't quit your day job, buddy."

I've finally figured out why some poems draw me in and some drive me away. It's the perception that the poems in question required no work. I'm not saying every verse has to be punctuated, metered and rhymed. But when a poem reads like a newspaper article or a dictionary, I can't help thinking the "poet" just scribbled down some random thought while waiting in line at the post office—no doubt applying for a government grant for his "art," but that's a soapbox for another day.

But part of the poet's work is putting me in position to work myself. I am more inclined to relate to David and confess my own sins by reading Psalm 51 than by just reading the account of his transgressions in 2 Samuel 11-12. The facts inform my mind, and then the poetry reaches my heart. The motivated Bible student wants both. As Solomon writes in Proverbs 1.5-6, "A wise man will hear and increase in learning, and a man of understanding will acquire wise counsel, to understand a proverb and a figure, the words of the wise and their riddles."

So read Bible poetry. Read slowly and repeatedly. Examine your own feelings as well as the text. Allow the words to take your heart where God wants it to go. Your life and service will be richer for the effort, I guarantee.

Word for Word

Hope

Some federal agency announced this week that 20 percent of Americans suffer from mental illness. Only 11 percent have what they call "a serious illness." That sounds like code for, "If you have ten friends, one will have a real problem, and one more will act like he does." Sounds about right.

I found it interesting that the highest levels of "mental illness" were in adults age 18-25. The lowest were among those 50 and older. Apparently I'm getting saner, not crazier, as I age. That's a relief. I'm out of wiggle room.

I don't want to minimize the legitimate problems of the mentally ill and their families. And "clinical depression" is a legitimate disorder that affects millions of people worldwide. But I'm going to get blunt here, okay?

Being "bummed out" is not a mental illness. If you're a college student or recent graduate and you are disturbed about being on your own for the first time, or about not finding a job, or about getting turned down for a date yet again, you don't need therapy. You don't need medicine. You need hope. And not an "If it could happen to Jed Clampett, it could happen to me" kind of hope. I mean a genuine confidence that the future is not determined by, and will be brighter than, the present.

And hope is in Jesus Christ. A good degree or marriage, however wonderful, can fail. The hope Jesus provides "does not disappoint" (Romans 5.5). It is a "living hope" (1 Peter 1.3-5) that tells you your earthly problems will not endure—if you will endure like Job (James 5.11). If it can happen for Job, it can happen for you.

Moths

Why are moths drawn to light? Scientists suggest the light may interfere with the moth's internal navigation system or pheromone sensors. Poets see it as a quest for greatness—an effort to live life to the fullest, despite the consequences. No one knows for sure.

I like the poets' theory. It is romantic to think that this lowly insect would crave a higher calling to such a degree that he would put his entire life in jeopardy in its pursuit. It inspires me to go climb a mountain—which I would do, of course, if it weren't for this chronic condition ...

The thing is, I have yet to read anything that would describe why moths are actually better off because they fly to the light. Light makes them more visible to predators, and therefore easier pickings. And of course, actually touching most light bulbs would prove fatal to most moths. What seems at the time to be a daring quest for a higher calling, when based on pure emotion rather than reason, can be catastrophic instead of empowering.

The moth population appears to be surviving this phenomenon quite nicely. But one human after another engages in the same sort of self-destructive behavior. And people applaud his daring. "At least he dared to live," we hear. Such empowering ones should be condemned as accessories to suicide before the fact.

Striving for greatness is a natural and good impulse. But it must be based on God's truth, not our (often tragic) impulses. "There is a way which seems right to a man, but its end is the way of death" (Proverbs 14.12, 16.25).

Word for Word

Gratification

I lost my grandfather, my final grandparent, more than 17 years ago. I like to think we were close. Certainly we spent a lot of time together, especially in my youth. About half of my Saturdays growing up were spent with Pawpaw, tending his garden, cutting his grass, feeding his cattle. I didn't like it much. Getting my hands dirty wasn't really my thing as a child. I would rather have been watching TV or playing basketball.

I see now the value of those hours. I learned how to back up a trailer and drive a stick. I learned how to plant potatoes and shell peas. More importantly, I learned about my family, about my heritage. I learned who I was.

I could have learned a lot more if I'd had a better attitude, if I'd given more of myself, asked more questions, listened better. I don't really blame myself; I was a kid acting like a kid. All the same, I'd give a lot today to have another afternoon with Pawpaw in his garden. A lot.

But we cannot back up time. All we can do is do the best with what we have, commit ourselves to being more conscientious now, and encourage the next generation to do better. Just like my father and grandfather did for me.

Tracie pointed out today that I could very well be a grandfather in a decade or so. It made me wonder what sort of legacy I am leaving for future generations. I can shout with Solomon, "Acquire wisdom! Acquire understanding! Do not forget nor turn away from the words of my mouth" (Proverbs 4.5). But will they listen? And will I have anything worth listening to?

I need to call my dad.

Decorations

Every year my wife, the queen of Christmas, manages to convince me to put the tree up one day earlier. This year it was two days before Thanksgiving. At this rate, in a few years I'll be telling my grandchildren how it has always been a family tradition to keep our Halloween candy under the tree.

Anyway, the holidays always makes me think of Proverbs 1.8-9—"Hear, my son, your father's instruction and do not forsake your mother's teaching; indeed, they are a graceful wreath to your head and ornaments about your neck." I'm not suggesting Solomon was a stockings-and-mistletoe sort of guy. But clearly he understood the importance of decorations. Whether one is adorning himself or his home, the extra effort shows one's appreciation for putting one's best foot forward in important situations.

And Solomon's idea of self-adornment, of course, is far more important than anything Martha Stewart could teach us. We drape ourselves daily, as it were, with the wisdom of our parents. It makes us more presentable, more equipped, and more pleasing to those with whom we come in contact.

My girls are rapidly exiting the stage in life when they think something is attractive simply because their mother and I say it is, whether the "something" is a new outfit or a new attitude. So while they are still listening, I need to remind them of passages like Psalm 119.9— "How can a young man keep his way pure? By keeping it according to Your word." Lessons like that will make them even more beautiful. And they will never go out of style.

Word for Word

Sunlight

Traditionally, armies attack at dawn. That has changed somewhat in the modern day, what with night-vision equipment and guided missiles. But even today, if the battle is to involve a large number of people trying to kill a large number of people, they attack at first light. And the reason is simple: the sun. Many things are flexible in this world—speed, effort, strategy, etc. But others are utterly inflexible. And right at the top of that list is hours of sunlight. The sun comes up when it comes up. The sun goes down when it goes down. Period.

That's what makes the story of the "long day" in Joshua 10 so encouraging. Joshua and the people were carrying out God's mandate to conquer the land of Canaan and subdue its inhabitants. God helped them, as He had promised (Joshua 1.5), even sending hailstones to crush their enemies. But Joshua needed more time. The setting sun would have allowed the enemy to escape, and presumably come back to fight another day. So he prayed. And God kept the sun from setting (Joshua 10.12-14). Amazing.

But then again, not so amazing. After all, God makes the sun rise and set every day anyway (Psalm 19.4-6); why shouldn't He be able to delay the sunset a few hours?

His point to Joshua, and to us, is that He will empower us to accomplish the task He assigns us. If we need a mountain moved, He will move it (Matthew 17.20). We do not have to worry about running out of sunlight; we only have to concern ourselves with properly utilizing the sunlight we have while it remains (John 9.4).

Fiction

I was about halfway through a book about a famous boxer during the Great Depression (somehow I find reading about boxing far more interesting than actually watching it), and I happened to turn to the copyright page and found this notice: *"This book is a work of fiction. References to real people, events, establishments, organizations, or locales are intended only to provide a sense of authenticity and are used fictitiously."*

Suddenly the book became a lot less interesting. The whole reason I was reading it was to give life to a *real* story. But if complete fabrications are interspersed freely with historic events, it's impossible for me to tell the difference. It might as well all be all fiction.

That's the main reason I react so strongly when people try to characterize the stories of Noah, Job and Jonah as allegorical—basically a fancy way of saying fictional. If we start picking and choosing which Bible events "really happened," the whole book loses credibility.

And who are we to decide which Bible stories are "improbable" anyway? To me, the most "improbable" story of all, Biblical or otherwise, is how Deity could take on human flesh and die for sinful mankind (Romans 5.6-8). Is that fiction? Is that just some writer's attempt to teach us a lesson about selflessness? Or did it really happen? If Jonah wasn't really swallowed by a fish, as Jesus Himself said (Matthew 12.40), how can I know for sure?

Bible stories really happened. They shouldn't lose credibility just because they're more interesting than anything that has ever happened to any of us.

Word for Word

Friend

People become "friends" on Facebook for all sorts of reasons. I do it so I can share the gospel with people all over the world, so I extend friend requests to all sorts of people—old high school acquaintances, preachers in far-off lands, minor celebrities, you name it. And if they agree to "friend" me, I don't read too much into it; they have lots of reasons to accumulate "friends," too—making business contacts, politeness, or even just accumulating numbers for the sake of numbers. I don't expect an invitation to Thanksgiving dinner, and I don't get offended if I don't get one.

I use the word "friend" very differently in other contexts—like when I need an attentive ear, or some advice, or $20. A true friend is not just someone who will acknowledge my existence; a true friend is one who will be there for me when I need him most, and vice versa.

Sometimes I wonder exactly what kind of "friend" some Christians want God to be. We read how Abraham was called "the friend of God" (James 2.23), and how "the Lord used to speak to Moses face to face, just as a man speaks to his friend" (Exodus 33.11). We want God to be our friend as well. But then we keep Him at arm's length, almost afraid of getting too close. That's not the action of a friend. Friends are givers, not just takers.

A Bible friend "loves at all times" (Proverbs 17.17). He "sticks closer than a brother" (Proverbs 18.24). He will "lay down his life for his friends" (John 15.13).

That's the kind of friend God is for us. What kind of friend do we want to be for Him?

Hal Hammons

Messes

At what point in a child's life does she become accountable for her own messes Adulthood? Graduation? Puberty? I suppose it depends on the mess in question. When a toddler learns the hard way that a coffee cup doesn't bounce, we tend to let that slide. If a teenager "forgets" to study and does poorly on a big test, that's different. Hypothetically.

But I must confess, a certain accountability has to be laid at my doorstep, regardless of my child's age. After all, I am the one who was responsible for teaching her responsibility. I will blame myself if something goes wrong, whether it's a bad grade in her teens, a bad marriage in her 20s, a bad child of her own in her 30s, or a bad moral choice in her 40s or 50s. I may console myself in that day, saying I did the best I could. But the fact is, I didn't. I've already made enough mistakes to fill the Library of Congress, and I'm not done yet. I can only pray my positive impact outweighs the negative, and that my girls are strong enough to cope with the rest.

My relationship with my heavenly Father is quite different. He makes no mistakes in His dealings with me. He gives me everything I need to succeed (2 Peter 1.3). He shelters me from forces beyond my control (1 Corinthians 10.13). He tells me, "Surely I will uphold you with My righteous right hand" (Isaiah 41.10). Any mess I make in my life is my fault. The sooner I accept that, the sooner I can get about the task of making fewer messes.

Word for Word

Sales

Phone sales is tough. I know firsthand. So I am polite when someone calls and tries to get me to change my electricity provider, or take out a Yellow Pages ad, or buy health insurance. I say I appreciate their time but I'm not interested.

The problem is, the good salesmen are like I was in high school with girls—perfectly willing to accept no for an answer, as long as "no" means, "not yet convinced but open to further attempts." Again, I don't blame the salesman; he's just doing his job. The more he talks, the more chance he has of saying something that resonates with me. If I don't want to buy, all I have to do is hang up the phone—which, of course, is what I do after two or three polite refusals. I have all the power, and he knows that.

Temptation works the same way. The devil doesn't need us to succumb right away. He just wants to keep a dialog going. He knows a "no" without conviction can become a "yes" with a little extra effort on his part.

Satan knows we have the power. We can flee the scene of the crime preemptively, as it were, like Joseph did (Genesis 39.7-12). And the Joseph strategy will work equally well for us. God will help (Matthew 6.13).

But for it to work, we must actually flee. Saying no to lust doesn't work too well if we keep watching the same movies. Saying no to gossip doesn't work too well if we keep associating with the same gossipy friends. Saying no to drunkenness doesn't work too well if we keep drinking.

Satan is a great salesman. The greatest. And if you listen to him long enough, you will buy. So don't listen.

Stereotypes

Living as close to the U.S.-Mexico border as we do, we see people of Hispanic descent constantly. Some of them speak Spanish to one another in the grocery story. Some fly the Mexican flag in their front yard. And yes, I'm sure some of them are in this country illegally. Not all, but some.

Some Americans rush to judgment in such cases, especially when illegals are perceived to be taking needed resources and jobs from legal residents. (I'm not sure just how many out-of-work white onion-pickers are out there, but that's another issue.) That raises the ire of Mexican-Americans, who resent the stereotype. And rightly so.

They're not alone; stereotypes are all around. Italians are mobbed up. Irish are hot-tempered. Southerners are stupid. Is it fair for entire demographic groups to be painted with the same brush? This Texan—who, by the way, owns boots but no cattle or oil wells—says no. But it happens. Even the apostle Paul wrote to Titus, who was preaching on the island of Crete, "One of themselves, a prophet of their own, said, 'Cretans are always liars, evil beasts, lazy gluttons'" (Titus 1.12). The sins of the fathers are sometimes visited upon the generations (to paraphrase Exodus 34.7 a bit out of context). We sometimes suffer for the actions of others. It's not fair. But it is life.

As a Christian, I resent being labeled as sanctimonious, Pharisaical and bigoted. But all I can do in response is, "be diligent to be found by Him in peace, spotless and blameless" (2 Peter 3.14). My neighbors may still think poorly of Christians. But it won't be because of me.

Word for Word

Black

Black used to be for gangs, funerals and formal wear. Not anymore. Everyone is wearing black these days, and for all occasions. Partly it's because black matches practically everything—a big plus for *What Not to Wear* candidates like me. But a lot of it is that black, we are told, is slimming. It's not only the new pink, it's the new Stairmaster.

And black clothes really can make you look thinner. I once had a black shirt that made me look gaunt to the point of emaciation. (Where is that shirt, anyway?) But there are some people who need a reality check. The color black has no magical properties. A black pup tent is not a cloak of invisibility. It's just black. And a pup tent.

Thankfully, there is an alternative. It tends to be more expensive, and it's *always* more trouble, than just buying an outfit. But it works a lot better, and you can go back to wearing colors if you like. It's called *losing weight.*

Now, before I am pelted with empty Chunky Monkey containers, let me emphasize my indifference toward how large my readers are or are not. I don't believe in abusing any of God's gifts, including the temple in which He dwells (1 Corinthians 6.19). But I'm not about to suggest 20 extra pounds will keep you out of heaven. I wouldn't do that. Believe me.

I'm more concerned with cosmetic "solutions" of a spiritual nature. Disguising a sinful life may appease our consciences and fool our friends. But God knows what's underneath. For true remedy, we must be truly sorry for our sorry state, and then truly repent (2 Corinthians 7.10). After all, it is better to be healthy than to look healthy.

Documentary

Hollywood just missed my family. If I had just thought to install cameras in my house during my girls' childhood, and hired a documentary filmmaker to sift through the footage, I could have produced hours and hours of heart-wrenching drama, perplexing mystery, and slapstick comedy worthy of the Marx brothers. The girls could have been catapulted into phenomenally successful careers. I could have been Joe Jackson to their Michael and Jermaine.

Okay, maybe it's just as well.

Anyway, I'm not too crazy about putting my private life on display. And I don't mean midnight trips to the fridge in my underwear (although we're all better off not seeing that in high definition, believe me). I mean my flaws. My errors. The things of which I am ashamed. I know God sees the things done in the dark (1 Corinthians 4.5). But you don't. And I'd like to keep it that way.

There may be no Bible principle I violate so regularly as the one found in James 5.16—"Therefore, confess your sins to one another, and pray for one another that you may be healed." I have no problem confessing my *sin*; we all have *sin* (Romans 3.23), so that doesn't really diminish me. Confessing *sins* is different. *Sins* is specific. Greed. Pride. Deceit. That's embarrassing.

But showing the whole documentary to my wife or a trusted brother in Christ does, in fact, heal. It has healed me before, and will again. It just takes faith in God. And God says, prayers are more heartfelt, more genuinely remorseful, more cleansing, when they are uttered in stereo.

Sealed

My proudest moment in home improvement was when my family returned from spring break one year to find I had tiled the kitchen. All by myself. Almost. I had chosen cream and green tiles and a buttery yellow grout. It was something to behold. For a few months.

Unfortunately, I didn't seal the grout. It seemed like a little thing at the time. But without the sealing step, the grout started collecting dirt like Larry King collects ex-wives. Before long it had turned dingy gray—not exactly ugly, but certainly not as beautiful as it once was.

The New Testament repeatedly refers to Christians as having been "sealed." An example is 2 Corinthians 1.21-22—"Now He who establishes us with you in Christ and anointed us is God, who also sealed us and gave us the Spirit in our hearts as a pledge." God not only saves us, He protects us for the future. This is done through the Holy Spirit, who guided the apostles into "all the truth" (John 16.13) and inspired them to preserve it in the Scriptures (2 Timothy 3.16-17). As long as we allow the Spirit to lead us, we remain in His fellowship (Romans 8.14).

But this seal is not permanent. It can wear off. It must be continually reapplied. God will supply all the sealant we could ever need. But we must choose to use it. Paul writes, "Do not grieve the Holy Spirit of God, by whom you were sealed for the day of redemption" (Ephesians 4.30). It would be tragic to let years of labor in His cause (to say nothing of His grace) go to waste because we were too lazy to make sure we were still sealed.

Relative

Will it take much longer? Is this shirt dirty? Do those pants make your wife look fat? These are subjective questions—questions where the proper reply depends on certain conditions. Specific circumstances may make a simple yes or no answer inadequate, or even misleading. "Long" may be defined differently by a "starving" child and the mother making his dinner. Neither one is right or wrong. It's relative.

Treating truth subjectively will serve you ill in certain disciplines. One plus one is not relative. The atomic weight of hydrogen is not relative. The definition of "is" is not relative. Such things are what they are, and that's that.

God's truth is not relative. It can't be. It doesn't depend on circumstances because He doesn't depend on circumstances. He is what He is, and that's that. And since His truth is a reflection of His mind, it must be determined and applied objectively.

Ironically, we sometimes find ourselves scrapping this concept on behalf of someone near and dear to us—a brother, a sister, a child. We're perfectly fine with objective truth when its object is a stranger. But truth becomes relative when its object is a relative.

It's a clear-cut example of putting family before the Lord—a practice Jesus says disqualifies one from His service (Matthew 10.37). He doesn't want us deciding on an ad hoc basis whether we will deign to obey. He does not want relatively submissive, relatively humble servants. Such are inadequate for a completely sovereign Lord.

Word for Word

Etymology

Etymology fascinates me. I don't mean I collect dead flies and moths; that's entomology (and sort of gross, if you ask me). No, etymology is the study of word origins. Words are the tools of my trade, and I have found I use them more effectively when I know where they came from.

Take the word *Christian*, for example. Obviously it is derived from *Christ*, and we all know who He is. Or do we? Have we delved into His character? Can we truly be following His example (1 Peter 2.21) if we have not examined it? How can we hope to copy the Mona Lisa (however inadequately) if we have not scrutinized the original?

People have different ideas about what a "Christian" is. My dictionary defines a Christian as a disciple of Christ, but it also says the word can mean a citizen of a nation where Christianity predominates, or simply a civilized human being. And I think that's where the problem lies. We have convinced ourselves that being a Christian is about who we are, where we live, what we do. In reality, being a Christian is all about Christ.

Getting back to the roots of the word is a good start. But we are simply involved in an academic exercise if we do not examine Christ with the purpose of copying what we find—His character, His priorities, His behavior. You can become a Californian by moving to California. You can become a Floridian by moving to Florida. If you want to be a Christian, you must move to Christ. Simply calling yourself a "Christian" isn't good enough.

Superstition

A century ago the British government determined to debunk the superstition that sailing on a Friday was unlucky. So the *H.M.S. Friday* was commissioned. Its keel was laid on a Friday. Its crew was hired on a Friday. And ultimately it was launched on a Friday under the command of Captain Jim Friday.

It was never heard from again.

I mention this not to alter your vacation plans, but rather to point out the power of superstition, and how we can utterly fail in our efforts to combat it. When we see things that defy explanation, we often find it convenient to ascribe it to unseen forces beyond our comprehension. It makes sense out of a nonsensical world. So we do all sorts of crazy things to get the forces of the universe on our side. Rub a rabbit's foot. Avoid the number 13.

Worship God.

Are these parallel? The atheist says so. I say no. I find it nonsensical to equate the order and intricacy of the universe (among other evidences) to a black cat or broken mirror. No, God has not personally introduced Himself to me and shown me video of the creation. I must be content with "the conviction of things not seen" (Hebrews 11.1). And the more I think about it, the more content I become.

I don't know if Stevie Wonder had God in mind when he wrote, "When you believe in things that you don't understand, then you suffer; superstition ain't the way." What I do know is, I don't understand God, and yet I believe. That's not superstition. That's faith.

Word for Word   **341**

Culture

I am a student of pop culture. I like knowing what's going on in the world of entertainment. Partly it's because I like being entertained. Partly it's to determine whether my children are complimenting me or cussing me out. But a big reason is to get ideas for this column. The latest misadventures of the Kardashians or Lindsay Lohan or the so-called "Real Housewives" (the "real" part escapes me) provide a treasure trove of ideas.

I worry, though, about missing my audience. A Justin Bieber reference may send many of my readers into a swoon (and others into convulsions), but someone with no pre-teen girls in the house may totally miss it. And as much as I would like to assume John Wayne and Andy Griffith connote certain images to people of all ages, I am finding out the hard way that such is not always the case.

That's one of the amazing things about the Lord's analogies. Yes, they are a bit dated; I don't know how many people out there today have literally misplaced a sheep or fretted over tares in their wheat fields. But the basics of human existence have not changed. People still go to war (Luke 14.31-32). Children still grieve their parents (Luke 15.11-32). Certainly the idea of stumbling across a huge treasure (Matthew 13.44) appeals today as much as it ever did. And so today's generations can have "ears to hear" (Matthew 11.15) as much as His contemporaries. His message transcends cultural boundaries.

I will never be the storyteller He was, and I'm okay with that. I just hope I can point people in the right direction, and not get in the Lord's way too much.

Lemonade

My daughter Kylie likes to drink Dr Pepper when we go out to eat. Tracie and I don't allow that—at least, not when we are hoping to get her to fall asleep (or allow us to) in the next 16 hours or so. So instead, she likes to get ice water with lemon. Then she'll mix some sugar in with the lemon and water, and voila! Lemonade!

Now follow me on this: The water is free, the ice is free, the lemon is free, the sugar is free; stands to reason, the lemonade should be free, right? But apparently, in some restaurants, they will charge you for lemonade if they catch you making your own. Hey, I thought that's what you're *supposed* to do when they give you lemons. It's a cliché, for crying out loud.

Bottom line, some people won't pass up a chance to tack a couple of bucks onto the bill. Well, far be it from me to tell someone how to run his business. But if they're going to charge for Kylie's lemonade, I want Kylie put on the payroll. And God's on my side here; Deuteronomy 25.4 reads, "You shall not muzzle the ox while he is threshing." (Not that Kylie resembles an ox; she's the shortest in her class and skinny as the proverbial rail.)

So should I file a child labor action over lemonade? Of course not. Paul was entitled to payment for his work, but pressing the point would interfere with a greater purpose (1 Corinthians 9.8-12). If I save two dollars by acting like a jerk, what have I accomplished? As Paul writes in 1 Corinthians 6.7, "Why not rather be wronged?" I'll take a good reputation over a quick buck any day.

Judge

You would think I would be qualified to judge a speech. I've been speaking professionally for 25 years. I've been arguing even longer than that. But when the local high school needed judges for a speech tournament, I had a hunch it would be more complicated than that.

Sure enough, the moment that 14-year-old boy stood up and started talking a mile a minute about how we'd be better off putting drug abusers in rehab instead of prison, I knew I was in trouble. I kept trying to find his pause button.

Fortunately I was supplied with a basic set of rules to judge the competitors. That gave me a basic framework of what was expected, what was valued, and what was prohibited. The rules didn't guarantee that I would do the job well, but at least it told me what the job was.

That principle keeps me balanced when I attempt to "judge with righteous judgment" (John 7.24) in spiritual affairs. No, I'm not supposed to judge hypocritically (Matthew 7.1) or judge beyond my purview (Romans 14.10). But to deny my responsibility to exercise judgment in any and all spiritual situations is to deny the Scriptures; after all, how can we avoid throwing pearls before swine (Matthew 7.6) without judging swine? Or pearls, for that matter?

The key is using God's rules for our judging criteria. If we condemn people for not meeting our own personal standards, shame on us. But if we measure them by God's word as best we can (however imperfectly that may be), we can help them become what God wants them to be.

Jogging

You never know when meditating on God's word can pay off. I'll give you an example. I was driving one early morning and saw a woman jogging with her dog. Out of nowhere, it came to me—"I know what Amos 3.3 means!" I practically shouted to myself.

The verse reads, "Do two men walk together unless they have made an appointment?" And it's talking about fellowship. If I had pulled over to the side of the road and started jogging with that woman, I likely would have gotten a face full of pepper spray and a leg full of dog teeth. It's not that I meant her or the dog any harm; obviously I didn't. But I didn't have an appointment. She had not agreed to run with me. I would not have been welcome.

Partnerships don't happen accidentally. Israel had chosen to walk with idols in Amos' day, not with the true God. Consequently, as the subsequent images in Amos' prophecy show, God would sound His warnings—not to ensnare Israel but to provide an opportunity to evade the snare, to again agree to walk with God. As verse 7 reads, "Surely the Lord God does nothing unless he reveals His secret counsel to His servants the prophets." He wanted to give them time and encouragement to repent.

We cannot blithely jog through life, assuming God is there with us. We have to make an appointment with Him—go in His way, on His terms. Because He already has an appointment with all of mankind that He intends to keep (2 Peter 3.11-12). And if we reject His fellowship now, He will reject ours then.

Word for Word

Barbecuing

You may want to write this down for cookout season next year. "Barbecuing" and "grilling" are not—repeat, *not*—synonyms. "Grilling" is cooking something, anything, on a grill. (Duh!) I prefer charcoal, but gas is perfectly acceptable. "Barbecuing" is cooking meat (in Texas, naturally, beef brisket is preferred, but anything from alligator to zebra will work) over indirect heat, fueled by hardwood, for several hours. Slathering K.C. Masterpiece on a grilled chicken breast doesn't make it barbecue any more than handing a microphone to a prepubescent girl makes her a Jonas brother.

You might get the impression from the previous paragraph that I am dogmatic on the subject. In fact, I have learned to be remarkably patient with people who offer me food. I have learned my chances of a second invitation go way up if I don't criticize the cook's terminology. So if I'm offered another plate of "barbecued" whatever, and it clearly does not merit the name, I just smile, say, "Yes, please," and stuff my face as quickly as I can.

Going to war over God's terminology is one thing; calling Bible things by Bible names is part of what it means to speak "as one who is speaking the utterances of God" (1 Peter 4.11). But going to war over our terminology is quite another. Such "disputes about words" (1 Timothy 6.4) are based in pride and lead to factiousness.

If we are not careful, we may find ourselves at war over our shibboleths like Jephthah did over his (Judges 12.5-6). And with similarly destructive consequences.

Sorry

As a culture, I must say, our apologizing stinks. If someone is accused of saying something offensive, he is likely to deny he said it at all. Then "I didn't say it" will yield to "I didn't mean it." Finally, if all else fails, he will say something to the effect of, "If you took what I said the wrong way, then I'm sorry." See how that works? The one "apologizing" is acting like he's building fences, but what he's really doing is accusing the other person of being too sensitive. He might as well say, "I'm sorry you're not intelligent enough to understand what I was saying."

The words "sorry" and "if" should never occur in the same sentence. "If" implies conditions. And if I'm really sorry (oops, I just put them together in two sentences in a row, didn't I?) for something I have said or done, it should be about my actions, not others' reactions.

In short, my judge is God (Romans 2.5-6), not my fellow man. And if I err, I err in His sight—regardless how my actions or inactions are viewed by others.

David's lament in Psalm 51 is a great example of true repentance. Certainly his actions caused offense to others (if it's fair to say he "offended" Uriah by having him killed). But how he was seen by others was the last thing on his mind. In verse 4 he writes, "Against You, You only, I have sinned and done what is evil in Your sight."

It's relatively easy to salve our own consciences with pseudo-apologies; if it doesn't fix the situation, we can just blame the other person. But if we want to mend fences with God, being genuinely sorry is the only way.

Word for Word

Bulls

My family loves watching *Mythbusters*. And it seems we're not alone; the show has quite a following. Is it the science? The witty banter? The explosions? My girls vote for the explosions, and I probably do too.

But one of our favorite segments is one where absolutely nothing was broken. They were investigating the old adage, "a bull in a china shop," and seeing if it really did describe abject chaos. And it absolutely did not! They ran one experiment after another—single bull, multiple bulls, slowed down, sped up. And the bulls just darted nimbly between obstacles. Not a single fragile dish was damaged. Turns out, a bull causes less damage in a china shop than, say, your average teen-ager.

So maybe destruction is not always as catastrophic as we anticipate. For instance, many Christians hesitate to speak up when the truth of God's word is challenged, thinking the aftereffects of such actions would be too messy. And that's certainly possible. Jesus warned us about the collateral damage that could come from standing with Him—trials and tribulations aplenty (Revelation 2.10). But that is not always the case. I recently heard of a college student who stood up (literally) and opposed his professor's pointless and repeated mockery of the Bible—and received a standing ovation from his peers. They were just waiting for someone to speak on their behalf.

"The fear of man brings a snare, but he who trusts in the Lord will be exalted" (Proverbs 29.25). Don't fall into in a trap that might not really be so scary after all.

Armadillo

Max may turn out to be not so much of a chicken after all. He encountered his first armadillo the other night, and all of a sudden he became Scooby-Doo's annoying little nephew, Scrappy—*"Lemme at him! Lemme at him!"* If dachshunds are bred to hunt badgers and beagles are bred to hunt rabbits, I guess miniature schnauzers are bred to hunt small, annoying varmints that are guaranteed to run for cover at the first opportunity and roll into a ball when cornered.

Maybe I shouldn't judge. I have yet to attack any member of the animal kingdom larger than a wasp that was likely to defend itself. And I admit, there is a sense of satisfaction in knowing I had a part in getting rid of some pesky little critter—however inconsequential and ultimately harmless that critter may have been.

However, I must admit these "victories" never really amount to much. Max will never catch an armadillo (and I think he knows that). And although chasing it away for one hour isn't exactly worthless, it doesn't do my lawn any real long-term good.

I guess I'm like Max sometimes, in that I find it easier to accumulate minor victories than do the work necessary for the major ones. Take prayer, for instance. If I thank God at every meal, that's a good thing. But if I never learn to pray for wisdom (James 1.5-8), or for my brethren (Hebrews 13.18), or for humility (Luke 18.13-14), I will never understand the power of prayer. And I will lose the fight simply because I never really fought it at all.

Word for Word

Oysters

How hungry must the first oyster-eater have been? I mean, the oyster is hidden underwater to start. Then if you happen to find one, it pretty much looks just like a rock; no evident nutritional value there. And if somehow you are motivated and innovative enough to crack one open, you find a little sliver of meat that looks like ... well, let's be charitable and just say it doesn't look much like food.

But someone, somehow, worked it out. And now oysters are a significant source of economy to thousands and of nutrition to millions. (By the way, don't count me among the millions. If someone slips an oyster into my gumbo, that's fine. But the whole slurping it raw out of the half-shell, I'll pass on that, thank you very much.)

My generation, I must say, seems to think that anything worthwhile in life will just be Fed-Exed to our doorstep; all we have to do is sign for it. And if work is called for, we either assume the item in question is not really of value, or we scour the internet for the appropriate agency to hear our complaint.

But God has been known to hide treasure in a field. It's not that He is trying to keep it from us, or make us work just to watch us sweat. He knows work is good for us—it is "the gift of God" (Ecclesiastes 3.13. So sometimes He asks us to put forth some extra effort—whether to understand a tough passage (2 Peter 3.16), or applying a tough concept (Hebrews 5.14), or conquering a tough trial (Hebrews 12.1). He promises, it is worth the effort.

Sometimes, you even find a pearl.

Hardened

If you make a pot out of clay and put it in an oven, it will harden. If you make another pot out of wax and put it in the same oven, it will melt. That does not mean your oven is faulty or that you are a poor pot-maker. Different elements will respond to the same stimuli in different ways, that's all.

I use this illustration to help people who are struggling with the idea that God hardens people with His message. He did it to Pharaoh (Exodus 10.20). He did it to the Israelites (Isaiah 63.17). And it happens to people in our day all the time. The more you preach God's word to them, the more determined they become to rebel against it.

Is there a problem with the message? After all, God says, "It will not return to me empty, without accomplishing what I desire, and without succeeding in the matter for which I sent it" (Isaiah 55.11). It doesn't take much effort to see that the gospel isn't saving everyone.

But it was never intended to save everyone. Yes, certainly He is saving those who want to be saved. But He is also exposing those who do not. It's why Jesus spoke in parables (Matthew 13.10-15). It's why false doctrine appears in the church (1 Corinthians 11.19). It's why He allows "the deception of wickedness" to become a "deluding influence" (2 Thessalonians 2.10-11). Jesus is doing exactly what John prophesied He would do—separating the wheat from the chaff (Matthew 3.12).

Certainly we do not rejoice in the loss of souls. And neither does God (2 Peter 3.9). But if God hardens us instead of melting us, that's not His fault. It's ours.

Word for Word

Drugs

As of now, I am not on any regular medication. With God's help, I'll keep it that way. But I sleep easier knowing, should I require drugs for blood pressure or an enlarged prostate or thinning eyelashes, a host of out-of-work actors (and a few minor celebrities) are ready to make critical decisions for me. *"I was in three episodes of* Chicago Hope *back in the '90s. So trust me when I say you should tell your doctor to change your prescription to Darcomax. Side effects may include dizziness, weight gain, liver dysfunction, memory loss, bleeding from eyeballs ..."*

Call me old-school, but I'd rather listen to my doctor about any chemicals I ingest. Amateurs are fine for painting houses or setting up stereos; I'm not likely to die from putting a subwoofer in the wrong place. If I'm laying electrical wiring or hooking up the gas, I'm going to go with an expert.

I suspect I could get 90 percent of America to agree with me on this point—that is, unless we are talking about the most important subject matter of all: our standing before God. For whatever reason, when it comes to the destiny of our immortal soul, we become do-it-yourselfers. And we're going to get ourselves killed. Eternally.

We have to quit trusting ourselves and start trusting Him. "I know, O Lord, that a man's way is not in himself, nor is it in a man who walks to direct his steps" (Jeremiah 10.23). His prescription for salvation will work. But only if we agree to swallow the pill, and our pride.

Plan

You know what I hate? I hate when people do despicable things to their fellow human beings, and when said humans somehow find a way to prosper, the offenders say, "Well, I guess it was all part of God's plan."

That is a horrible misuse of Romans 8.28—"And we know that God causes all things to work together for good to those who love God, to those who are called according to His purpose." Brushing off one's own misbehavior in the name of being a part of God's plan is reckless, if not blasphemous. It would be like Joseph's brothers showing up in Egypt, seeing the brother whom they gave up for dead alive and well, and saying, "I suppose it worked out for the best." Somehow I doubt Joseph would have considered that to be an adequate apology.

Romans 8.28 simply means that God has a plan for our lives—which is, as the next verse indicates, conformity with the image of Jesus Christ. He calls us through the gospel (2 Thessalonians 2.14) to participate in that plan. And when we accept His invitation, He begins working out that "good" in our lives. Success, misfortune, loss—all of it is used to make us more like Christ.

Yes, God uses sinners to work good in His people—maybe by testing our patience, or by increasing our dependence on Him. But that doesn't make the sinners' acts any less evil. Judas' sin, Pilate's sin, Caiaphas' sin all were used by God for His purpose. And all were still sin.

God's plan is for your brother to be saved. It is not for you to "help" him along the way by causing him harm.

Word for Word

Keys

We have two key chains in the Hammons household. One per car, one per driver. (Taylor is convinced that will change in a year or so. We'll see. When she can get from the front door to the driveway on foot without running anyone over, then we will talk about getting her a driver's license.)

Anyway, we have only one key to my office. And I have a bad habit of leaving the house with the wrong key chain, and then having to return home to get the right one. Thankfully, it's about a two-minute drive. But still, it's the principle of the thing. No keys, no entrance.

I should know that by now—especially since I preach about keys and their spiritual significance quite frequently. For instance, Jesus tells Peter in Matthew 16.19, "I will give you the keys of the kingdom of heaven; and whatever you bind on earth shall have been bound in heaven, and whatever you loose on earth shall have been loosed in heaven." Peter would "open the door" to the kingdom, as it were. The Holy Spirit would empower him to tell us how to enter. And the judgments he made would be reflections of the Divine mind—not just his ideas of what would be necessary, but rather God's ideas.

So when he told the people at Pentecost, "Repent, and each of you be baptized in the name of Jesus Christ for the forgiveness of your sins" (Acts 2.38), he was using God's keys. He was telling us God's will. He was showing us God's way. And he and God were telling us how to follow. No keys, no entrance.

Contentment

I have a friend. A brother in Christ. He's in a bad place right now—a place not of his choosing, but that is a result of poor choices in his past. He says he has made his life right with God, and I believe him. But now his situation is making it difficult for him to find his contentment. So he has decided to wallow in his unfortunate status until other people start acting differently, and then he will get back to being happy.

But then, isn't our contentment supposed to be independent of our situation? Paul wrote in Philippians 4.12, "I know how to get along with humble means, and I also know how to live in prosperity; in any and every circumstance I have learned the secret of being filled and going hungry, both of having abundance and suffering need." And he wrote that from prison, remember. His "means" were about as humble as means could get at the time—no family, few friends, no freedom, no money. And yet he is moved to use the words "joy" and "rejoice" 15 times in four short chapters in his letter to the Philippians.

We would do well to remember Paul's "secret," which he reveals in the next verse—"I can do all things through Him who strengthens me." As long as we are looking at ourselves, we will find something that will dissatisfy, that will discourage, that will make us discontent. I certainly do. But when we look at Jesus, remembering what He has done for us, what He is doing, what He has promised to do in the future, we find our lesser feelings banished.

We won't find contentment in what others do for us. We will find it in what we can do for the Lord.

Word for Word

Examine

Taylor aspires to be a writer when she grows up. She very well may make it. She's a much better writer than I was at 14. Kylie's not bad either, for an 11-year-old. When I examine their work, I take their age into account. I let a lot slide.

When Tracie writes something (she's the real talent in the family), I examine her work differently. She wants me to catch mistakes. Her work is usually for Bible studies, and therefore much more serious. It calls for a serious critique. But I still restrain myself somewhat. Not every point is worth making. I may suggest a change based on personal preference, but I don't press it.

I'm much harder on myself. My writing could be read by hundreds or even thousands of people. It could be saved and reread multiple times, shared with others far beyond my personal reach. That's serious. So I edit five or six times, maybe more. I triple-check all my Scripture references. I scan it for words, phrases or points of application that may be pointlessly repetitive. I read it to myself multiple times to see if it flows well, if my logic holds, if my references are still timely. I will scrap hours of work entirely if it does not serve the intended purpose. My writing is how I present myself to the world. I want it to be as close to perfect as I can manage.

Examining others is more comfortable, but Paul says, "examine yourselves" (2 Corinthians 13.5). And if Paul could fail the test (1 Corinthians 9.27), I certainly can. I should definitely help others along the way. But I should always reserve my harshest examinations for myself.

Technology

My girls are astonished when Tracie and I tell them about our youth. *"How did you get picked up from after-school activities without cell phones? How did you make popcorn without microwaves? How did you eat without forks?"* (Okay, you caught me on the last one.)

The fact is, our lives are shaped by available technology. We became accustomed to electricity, then cars, then computers, then texting. I'm sure if teleportation ever becomes a reality, we'll immediately wonder how we ever tolerated rush-hour traffic or lines at the grocery store.

Technology can be defined as man's efforts to alter his environment. Its development is wholly within the mandate given mankind in the garden to subdue the earth (Genesis 1.28). But the greater our dependence on technology, the more pride gnaws away at our faith. We come to think of ourselves as solution-makers instead of faith-walkers. We begin to believe that mankind has an almost complete control over the world. If we cannot yet prevent tornadoes or wean ourselves off oil dependency, well, that's just a couple of inventions away.

It might do us good to revisit the days of old. Most or all of the pre-flood technology (and there was plenty of it—read Genesis 4.17-22) was washed away. Noah and his family stepped off the ark with little more than their faith to sustain them. And as always, faith was enough.

"The fear of the Lord is the beginning of wisdom" (Psalm 111.10, et al). Whatever we learn in this life, we cannot afford to forget that.

Word for Word

Portion

To me, the holidays are all about pumpkin pie. I love turkey, football and ugly sweaters as much as the next man. But I do not consider the season to be properly started until I bite into a generous wedge of orange-brown goodness.

That's my portion. And if I get it, the rest of the holiday will be just fine. And if I don't get it, the rest of the holiday will be just miserable. And if you think I'm going to suffer in silence, just ask Tracie.

I exaggerate a bit. But whenever I tuck into this, the most delectable offering of autumn, I really do think of Lamentations 3.24—"'The Lord is my portion,' says my soul, 'Therefore I have hope in Him.'" Jeremiah, writing in the rubble that once was the city of David, had watched his nation crumble around him—first spiritually, then politically, and finally physically. He had been placed in stocks (Jeremiah 20.2), been condemned to death (Jeremiah 26.8-11), had the king throw his prophecy into the fire (Jeremiah 36.20-23), been thrown down a muddy well (Jeremiah 38.6), and suffered numerous other indignities. (How is your life going these days, by the way?)

How could it be that, here at the culmination of all his work, as every despairing word he had uttered had come true, he was able to go on? Because his security was not defined by his circumstances, but rather by his relationship with God. And having that, he could be content.

The Lord is my portion. And if I have Him, the rest will be just fine. And if I don't have Him, the rest will be just miserable.

Receiving

From my youth, I was taught that Christmas was all about giving. And I'll confess, I didn't really buy it. The receiving part, I got. Ask Santa for something, then open it up and enjoy it. A 6-year-old can wrap his little mind around that idea.

That might not be the noblest holiday sentiment you've ever heard. But it's not as horrible as it might sound. The way I see it, we have to learn how to appreciate receiving before we can appreciate giving. If we can be properly grateful, we can start developing a desire to be more worthy of the gift, and to be more giving ourselves.

It works that way with Jesus, too. We give everything to Jesus— our devotion, our energy, our very lives. Being a Christian is all about giving. But before we start giving, we have to receive. I'm not suggesting for a moment that we have no obligation to put ourselves in the path of His grace. But salvation is ultimately about what God does for us, not what we do for God. Grace is all about letting Jesus wash our feet (John 13.8). We learn to be loved before we learn to love.

The poor in spirit, the ones who mourn, those who hunger and thirst for righteousness, the pure in heart—these are the ones who are fit for the kingdom (Matthew 5.3-12). These are the ones of whom it is said in John 1.12, "But as many as received Him, to them He gave the right to become children of God, even to those who believe in His name." Once we learn to receive from Him, we can start giving back to Him what is rightfully His—our praise, our service, our loyalty, our love.

Word for Word

Scars

When I was six, I tripped over a sprinkler head and gashed my knee open. It took 11 stitches to close. I still have the scar. To this day, thank God, it's the most serious physical trauma that has befallen me in my life.

My knee is fine now, of course. God's creation is astonishing in every way—truly we are "fearfully and wonderfully made" (Psalm 139.14)—but particularly in its way of healing itself. Virtually every part of the body has regenerative power. Wounds may leave scars, but they will usually heal.

Perhaps it's significant, then, that brain cells do not regenerate. Damage done to the brain—whether through injury, illness, or abuse—is done. It can be true in a metaphoric sense as well. We have all been through trials that have tested us to the utmost. The events themselves may be over, but the damage left behind is permanent.

So what do we do with our scars? Do we brag about them, as if enduring hardship makes us better than others? Do we hide them, as though past events (even those beyond our control) make us worse? No, we move past them. We accept them as part of our current lives. And occasionally we reflect on the events that caused them, so we can avoid similar events in the future.

Solomon wrote the Proverbs "to give prudence to the naïve, to the youth knowledge and discretion" (Proverbs 1.4). By grace, we have survived thus far. Hopefully we have learned enough lessons in so doing that we won't have to learn the next one the hard way.

Time

Albert Einstein wrote, "The only reason for time is so that everything doesn't happen at once." As a writer, reading that sentence annoys me. To not only have truly brilliant thoughts, but also be able to put them in simple, readable terminology—I wish I could write like that. (I've long since given up thinking like that.)

Anyway, time. God has a wealth of experiences waiting for us in this life. Ecclesiastes 3.2-8 lists a few of them—giving birth, dying, killing, healing, weeping and laughing among them. And, as he writes in verse 11, each one of them is "appropriate in its time." Our minds would explode if we got them all simultaneously. We need time to process them all. So He distributes them as He sees fit throughout our threescore and ten.

As we travel through time, we tend to characterize the days and years in terms of those experiences—did we enjoy them, did we suffer through them, etc. If the days were pleasant, we might say we "had a good time." But the time—all of it—was a gift from God, the Giver of "every perfect gift" (James 1.17). And therefore by definition, it was all good.

We may value the pleasant days more than the unpleasant ones, but God does not. Each one, with whatever blessing or burden it may, is designed to hone our character. God is teaching us the lessons we need to successfully navigate the passage from this life to the next.

What a tragedy it would be if we used His time in pursuit of a purpose less noble than that.

Word for Word

Tyrannical

Athena was never a child. In Greek mythology, she sprung from her father Zeus' head fully grown, fully functional in every sense. Once in a while I have a sermon idea like that. I absolutely love those weeks. I'd love to claim they are the product of a well-developed intellect. But most of the time, I must admit, the credit goes to a passage of Scripture that's particularly easy to put into a neat outline.

Take the "tyrannical city" of Zephaniah 3.1-2. Jerusalem stood condemned. Its citizens were "tyrannical" in that they usurped their true King's authority. And we do the same when we fall under the same condemnation.

"She heeded no voice." God sends His call out to the whole world (Mark 16.15-16). Those who choose not to listen have no hope.

"She accepted no instruction." Listening to His word is of no value if we do not obey. James likens it to one who cares enough about his appearance to look in a mirror, but not enough to fix what is amiss (James 1.23-24).

"She did not trust in the Lord." Some listen to God's word and make efforts to implement it, but never really believe in it, or in Him. James calls this one "a double-minded man, unstable in all his ways" (James 1.5-8).

"She did not draw near to her God." God doesn't want lackeys; He wants children (Hebrews 2.10). We miss the point of submission if we find no comfort in it.

Preachers, feel free to pilfer. And all, do not be satisfied with anything less than full compliance. You owe that to your King. And to yourselves.

Gluttony

If you are feeling bad about your calorie intake over the holidays, consider Donna Simpson. In two hours this Christmas she put away two turkeys, two hams, 15 pounds of potatoes, five loaves of bread, five pounds of stuffing, four pints each of cranberry dressing and gravy, plus dessert. But don't think she was eating poorly; she also ate 20 pounds of veggies.

Already the biggest woman to have given birth, she plans to become the biggest, period. At around 650 pounds, she has about 350 to go. I like her chances.

I cannot begin to justify this sort of gluttony—from the 30,000 calories to the $230 cost of the meal. But she can. She says she enjoys food. She says visitors to her web site enjoy watching her eat. (They probably do, in a William Hung sort of way.) She insists her health is fine, "I love eating," she says. "I'm not hurting anyone."

Yes, you are. You are hurting yourself by robbing yourself of a real life. You are hurting your children by showing them an example of self-centeredness and lack of restraint. You are hurting the needy in your community whom you could be helping. Shame on you.

And shame on us when we act selfishly. When Paul spoke of those "whose god is their appetite" (Philippians 3.19), he did not refer to gluttons particularly; he meant anyone more concerned with their own short-term interests than others. When God's blessings move us first to indulge deeper instead of offering thanks and/or service, we worship the oldest idol of all—self (Colossians 3.5). And that idol, like all others, will be torn down one day.

Word for Word

Cancer

One thing I love about late John Wayne movies is how his battle with cancer was lived out on the big screen. For instance, he made *Big Jake* while his early efforts to fight it off were relatively successful. I can't help thinking it's a big inside joke that everyone who sees Jacob McCandles tells him, "I thought you were dead." And he stares them down in classic Duke style and says, "Not hardly."

But in *The Shootist*—his final film, shot when it had become evident his years were numbered—he plays an aging gunfighter who is himself dying of cancer. Robbed of any opportunity to live the life he wants, J.B. Books chooses to die as he lived—facing down his enemies with a six-shooter in each hand.

We all stare down death's gun barrel eventually. It is part of Adam's curse. But the other part is even worse—spiritual death, eternal separation from God, a consequence of the sin Adam introduced and of which we all partook (Romans 5.12). This spiritual cancer is terminal. We may feel like we are making headway. We may even feel we have beaten it. But it will get us in the end.

Thanks be to God, Jesus offers us a cure. "So then as through one transgression there resulted condemnation to all men, even so through one act of righteousness there resulted justification of life to all men" (Romans 5.18). Struggling won't help. Ignoring the problem won't help. Only prostrating ourselves before the Lord will help.

We can go out on our feet, or we can go out on our knees. It's our choice. But it's not much of one.

Finished

There is something truly thrilling about setting an objective for yourself, the more lofty the better, and then achieving it. All the stress involved in the task is alleviated, and you are free to look at the effort in retrospect and see every bit of it (even the parts that were not too enjoyable in isolation) as a necessary and valuable part of the whole. Everything is put in perspective. I know it's a cliché, but then again, clichés become clichés for a reason.

The apostle Paul saw his entire life as an opportunity to serve his Maker. For far too long he kicked against the goads (Acts 26.14), but eventually he realized submitting to God meant submitting to Jesus Christ, and he did so. And every day after that he spent in that pursuit: "one thing I do: forgetting what lies behind and reaching forward to what lies ahead, I press on toward the goal for the prize of the upward call of God in Christ Jesus" (Philippians 3.13-14). He never considered himself to be finished. Even as he prepared for his certain and pending execution, he was asking Timothy to bring him books, parchments and fellow workers (2 Timothy 4.11-13). Clearly he did not intend to spend his final days idle.

Even so, he delighted in the end that drew nearer. He had not technically "finished the course" quite yet; but like a marathoner nearing the goal, he could almost feel the crown of victory resting on his forehead (2 Timothy 4.7-8). What a marvelous feeling that must have been.

Word for Word

Another Deward Daily Devotional

Flight Paths
A Devotional Guide for your Journey

When encroaching blindness took her music teaching career away, Dene Ward turned her attention to writing. What began as e-mail devotions to some friends grew into a list of hundreds of subscribers. Three hundred sixty-six of those devotions have been assembled to form this daily devotional. Follow her through a year of camping, bird-watching, medical procedures, piano lessons, memories, and more as she uses daily life as a springboard to thought-provoking and character-challenging messages of endurance and faith. 475 pages. $18.99 (PB)

Glimpses of Eternity: Studies in the Parables of Jesus
Paul Earnhart

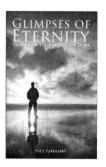

The parables of Jesus are the compelling stories and illustrations from our familiar world which the Lord used to open windows for us into heaven. They help us to understand the heart of God and the nature of the spiritual kingdom which His Son has brought into the world at such an awful cost. There are messages of comfort in the parables and some stern warnings too. These studies are the compilation of a series of articles written for *Christianity Magazine*. 198 pages. $11.99 (PB)

Two Men: Articles on Practical Christian Living
Bill Hall

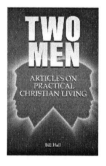

Brief articles contrasting different characters fill about one-fourth of the book, thus the title, *Two Men*. The men described remind us of people we know, and sometime of ourselves, as we see qualities both good and bad so graphically described. Such portraits should encourage self-improvement. The remaining articles are equally practical, dealing with such subjects as family, church, doctrinal questions and Christian living, providing godly wisdom for dealing with real life situations.

Just Jesus: The Evidence of History
James T. South

Few people are able to ignore Jesus. He has devotees and detractors, but hardly anyone is neutral about him. But how much do we know about him? Whether we love him or loathe him, it only makes sense that we know what and whom we're talking about. *Just Jesus* is about what we can know about Jesus. Jesus isn't just a religious idea but a phenomenon of history. That means we can and should ask about him all of the historical questions we can think of and see which ones can and can't be answered. Fortunately, we're able to learn a lot more about Jesus than most people think. 152 pages. $9.99 (PB)

CPSIA information can be obtained at www.ICGtesting.com
Printed in the USA
BVOW080924191112

305892BV00001B/1/P